W9-BCV-474

THE COMEDY OF MANNERS

WILLIAM CONGREVE.

From a painting by Sir Godfrey Kneller in the National Portrait Gallery.

THE COMEDY OF MANNERS

BY

JOHN PALMER

SOME TIME SCHOLAR OF BALLIOL COLLEGE, OXFORD

> Your judge-wit or critic . . . He rails at all the other classes of wits, and his wit lies in damning all but himself:—he is your true wit.

NEW YORK

RUSSELL & RUSSELL · INC

1962

First Published in 1913 by G. BELL & SONS LTD., *London*
Published in 1962 by RUSSELL & RUSSELL, INC., *New York*
By Arrangement with G. BELL & SONS, LTD.
L. C. Catalog Card No.: 61 – 13782

PR
691
P3
1962

PRINTED IN THE U.S.A.

INTRODUCTION

THERE is no History of the Comic Dramatists. There are competent memoirs scattered through various editions of the plays of Etherege, Wycherley, Congreve, Vanbrugh and Farquhar. Leigh Hunt, Macaulay, and Dr. Johnson have dealt monographically with men of the period. Hazlitt and Lamb have approached Restoration drama as critics of the theatre. Mr. Edmund Gosse, Mr. W. C. Ward, Mr. G. S. Street, and Mr. A. W. Verity, in studies of Etherege, Wycherley, Congreve, and Vanbrugh, have in the last thirty years written historically and critically of the dramatic literature of the late seventeenth century. But there has, as yet, been no attempt to present an historical view of the rise and fall of the comic dramatists of the Restoration.

What is the reason of this neglect? It is surprising that a generation of English men of letters should have left the unhistorical estimate of Macaulay as the accepted introduction to a study of the great age of English comedy. No intelligent estimate of the comic dramatists as a literary group has appeared since Leigh Hunt published his prefatory memoirs in 1849. Macaulay has remained secure in his critical triumph for over half a century. Every line of his essay upon the Leigh Hunt edition is, in all but literary glitter, conspicuously inferior, as history and criticism, to the amiable and just appreciations of his victim. Macaulay's immunity is in part due to the hard common sense of his estimates. All that he has to say seems so conspicuously reasonable that for fifty years we have been content to regard Leigh Hunt as an ineffectual enthusiast; Charles Lamb as an amateur of paradox; and Wycherley as an author whose "indecency is protected against the critics as a skunk is protected against the hunters."

But Macaulay's common sense would not have protected him from his able critical successors if he had not a stronger shield for his fame. Macaulay, as we shall see, treated the reputation of the comic dramatists from an ethical point of view. He, of course, admitted that they were brilliantly witty; that they had astonishing gifts of style. But these qualities were accidents of fortune. The main point for Macaulay was that they were immoral men, who wrote plays wherein husbands were made ridiculous; that they lived about town; and perversely disposed of their property at death. His important final conclusion about Congreve and Wycherley was that their plays were not founded upon the moral values of the middle nineteenth century. Macaulay, in fact, like too many of the critics who have dealt with this period of English literary history, ended where he should have begun. He said in effect, "These men have literary merit, but it is more important to observe that they are wicked." More wisely he would have said, "Let us agree that these men

are, according to the standard of our time, wicked.
But what is their position in English dramatic
literature ? "

The present volume is an attempt to fill a gap
in English dramatic criticism ; and, if it be possible,
to reform our point of view as to the drama of the
Restoration. It would be impudently ungracious
to claim that this is pioneer work of the backwoods.
Mr. George Street, Mr. Edmund Gosse and other
critical essayists upon the period in general, and
the Restoration dramatists in particular, have
already prepared the way for an estimate of these
men and their work, viewed in perspective with
their period, measured by standards of morality
and taste which they themselves would have accepted. But this is the first attempt by a writer
who has *en bloc* digested the historical evidence to
put right the injustice of over two centuries. Since
Jeremy Collier discovered that the Restoration
dramatists were profane, wicked, and subversive
of good manners, nearly every printed opinion, with
one or two celebrated and conspicuous exceptions,
leaves the impression that these writers have been
measured by standards they would neither have
respected nor understood.

This volume is a compromise. It is addressed
to the merely literate. It is not written for the
specialist in Restoration literature. At the same
time the author has omitted no labour that might
make his criticism historically just and accurate.
The text is so written that the precise origin of
cardinal and important statements is given the
reader *currente calamo*.

CONTENTS

LIST OF ILLUSTRATIONS

THE
COMEDY OF MANNERS

CHAPTER I

CRITICAL PRELIMINARIES

WHO are the comic dramatists of the Restoration?
Dryden wrote comedies; Shadwell's *Squire of
Alsatia* was as popular in its day and regarded
as of equal importance with *The Country Wife;*
Sir Charles Sedley, Buckingham, and Rochester,
have a claim to be included; Aphra Behn, Crowne
and Settle could not very well be omitted in an
exhaustive study of the comedy of the period;
Otway was the author of no fewer than three
original comedies; Colley Cibber was a formidable
contemporary rival of Vanbrugh and Farquhar.
But it is obviously impossible within the limits of
a single volume to include every author of a
comedy who wrote within a period of fifty years.
What shall be our principle of selection?

The Leigh Hunt edition of the comic dramatists
is a collected edition of the plays of Wycherley,
Congreve, Vanbrugh, and Farquhar. Apparently
Macaulay had no fault to find with the selection of

these four authors as the principal comic writers of the period. Hazlitt agrees. These are the four undoubtedly great figures in our comic literature between Shakespeare and Sheridan. Further selection is difficult. If we admit Etherege, should we not also admit Shadwell and Mrs. Behn ? What are we to do with Dryden ? Is not Cibber almost as important as Farquhar ?

All hangs upon our intention. If we are aiming merely at the personal distinction of the author, it would clearly be necessary to include Dryden. On the other hand, in a general history of the stage, Cibber is a more interesting historical figure than Dryden ; and, if it were here intended to use the comic dramatists as cover for a collection of scandalous anecdotes, Rochester and Sedley would easily defeat the claims of Captain Vanbrugh. But we are here to be concerned with the origin and development of the English Comedy of Manners. To the main course of this development Dryden was as unnecessary as Shadwell, or Mrs. Behn ; and, from this point of view, Cibber is less important as a dramatic author than as a critic and an actor. But Sir George Etherege is strictly necessary. He becomes, in fact, historically more important than Wycherley.

To anticipate the theme of this history, the English comedy of manners began with Etherege ; rose to perfection in Congreve ; declined by easy stages with Vanbrugh and Farquhar ; and was finally extinguished in Sheridan and Goldsmith. We have to study its rise in the plays of Etherege, Wycherley and Congreve, and the influences which prepared its declension in Vanbrugh and Farquhar. All that is of permanent importance in this story of the rise and fall of English Comedy may be studied in the lives and plays of these five principal dramatists. It is impossible to omit any one of them; it is unnecessary—except, of course, by way of allusion and illustration—to include their contemporaries.

Perhaps the first and most striking fact as to these five selected authors is that only two of them can be said to belong in any sense to the period of the Restoration. It is one of the astonishing results of their neglect, and of the false perspective in which their contribution to English literature has continually been presented, that even the date of their flourishing is confused in the popularly-educated mind. Every one has by heart the historical commonplaces about the immorality of Restoration life and literature during the reaction which followed the Puritan supremacy. These commonplaces, so brilliantly insisted on by Macaulay, have been loosely accepted for an explanation of the "indecency" of the comic dramatists. Restoration drama is deeply associated in the general mind with Charles II. and Mrs. Gwynn. Unfortunately for Macaulay's generalisation the comic drama of the Restoration neither began nor ended with the moral reaction against the Puritans. For four complete years of the reign of Charles II., at which time we are presumably to imagine that the moral reaction was at its height, the English theatre was the theatre of Charles I. restored. Not until Etherege's *Love in a Tub* was producd in January, 1664, was the theatre of Charles II. afflicted with the sort of comedy that Macaulay has so solemnly deprecated. We are asked to believe that for four years the comic dramatists of the Restoration successfully refrained from indulging their reactionary impulse to write intentionally lewd and scandalous comedy ; and that this same comedy of the reaction continued to develop and reached perfection at a period when its historical explanation was thoroughly exhausted. Congreve's first comedy *The Old Bachelor* was first produced five years after the Revolution of 1688. To describe Congreve's comedies as the fruit of a reaction against the Puritan severities of Cromwell is absurd. Congreve was nine years old when Charles II. was restored. He had neither personal nor literary connexion with the Court life that included Nell Gwynn and Mrs. Palmer. Macaulay, in fact, has explained the comic dramatists by historical influences with which they were, neither in the beginning nor the end, contemporary. Of the four great dramatists of the Restoration accepted by Macaulay as typical of the group, only Wycherley belonged to the period of the Restoration proper ; and the plays of Wycherley were first produced twelve years after the accession of Charles II. Congreve is a dramatist of the Orange period. Vanbrugh and Farquhar were contemporary with Addison, Swift, and Steele.

Midway through the period we are setting out to examine is the year in which Jeremy Collier published his *Short View of the Profaneness and Immorality of the English Stage*. This was the monstrous blast from which the comic dramatists have to this day not entirely recovered. There is a striking contrast

JEREMIAH COLLIER.

From a mezzotint by Wm. Faithorne, after a painting by Edmund Lely.

between the attitude of critics and publicists towards the drama of the Restoration before the publication of Collier's *Short View* and afterwards, Collier set the fashion of applying to the comic dramatists the test of propriety as we understand it to-day. No one whose opinion counted had as yet dreamed of doing so. After Collier, with one or two exceptions, propriety is the final criterion.

Jeremy Collier invented the moral test. The controversy that raged for several years between Jeremy Collier and the dramatic authors must needs be dealt with at the end of this inquiry. But it is impossible even to begin an examination of the period without clearly realising the importance of the revolution in critical opinion in the period which immediately followed the publication of the *Short View*. In the period that preceded Collier's celebrated pamphlet it is almost impossible to find any sense in the contemporary public of the perilous indecency of the Restoration theatre. Pepys may reasonably be taken as a typical playgoer of the Restoration. Now Pepys was quite conscious, as a citizen of the respectable middle state, of the blemishes upon the life of his time. We read in the *Diary* (29 January, 1665–6) how he improves the hour with Mr. Evelyn in "excellent discourse till we come to Clapham talking of the vanity and vices of the Court which makes it a most contemptible thing." Evelyn himself was a monument of the just man suffering the iniquities of his generation. But neither Pepys nor Evelyn, though they deplore the extravagance and vanity of the Court, is distressfully disturbed by the improprieties

afterwards discovered by Collier and his successors
in the theatre. Evelyn has no particular fault to
find with the comedies of Sir George Etherege.
Love in a Tub he finds merely a " facetious " comedy
in 1664. Pepys criticises the plays he so loved to
frequent from almost every other point of view than
the moral. Dryden's *The Rival Ladies* he terms
" a very innocent and most pretty witty play," a
criticism which few playgoers of the post-Collier
period would endorse. All the evidence agrees as
to the blindness of the period to the enormous
sinfulness of its theatre. Queen Mary was the
avowed patron of Congreve. She commended
The Double Dealer; ordered a revival of *The Old
Bachelor;* and Dr. Payne in his funeral elegy
praised her for love of play-going and other gentle
amusements. One recalls also the surprising eulogy
of Bishop Burnet upon the Earl of Rochester : " I
do really believe that if God had thought fit to
continue him longer in the world, he had been the
wonder and delight of all that knew him."

But Jeremy Collier in 1698 trumpeted a revolution. The force of his delivery was the result
partly of his genius for controversy, partly of the
ripeness of the time. His contemporaries were
just ready to discover that they were better men
than their predecessors. Richard Blackmore, in a
preface to his *Epic of Prince Arthur*, had already
warned his fellow poets that, if they were not
careful to reform, they might come to be regarded
in after ages as " the dishonour of the morals and
the underminers of the public good." A few months
previous to the publication of Collier's *Short View*

there had appeared the violent pamphlet of Merriton castigating the "morality, debauchery and profaneness" of the theatre and the age. The public was ready for Collier.

The controversy that followed upon the publication of Collier's little book is one of the most amusing and instructive literary controversies in the whole body of English literature; and it will hereafter be very particularly considered. We will for the time being be content to notice that a few years after the appearance of the *Short View*, Steele in the *Tatler*, and Addison in the *Spectator*, were testing the contemporary theatre by standards which would have seemed impertinent to their function as critics in the view of their immediate predecessors. Collier had completely changed the point of view of critics and public alike. The new critics were vigilant moralists. Very speedily London was honeycombed with societies for the reformation of manners. A little later Defoe tells of a *Society for London and Westminster*, that drew down penalties upon the heads of over 3000 " lewd and scandalous " persons.

The attitude and criticism of Dick Steele is a reasonable measure of the change in public opinion. Steele's commendation is even more significant than his hostility. Writing in the *Tatler* (16 April, 1709) he says of *The Country Wife* that Wycherley has "shown the gradual steps to ruin and destruction which persons of condition run into without the help of a good education how to form their conduct." We can but faintly imagine Wycherley's amazement at finding himself credited with this agreeable intention in writing *The Country Wife*. Steele's test for the theatre, following Collier, was invariably a moral test—precisely the test which no one before Collier had ever dreamed of applying. "A good play acted before a well-bred audience," says Steele, "must raise very proper incitements to good behaviour and be the most quick and most prevailing method of giving young people a turn of sense and breeding." In the *Tatler* for 26 November, 1709, we further read, "My old friends, Hart and Mohun, the one by his natural and proper force, the other by his great skill and art, never failed to send one home full of such ideas as affected my behaviour, and made me insensibly more courteous and humane to my friends and acquaintances. It is not the business of a good play to make every man a hero; but it certainly gives him a livelier sense of virtue and merit than he had when he entered the theatre." In June, 1710, Steele tells us how he has discovered the play of a young author wherein he finds "all the reverent offices of life, such as regard to parents, husbands, and honourable lovers, preserved with the utmost care; and at the same time that agreeableness of behaviour, with the intermixture of pleasing passions as arise from innocence and virtue, interspersed in such a manner, as that to be charming and agreeable shall appear the natural consequences of being virtuous." Here we are in a different world from that of Mr. Horner and Sir Fopling. It is not a comparison between two worlds more virtuous or less that suggests itself. The whole scheme of values is changed. To suggest that Mr. Horner is a wicked man is not to suggest that his conduct might conceivably be improved.

The suggestion utterly destroys him. As soon as we attempt to drag him before the expert moral tribunal of Collier and Steele, Mr. Horner turns to simple moonshine. The tribunal is left to pass judgment upon a wraith. Criticism of the Restoration dramatists on the lines suggested by these sentences of Steele is beating the air.

In *Spectator* 51, Steele writes particularly of Sir George Etherege : "If men of wit who think fit to write for the stage . . . instead of this pitiful way of giving delight, would turn their thoughts upon raising it from such good natural impulses as are in the audience, but are choked up by vice and luxury, they would not only please but befriend us at the same time. If a man had a mind to be new in his way of writing, might not he who is now represented as a fine gentleman, though he betray the honour and bed of his neighbour and friend, and lies with half the women of the play, and is at last rewarded with her of the best character in it ; I say, upon giving the comedy another cast, might not such a one divert the audience quite as well, if at the catastrophe he were found out for a traitor, and met with contempt accordingly ? " " Why not have virtuous and moral people for heroes and heroines ? " continues Dick Steele. " Such characters would smite and reprove the heart of a man of sense, when he is given up to his pleasures. He would see he has been mistaken all the while, and be convinced that a sound constitution and an innocent mind are the true ingredients for becoming and enjoying life. All men of taste would call a man of wit who should turn his ambition that way a friend and benefactor to his country ; but I am at a loss what name they would give him who makes use of his capacity for contrary purposes." From the writer's point of view this is all so extremely obvious that it scarcely needed to be set down. But it would merely have puzzled Sir George Etherege. As criticism it does not touch the merits of his work. It is irrelevant.

Steele's attitude towards Restoration comedy particularly repays examination. It is representative of the entire century which followed—the attitude from which literary criticism of the English stage has not even yet recovered. More than a century later Hazlitt, Lamb, and Leigh Hunt rescued the seventeenth century dramatists for a brief and brilliant moment from the abyss into which Collier's successors had plunged their reputation. But at this point Macaulay repeated the success of Collier. Scarcely had they risen in polite estimation to the dignity of a collected edition of their four great representatives than they were immediately flung back into disrepute. It is a fascinating chapter in the history of criticism.

In the period of eclipse between Collier and Leigh Hunt, perhaps the two greatest names in English literature are Dean Swift and Dr. Johnson. Swift in 1709, writing of the comic dramatists, is the absolute echo of Steele : " I do not remember that our English poets ever suffered a criminal amour to succeed on the stage till the reign of Charles II. Ever since that time the alderman is made a cuckold, the deluded virgin is debauched, and adultery and fornication are supposed to be

committed behind the scenes as part of the action."
This is Macaulay's essay in parvo. Swift knocks
his victim on the head with the identical bludgeon.

Dr. Johnson in his memoir of Congreve, dealing with the Collier controversy, falls into line with
Swift. "The cause of Congreve," he writes, "was
not tenable: whatever glosses he might use for
the defence or palliation of single passages, the
general tenour and tendency of his plays must
always be condemned. It is acknowledged with
universal conviction that the perusal of his works
will make no man better; and that their ultimate
effect is to represent pleasure in alliance with
vice, and to relax those obligations by which life
ought to be regulated." Dr. Johnson, in fact,
assumes that Congreve and his contemporaries
should have accepted the standards whereby Collier
misused them. There is nowhere in his memoir
a clear sense that no body of literature can be
intelligently approached without a careful reference
to its historical origin; or that the moral test of
the publicist may conceivably be, in the literal sense
of the word, absurd, applied to the creatures of a
poet.

In the first half of the nineteenth century some
necessary commonplaces of history and criticism
were recovered on behalf of the comic dramatists.
Leigh Hunt's edition of 1849 is the pinnacle of
their reputation. We have not only the excellent
memoirs and sound opinions of the Editor himself,
but also the essays of Hazlitt and Lamb, printed
in extenso as models of criticism. For the first
time Jeremy Collier is squarely met. Leigh Hunt

does not apologise for the comic dramatists: he
retorts upon Collier. Quoting Vanburgh's famous
saying as to Collier—that he makes debauches
in piety as sinners do in wine—Leigh Hunt
continues: "Conceive the horror of Collier at
seeing Vanbrugh saying in print that he was
really not aware of the indecencies imputed to
him, and that he could very well fancy a virtuous
woman laying his plays by the side of her Bible. . . .
Collier did not suspect that one profession might
have its privileged ' indecencies' as well as
another, and that a clergyman of those times might
be solemnly and furiously vicious—indecent for
want of the decorum of charity, and wicked for
want of charity itself. Yet we have now lived
to see that if the stage at that time was one half
licentious, in the other half it was not only innocent
of all evil intention, but had a sort of piety in the
very gaiety of its trust in nature; while Jeremy
Collier, if he was one half of him pious and well-
intentioned, was the other half little better than
a violent fool."

Leigh Hunt, in fact, has a very clear suspicion
that Collier's was not the final word as to the
comic dramatists; and he goes on to plead that
they shall at least be viewed in relation to their
period. The plea seems to us almost ridiculously
obvious to-day; in 1849 it was almost a paradox.
"Future ages," he tells the people of 1849, "will
think us perhaps more honest in some things than
we suppose we are; but most certainly they will
attribute vices, or at least barbarous follies, to us in
others of which we have no conception. . . . Yes;

and by the same token many things are done this moment, and thought very little of—nay, reckoned creditable to the wit and knowledge and conventional respectability of the doers—which two hundred years hence will be thought as immoral and ridiculous as we now think the immoralities and absurdities of the days of Charles II. And if these or some of them do not immediately present themselves to every intelligent reader's mind, it only shows how far we are gone in them, and how far we are blinded in their gulf; fortunate still, if we do but know this, that times will improve after us as well as those that have gone before us; and that those will see their own way through error best and cheerfullest who think the best and kindest of whatsoever nature has done." We shall soon see how cleverly Macaulay has seemed to accept this warning of Leigh Hunt, and how brilliantly he disregarded it.

Hazlitt attacks Collier with an equal zest, and an irony which the amiable Editor was unable to command. Hazlitt seems to have realised more clearly than any critic before or since the precise character of the injustice Collier inflicted upon the comic dramatists, and the mischief he wrought upon the English stage. "We may date the decline of English comedy," Hazlitt concludes, " from the time of Farquhar. For this several causes might be assigned in the political and moral changes of the times ; but among other minor ones, Jeremy Collier, in his view of the English stage, frightened the poets, and did all he could to spoil the stage, by pretending to reform it ; that is, by making it an echo of the pulpit; instead of a reflection of the manners of the world. He complains bitterly of the profaneness of the stage; and is for fining the actors for every oath they utter, to put an end to the practice; as if common swearing had been an invention of the poets and stage-players. He cannot endure that the fine gentlemen drink, and the fine ladies intrigue in the scenes of Congreve and Wycherley when things so contrary to law and gospel happened nowhere else. He is vehement against duelling, as a barbarous custom, of which the example is suffered with impunity nowhere but on the stage. He is shocked at the number of fortunes that are irreparably ruined by the vice of gaming on the boards of the theatres. He seems to think that every breach of the ten commandments begins and ends there. He complains that the tame husbands of his time are laughed at on the stage, and that the successful gallants triumph, which was without precedent either in the city or the court. . . . He forgets, in his over-heated zeal, two things : First, that the stage must be copied from real life, that the manners represented there must exist elsewhere, and 'denote a foregone conclusion,' to satisfy common sense ; Secondly, that the stage cannot shock common decency, according to the notions that prevail of it in any age or country, because the exhibition is public. If the pulpit, for instance, had banished all vice and imperfection from the world, as our critic would suppose, we should not have seen the offensive reflection of them on the stage, which he resents as an affront to the cloth, and an outrage on religion.

On the contrary, with such a sweeping reformation as this theory implies, the office of the preacher, as well as of the player, would be gone ; and if common peccadilloes of lying, swearing, intriguing, fighting, drinking, gaming, and other such obnoxious dramatic commonplaces, were once fairly got rid of in reality, neither the comic poet would be able to laugh at them on the stage, nor our good-natured author to consign them to damnation elsewhere."

Hazlitt here insists upon the necessity for an intelligently historical and critical point of view. Restoration comedy must be judged as an honest reflexion of contemporary manners ; it cannot be intelligently approached as a question of morality *in vacuo*, or as an hortation to be vicious by the devil's advocates. Continually, too, in reading Hazlitt's essay, we are asked to appreciate the folly of an extremely common habit of criticism. The first word of competent criticism is not yet uttered upon a piece of literature, though the last word is exhausted upon its subject and object. To say of the plays of Wycherley that they deal with the intrigues of lecherous young men and incontinent young women is perfectly true in fact ; but it is not a critical opinion. In this, as in other regards, we shall return to Hazlitt's essay when in our critical conclusions we discover that the successors of the comic dramatists of the Restoration, even when morally considered, become steadily less palatable as they become steadily less responsive to the vices and follies of the time.

Lamb's essay upon artificial comedy is one of the most delightful and characteristic of his papers.

Like Falstaff it is as well known as Paul's, but cannot for that reason be wholly omitted here. Macaulay's treatment of " Mr. Lamb" in this matter of artificial comedy is a classical study of a successfully misdirected effort. Lamb's essay is an inimitably urged plea for giving the Nonconformist conscience a rest. He throws off in brilliant paradox an accepted commonplace of criticism, namely, that the creatures of a play are not necessarily to be weighed according to the strict moral values of life, and that the critic must begin by accepting the conventions and postulates of the poet whose work he contemplates. For Charles Lamb the world of Mr. Horner and Sir Fopling is fairyland. The life into which he enters in their company bears no relation to the life he knows ; but he is imaginatively quick to accept the revolution and to delight in the manners and customs of a strange folk. This world of Mr. Horner and Sir Fopling was once the poetic reflexion of a world that actually lived and moved. It is a poetic image that has survived the dead original. "Why," ask Lamb in effect, "worry about the morality of this original, when we may enjoy the image?" Art and life, though they grow one from another, are different kingdoms. In Wycherley's *The Country Wife*, you may enjoy the adventures of Mr. Horner, though in the flesh you might steadily refuse to be acquainted.

Some lines of the essay itself are an excellent foil to the blindman vigour with which Macaulay attacked it. "The artificial comedy, or comedy of manners," says Lamb, "is quite extinct on our

stage. Congreve and Farquhar show their heads
once in seven years, only to be exploded and
put down instantly. The times cannot bear them.
Is it for a few wild speeches, an occasional
licence of dialogue? I think not altogether.
The business of their dramatic characters will
not stand the moral test; we screw everything
up to that. Idle gallantry in a fiction, a dream,
the passing pageant of an evening startles us in
the same way as the alarming indications of profligacy in a son or ward in real life should startle
a parent or guardian. We have no such middle
emotions as dramatic interests left. We see a
stage libertine playing his loose pranks of two
hours' duration, and of no after consequence, with
the severe eyes which inspect real vices with their
bearings upon two worlds. . . . All that neutral ground
of character, which stood between vice and virtue,
or which in fact was indifferent to neither, where
neither properly was called in question ; that happy
breathing place from the burthen of a perpetual
moral questioning—the sanctuary and quiet Alsatia
of hunted Casuistry—is broken up and disfranchised,
as injurious to the interests of society. The privi-
leges of the place are taken away by law. We dare
not dally with images, or names of wrong. We
bark like foolish dogs at shadows. We dread infection from the scenic representation of disorder, and
fear a painted pustule. In our anxiety that our
morality should not take cold, we wrap it up in a
great blanket surtout of precaution against breeze
and sunshine."

Note that Lamb has nowhere distinctly said that

the dramatic picture of society in the plays of the comic dramatists never had any historical connexion with the life of their time.   He merely pleads that as critics we must approach Mr. Horner and Sir Fopling in a different spirit, since these are the creatures of a poet, from that in which the moralist approaches the conduct of their originals.   We will grant Macaulay in advance that the comic plays of the Restoration were a reflexion of the morals and manners of the Restoration.   But that is no reason why the two should be critically confused.

Let the incomparable Elia describe for us his own delightful sense of escape into a world which Macaulay never really entered.   " I confess for myself," Elia continues, " that (with no great delinquencies to answer for) I am glad for a season to take an airing beyond the diocese of the strict conscience, not to live always in the precincts of the law courts, but, now and then, for a dreamwhile or so, to imagine a world with no meddling restrictions, to get into recesses whither the hunter cannot follow me—

> . . . Secret shades
> Of woody Ida's inmost grove,
> While yet there was no fear of Jove.

I come back to my cage and my restraint the fresher and more healthy for it.   I wear my shackles more contentedly for having respired the breath of an imaginary freedom.   I do not know how it is with others, but I feel the better always for the perusal of one of Congreve's—nay, why should I not add even of Wycherley's—comedies.   I am the gayer at least for it ; and I could never connect those

sports of a witty fancy in any shape with any result
to be drawn from them to imitation in real life. They
are a world of themselves, almost as much as fairyland. The Fainalls and the Mirabells, the Dorimants
and the Lady Touchwoods, in their own sphere do
not offend my moral sense ; in fact, they do not
appeal to it at all. They seem engaged in their
proper element. They break through no laws or
conscientious restraints. They know of none. They
have got out of Christendom into the land of—what
shall I call it?—of cuckoldry—the Utopia of gallantry,
where pleasure is duty, and the manners perfect freedom . . . We are not to judge them by our images.
No reverend institutions are insulted by their proceedings—for they have none among them. No
peace of families is isolated—for no family ties exist
among them. No purity of the marriage-bed is
stained—for none is supposed to have a being. No
deep affections are disquieted, no holy wedlock bonds
snapped asunder—for affection's depth and wedded
faith are not of that soil. There is neither right nor
wrong—gratitude or its opposite—claim or duty—
paternity or sonship."

In fact, as Charles Lamb might have concluded,
but did not think fit to conclude, here was a perfect
reflexion of the genius of early Restoration society.
But that historic point, on which Macaulay bases
his whole indictment of Lamb, is not really important in the critical argument with which Lamb
was concerned. Lamb was brilliantly pleading
against the habit of mind in which a whole
century of critics and playgoers had approached
the artificial comedy. In his own phrase : " We

dare not contemplate an Atlantis, a scheme out of which our coxcombical moral sense is for a little transitory ease excluded. We have not that courage to imagine a state of things for which there is neither reward nor punishment. We cling to the painful necessities of shame and blame. We would indict our very dreams." This essay, at the time of writing, as still to-day, is a perpetual necessary protest against the final reference of the poet's work to the merely sensible standards of contemporary morality. Its necessity was never more clearly shown than in Macaulay upon " Mr. Lamb."

That Leigh Hunt's edition of the comic dramatists fell to be reviewed by Macaulay is one of the tragedies of literary history. Macaulay's review undid all that the best critical intellect of his time had achieved for the reputation of English comedy. Macaulay talked sense for sensible people ; and, since he talked brilliantly as only Macaulay could, and since his wit was sharpened to the enterprise by the vigour of all his accumulated prejudices, political and sentimental, he was easily able, in the view of his contemporaries, to thrust his victims back into disrepute.

Macaulay starts, in the manner of an able advocate, granting points to the enemy with a splendidly affected generosity, that he may at a later stage of the argument fall upon him with all the more crushing effect. Macaulay has a "kindness for Mr. Leigh Hunt," and he expresses this kindness in a way that must have been extremely gratifying to the friend of Coleridge, Byron, Shelley, Keats— not to mention Hazlitt and " Mr. Lamb." Macaulay

continues : " The plays to which he (Mr. Leigh
Hunt), now acts as introducer are, with few exceptions,
such as, in the opinion of many very respectable
people, ought not to be reprinted.   In this opinion
we can by no means concur.   We cannot wish
that any work or class of work which has exercised
a great influence on the human mind, and which
illustrates the character of an important epoch in
letters, politics, and morals should disappear from
the world."

Could anything be more superbly impertinent ?
Here was a reviewer deliberately sitting down to
castigate the impurities of a body of English literature entirely from the standpoint of his personal
prejudices as to the correct conduct of contemporary
family life, and he artfully begins with a careful
demonstration of the " broadness " of his mind, and
a discreet difference of opinion with " many very
respectable people."   No one knew better than
Macaulay that this was the irresistible approach
to the hearts of his contemporaries.   Nay, is not
the attitude always with us ?   " I am not a narrow-
minded person ; but I really do draw the line
at these comic dramatists."   It is a consecrated
formula.

Virtually disclaiming the moral test as final
in this opening passage, Macaulay employs it,
in summing up, as the touchstone of his critical
estimate.   He has misunderstood the protest of
Charles Lamb and turned his thunder upon the
mists.   Macaulay should have first distinguished
between what was obviously false in Lamb's contention (if Lamb actually intended it, which is not clear,

and scarcely relevant), and what was obviously true.
If Lamb really intended to suggest that the manners
of Restoration comedy had no pattern in Restoration
life, he was wrong ; and, here, Macaulay's criticism
is pertinent and just.   The excellence of Restoration
comedy is, in fact, directly due to the honest fidelity
with which it reflects the spirit of an intensely
interesting phase of our social history.   But Lamb
would certainly have acknowledged that Macaulay,
on the historical side, was right ; nor would he
thereby have lost a jot of his argument.   " Mr.
Horner," says Charles Lamb in effect, "is a fairy."
" He is not a fairy," answers Macaulay, "he is an
impudent debauchee.   He betrays his friends and
seduces his friend's wife.   People actually behaved
like that in the time of Charles II.   Therefore Mr.
Horner is an actual live person.   We must detest
him   accordingly."   Lamb   might   simply   have
answered : " Every one, seen through the imagination of a poet, is a fairy."   To which Macaulay may
be conceived as replying : " That is a hard saying ;
please put it in terms of common sense."

The fraudulent character of Macaulay's preliminary concessions appears throughout.   He dis-
claims the moral test as final ; but he applies
none other.   He examines *The Country Wife*,
perhaps the most perfect farce in English dramatic
literature ; but he never even begins to examine it
as a critic.   His paragraph as to this play is typical
of the whole essay.   Note how throughout he deals
with the subject-matter of Wycherley's play ; not,
as a true critic would, with the play itself.   " The
only thing original about Wycherley,"—Macaulay is

writing apropos of Wycherley's indebtedness to
Molière—" the only thing which he could furnish
from his own mind in inexhaustible abundance, was
profligacy. ʃIt is curious to observe how everything
that he touched, however pure and noble, took in
an instant the colour of his own mind. Compare
the *Ecole des Femmes* with *The Country Wife*.
Agnes is a simple and amiable girl, whose heart
is indeed full of love, but of love sanctioned
by honour, morality and religion. Her natural
talents are great. They have been hidden, and, as
it might appear, destroyed by an education elaborately bad. But they are called forth into full energy
by a virtuous passion. Her lover, while he adores
her beauty, is too honest a man to abuse the confiding tenderness of a creature so charming and in-
experienced. Wycherley takes this plot into his
hands; and forthwith this sweet and graceful courtship becomes a licentious intrigue, of the lowest
and least sentimental kind, between an impudent
London rake and the idiot wife of a country squire.
We will not go into details. In truth, Wycherley's
indecency is protected against the critics as a skunk
is protected against the hunters. It is safe because
it is too filthy to handle, and too noisome to
approach." There is a good deal hereafter to be
said as to Macaulay's view of Mr. Horner as an
" impudent London rake"; and of Mrs. Pinchwife
as "the idiot wife of a country squire." How it
would have puzzled " Mr. Lamb," and how it must
have puzzled Mr. Leigh Hunt for whom " we have a
kindness," to see Macaulay rising to moral solemnity
over the doings of Wycherley's puppet-folk. All

possibility of rejoinder from either of these accomplished critics—not to mention Hazlitt—would have
been extinguished in delighted laughter.

One other point as to Macaulay's critical methods
in this essay clamours to be exposed. Just as he first
deprecates the finality of the moral test, that he may
the more effectively apply it later on ; so he begins
with an appeal for an historical treatment of the
comic dramatists, and ends by falling into the worst
blunder possible in a serious historian. He begins
by pleading that all bodies of literature must be
judged by the moral standards contemporary with
their production ; he ends by assessing the comic
dramatists in every line of his commentary by the
standards of 1849. Here again, in the trained
manner of the advocate, he is splendidly generous
to the object of his attack. " The worst English
writings of the seventeenth century," he handsomely confesses, " are decent compared with much
that has been bequeathed to us by Greece and
Rome. Plato, we have little doubt, was a much
better man than Sir George Etherege. But Plato
has written things at which Sir George Etherege
would have shuddered. Buckhurst and Sedley,
even in those wild orgies at the 'Cock' in Bond
Street, for which they were pelted by the rabble,
and fined by the Court of King's Bench, would
never have dared to hold such discourse as passed
between Socrates and Phædrus on that fine summer
day under the plane-tree, while the fountain warbled
at their feet, and the cicadas chirped overhead."
This is admirable in sentiment and expression—
a plea that as Plato must be judged at the bar

of B.C. 500, so Etherege and Wycherley must be judged at the bar of 1664. When, however, we turn to the judgments of Macaulay we find that Etherege and Wycherley are at the bar of 1849.

"The morality of *The Country Wife* and *The Old Bachelor*," says Macaulay, "is the morality, not, as Mr. Charles Lamb maintains, of an unreal world, but of a world which is a great deal too real. It is the morality, not of a chaotic people, but of low town rakes, and of those ladies whom the newspapers call 'dashing Cyprians,' and the question is simply this, whether a man of genius who constantly and systematically endeavours to make this sort of character attractive by uniting it with beauty, race, dignity, spirit, a high social position, popularity, literature, wit, taste, knowledge of the world, brilliant success in every undertaking, does or does not make an ill use of his powers. We own that we are unable to understand how this question can be answered in any way but one."

Now, the obvious implication of this passage is that the comic dramatists of the seventeenth century deliberately set themselves to corrupt the taste and morality of their generation. Macaulay assumes that they really were capable of better things; that they saw the good and systematically chose the worse. Macaulay is not regarding them as echoes or reflexions of their period. He is not judging them, even from the purely moral point of view, by the standards of their time. He instinctively conceives them as gentlemen of 1850, fully alive to the iniquity of their dealings, and deliberately pandering to the worst instincts of the period in

which they lived.   He is judging them not on the
merits they had, but on the merits he thinks they
ought to have had.   Macaulay's prejudices, moral and
political, are so ungovernably violent that he, one of
the greatest of our English chroniclers, instinctively
falls into the blunders of a prize-essayist.

Macaulay was writing for the majority.   Of the
main host of his educated generation that felt the
weight of Macaulay's logic, and delighted in
the vigour of his thrust, few could catch the more
difficult message of Hazlitt and Lamb.   Macaulay
finally determined in 1849 that, in popular estimation, the inevitable first thought as to the comic
dramatists should be of their immorality and offen-
siveness to contemporary taste.   No two writers in
the following period had better title to talk of
comedy and the comic spirit than Thackeray and,
after Thackeray, Meredith.   Both these writers go
back, almost, to the view of Johnson and Swift.

"Congreve's comic feast," says Thackeray in
his lectures on the English Humorists, "flares
with lights, and round the table, emptying their
flaming bowls of drink, and exchanging the wildest
jests and ribaldry, sit men and women, waited on
by rascally valets and attendants as dissolute as
their mistresses—perhaps the very worst company
in the world.   There does not seem to be a pretence
of morals.   At the head of the table sits Mirabell
or Bellmour (dressed in the French fashion and
waited on by English imitators of Scapin and
Frontin).   Their calling is to be irresistible, and to
conquer everywhere.   Like the heroes of the chivalry
story, whose long-winded loves and combats they

were sending out of fashion, they are always splendid
and triumphant—overcome all dangers, vanquish all
enemies, and win the beauty at the end. Fathers,
husbands, usurers are the foes these champions
contend with. . . . All this pretty morality you
have in the comedies of William Congreve Esquire.
They are full of wit. Such manners as he observes,
he observes with great humour ; but, ah ! it's a
weary feast, that banquet of wit where no love is.
It palls very soon ; sad indigestions follow it, and
lonely blank headaches in the morning."

This is the criticism of Steele, Swift, and Johnson in the manner of Thackeray. Nor is Meredith less uncritical. He falls upon Lamb directly.
" Elia," he writes in the Essay on Comedy, " whose
humour delighted in floating a galleon paradox
and wafting it as far as it would go, bewails the
extinction of our artificial comedy, like a poet
sighing over the vanished splendour of Cleopatra's
Nile barge, and the sedateness of his plea for a
cause condemned even in his time to the penitentiary
is a novel effect of the ludicrous." The fan behind
which " ladies present in the theatre retired at a
signal of decorum," Meredith elsewhere continues,
may be regarded as " the flag and symbol of the
society giving us our so-called Comedy of Manners,
or Comedy of the Manners of South Sea Islanders
under city veneer ; and as to comic idea vacuous
as the mask without the face behind it."

Yet Meredith himself has diagnosed the disease of which he is, in these passages, conspicuously a victim. The inflamed Puritan conscience
of which, in this matter of the comic dramatists,

Jeremy Collier, despite his nonjuring politics, and
Lord Macaulay, despite his decorous whiggery, are
the champions and historical indices, is the explanation of the reputation in which Congreve, Wycherley,
Vanbrugh, and Farquhar are held to-day. To quote
the words of Meredith himself, perverting their
intention, " our tenacity of natural impressions has
caused the word ' theatre ' . . . to prod the Puritan
nervous system like a Satanic instrument ; just as
one has known anti-Papists, for whom Smithfield
was redolent of a sinister smoke, as though they
had a later recollection of the place than the lowing
herds. Hereditary puritanism, regarding the stage,
is met, to this day, in many families quite undis-
tinguished by arrogant piety. It has subsided
altogether as a power in the profession of morality ;
but it is an error to suppose it extinct, and [here,
of course, Meredith separates himself from the contentions of this book] unjust also to forget that it
had once good reason to hate, shun, and rebuke our
public shows."

These critical preliminaries will, perhaps, have
suggested the necessary gap to be filled in an
account of the comic dramatists. First, it is due
to their reputation that we view them—as Macaulay
professed, but neglected, to do—historically. What
sort of men were they in the face of their period?
Is their work a true mirror of life as they followed
it ? Is there anything spiritually of value in the
truths that they wrested from the passing of their
generation, and moulded imperishably in their art ?
Second, what is the literary value of those masterpieces of comedy they have left us, viewed, not

after the criteria of the publicist, but according to
the laws of imagination ?   Hazlitt and Lamb knew
and tested the work for themselves ; and left their
impressions where we may to-day recapture them.
But are we æsthetically, or even morally—for,
though it is not the final test by which the works
of the imagination are to be viewed, we are not
going to shirk the moral issue—justified in accepting Hazlitt and Lamb in the teeth of the giants—
Johnson and Swift, Thackeray and Meredith ?
Have we, as a nation, consistently misjudged the
comic dramatists owing to an inflamed " Puritan
nervous system," or is their degradation in the
popular mind due to a deeper falsehood in their
work than Jeremy Collier was able to discover ?
In a word, is all that they wrote palpably a lie ?—
false to the truths that go deeper than the pulpit
fashions of this or that particular generation ?   Was
it a legitimate defence, or mere ruffling blasphemy,
when Captain Vanbrugh said of his plays that he
could fancy a virtuous woman laying them by the
side of her prayer-book ?

CHAPTER II

THE LIFE AND LETTERS OF SIR GEORGE ETHEREGE

THIRTY years ago it was possible to say of Sir George Etherege, as Lord Rosebery said of Shelburne, that he was one of the suppressed characters of English history. But in 1883 Mr. Edmund Gosse published his *Seventeenth Century Studies*. Some one had happily re-discovered for Mr. Gosse in the British Museum a manuscript letter - book containing drafts of over a hundred letters from Etherege while he was ambassador at Ratisbon in the service of King James. This letter - book, like Etherege himself, seems somehow to have been mislaid from the time it was used by Macaulay for his *History*, and reclaimed by Mr. Gosse for his *Seventeenth Century Studies*. The contemporaries of Etherege were fully aware of his literary importance, both as the founder of a new school of English comedy, and the first prose stylist of his day. The Kit-cat critics of the early eighteenth century cherished his reputation; and Hazlitt celebrated him as the first in date of the comic dramatists. But in the period after Macaulay Etherege was almost entirely lost; and the first complete edition of his plays did not appear until Mr. A. W. Verity introduced them in 1888. It is

difficult to be sufficiently astonished at this neglect.
Etherege is historically more important than Dryden
in three ways, only one of which really concerns us
here. He was the first English dramatic author to
substitute the heroic couplet for blank verse; he
was as a prose writer the necessary link between
the architectural and euphuist styles of the early
seventeenth century and the nimble essayists of the
eighteenth; he was the actual founder of the English
comedy of manners.

Literary importance apart, there is a further significance in the life and character of Sir George
Etherege. He was typically a figure of the time.
It is extremely important that we should as soon
and as intimately as possible realise the habit of
thought and of temperament in which the comedy of
manners was formed and developed. Happily we
may with advantage pause, in this regard, upon the
first portrait of our selected gallery. Sir George
Etherege was a familiar of the Court: he was
personally acquainted with the politicians and the
wits; with the men of affairs and of fashion; with
all that was best and worst in the life of his time.
Moreover, he is, of all the men with whom we are
in this volume to deal, the most accessible to our
fancy. It is true that many details, precious to the
formal biographer, are lacking. We know neither
where nor when precisely he was born; the date
and circumstances of his death have yet to be discovered; we must rely upon mere literary gossip to
determine his parentage, education, fortunes, and
achievements up to the time of the publication of
his first play; when and whom he married is a

problem ; when and how he entered diplomacy is
mysterious. But, what is more important, we do
know how and upon what topics he wrote to his
friends ; what his amusements were ; what books
he was in the habit of reading ; how he bore himself, as an English gentleman, in a difference with
Lady Etherege, or with the burgher precisians of
Ratisbon. Dryden is but a mythical figure beside
the living personality of Etherege as revealed for us
in his correspondence, and in the notes of Oldys
and of Gildon.

Etherege was born in 1635 or 1636. "About
the year 1636," Oldys says ; and Dryden addresses
him at Ratisbon in 1686 :

> To you who live in chill degree,
> As map informs, of fifty-three,
> And do not much for cold atone,
> By bringing thither fifty-one.

The arithmetic is conclusive. Gildon and Oldys
between them derive Etherege from an Oxfordshire
family ; place him at Cambridge University ; and
afterwards put him to law at the Inns of Court.
We may believe as much of this as pleases us.
Gossip aside, the documentary story is blank, prior
to the production of *Love in a Tub*, in 1664. It
would seem that at about thirty years of age
Etherege was an unknown man of uncertain profession ; possibly of good family ; probably of good
means ; and certainly with a personal knowledge of
Paris, and of French contemporary literature.
Other fixed points of his career are that his three
comedies were successively produced in 1664, 1667,

and 1676 ; that in 1676 he brawled at Epsom with Rochester, and had to go into hiding from the law ; that he was knighted and married somewhere about 1680 ; that in 1685 he went for King James II. as English Envoy to Ratisbon ; that he absconded to Paris at the Revolution ; and that in February, 1690, he was only recently dead. These are the dry bones.

In December, 1687, Etherege wrote home to England : " I wear flannel, sir ; therefore pray talk to me no more of poetry " ; and in this same letter we read : " Here are two very handsome young ladies ; but their unconscionable price is marriage. Nevertheless, were I as capable of a belle passion as some at my age, they would cost me many a billet, and much time in tying my cravat at 'em ; but I cannot think of laying a siege, wanting a stock of things necessary to carry it on, and strength sufficient to maintain the place in case I should take it." Men of the Restoration were old at fifty ; and Etherege is past the racket of his prime when first we come to know him. His years are for him a melancholy subject. In March, '87, he writes to the Lord Chamberlain : " The pleasure you have given me makes me forgive the malice you have showed in reminding me of my being old." But his philosophy was equal to his need. In September, 1687, he writes to an unknown correspondent : " J'étais peripatetique et j'aimais le promenade, mais tout d'un coup je suis devenu disciple d'Epicure. Je me tiens dans ma petite retraite et je me suis établi pour maxime que la plus grande volupté consiste dans une parfaite santé. Le transport d'un débauche ne

paye pas le mal au cœur qu'on sent le lendemain
au matin."

Etherege grows old more gracefully than might
be expected of the companion of Rochester and
Sedley, men who, in his mischievously ironical
phrase, "have by long experience of the frailties
of the sex almost acquired a perfect chastity."
Etherege had a horror of the vices of age. " Let
us take care," he writes to Mr. Grey in October,
1687, "that our years do not sour us with any
of the common vices of age. Let us still preserve our good humour and our good nature to
make us welcome near those young people who
possess that plentifully which we have pretty well
run out of." A little later he writes to an unknown correspondent : " The women need not rail
at our changing. Few of us have the gift to be
constant to ourselves. Sir C. S. (Charles Sedley)
sets up for good hours and sobriety. My Lord D.
(Dorset) has given over variety and shuts himself
up within my lady's arms." The mournful ring is
perceptible here, as also in Etherege's warning to
my Lord Arran against too much ardour in marriage :
" That sort of courage is a little too violent for the
present purpose. The business that you have now
on your hands is to be spun out in length, and not
to be ended at once."

The reflective resignation of these passages is
indirectly a light upon the period. When the man
of pleasure has the conscience of the community
against him he cannot quite so decently grow old.
The letters of Etherege are those of a man at one
with his time—his conscience unpricked. He is

the perfect man of his particular world. Neither
Etherege, nor the society in which he moved,
was troubled with conviction of sin. Reading the
letters of his mellow years, we begin to understand
the Eulogy of Bishop Burnet upon Rochester,
and the habitual attendance of Queen Mary at
the play.

The first manner of Restoration Comedy was
formed at the moment when Etherege was fre-
quenting the Mulberry Garden, the ordinaries and
the playhouse with Rochester and Dorset. These
men were of a lazy, indifferent world; "Gentle"
George and "Easy" Etherege was the author of
Sir Fopling Flutter. The adjectives are an illu-
mination upon the Court of Charles II. Where his-
torians have seen a national reaction against the
severities of the Puritans bursting ferociously forth
in 1660, it seems more reasonable to assume that
there gradually emerged in the period between
1660 and 1700 a *fin de siècle* spirit in letters and
society—a spirit which found nothing exception-
able in the career of Sir George Etherege; that
allowed him to grow in honour and in years without misgiving; and, in his flannel days, to write
in the untroubled manner of the letters we have
quoted.

Let us, for the moment, turn for light to a
diagnosis of Etherege's most celebrated quality—
his laziness. In February, 1687, he writes back
to Dryden: "You know I am no flatterer, and,
therefore, will excuse me when I tell you I cannot
endure you should arrogate a thing to yourself you
have not the least pretence to. Is it not enough

you should excel in so many eminent virtues, but
you must be putting in for a vice which all the
world knows is properly my province? If you
persist in your claim to laziness, you will be
thought as affected in it as Montaigne is when
he complains of the want of memory. What soul
has ever been more active than your own? . . . I
(whose every action of my life is a witness of my
idleness) little thought that you who have raised
so many immortal monuments of your industry durst
have set up to be my rival. But to punish you I
will distinguish. You have no share of that noble
laziness of the mind which all I write makes out my
just title to; but as for that of the body, I can let
you come in for a snack without any jealousy."

It was precisely this "noble laziness of the
mind" which determined the quality and temper
of Restoration Society. Here King Charles II. was
supreme. An interesting monograph might be
written of the effect upon policy and administration
of the "noble laziness" of Charles II. The young
prince, like Prynne of *Histriomastix*,

> So strangely tossed
> From pillar to post,

had come home not so much intending to be wicked
as intending to rest. Idleness is the keyword of the
Restoration. Charles roused himself by fits and
starts, making sudden and unexpected incursions
into policy. Sometimes he showed an energetic
preference for a friend or a mistress. But, as a rule,
he accepted his women as he accepted his policy—
to avoid the energy of refusing. Moreover, there
was something of the camp or bivouac about the

Court of Charles. The days of his adventuring left their mark upon him, and upon the friends of his exile. Their readiness to take what life had to offer at the moment was the legacy of nomad years upon the continent. It was the spirit that returned with Charles rather than the conditions which he found in England upon his arrival, that determined the so-called "excesses" of the period. They were excesses of the camp—of a camp of witty, intellectual captains taking their ease between stricken fields. Though Charles was resolved not to go again upon his travels, his conduct and temperament were by habit those of a man ready to do so at a moment's necessity. Men of the Restoration took what was offered with a cheerful indifference. The spirit abroad was opportunist. Religion was opportune; philosophy and manners were opportune. Etherege was the perfect opportunist, which explains why he was able to grow old without losing his character, and turn from playwriting to diplomacy in middle life. For Etherege and his friends pleasure was a wise young man. They based their conduct upon inclination; and squared religion and morality with life of the twenty-four hours. There was never in English history a time when the conscience of society was more at ease; when precept and practice were so clearly connected. To this is due what merit we shall discover in the comedy that sprang to life in these years; and it faded almost as soon as the connexion was broken.

But it is scarcely reasonable to base these contentions upon a single passage from a single letter of a single gentleman who knew the King who was himself the glass of fashion. The turn of Wycherley and of Congreve—heirs of the Restoration—will come in due course to be considered from this point of view. We have yet to be better acquainted with Sir George Etherege.

Like Congreve and Wycherley, Sir George Etherege regarded his plays as the accidental fruit of his leisure. It was an affectation of the time that life itself was casual, entered in a fit of absent-mindedness, and thrown off with apology. Charles II.'s dying speech could only have been uttered or invented in the late seventeenth century. It was one of those startling affectations that suddenly throw into relief the social attitude of a period. One of the amusing features of post-Collier criticism has been the solemn discussion by essayists and monographers as to whether the plays of Wycherley were really a freak of his youth, as he stubbornly maintained. This point will be noticed more particularly in a later chapter, as will Congreve's splendid affectation in the celebrated meeting with Voltaire that he was prouder of his reputation as an English gentleman than as a dramatic author. The point for emphasis here is that Congreve and Wycherley, like Sir George Etherege, were—or affected to be—amateurs. They wrote plays in the idle fashion of the period in precisely the same spirit in which they understood an equipage, or tied a riband.

Sir George Etherege, as is fitting in the man nearest the Court of Charles II., was reputed the idlest poet of his time. *Love in a Tub* was produced in 1664. Etherege was silent for three years,

and then wrote *She would if She could.* His next
play, *Sir Fopling Flutter,* followed upon an eight
years' interval; and it was his last. Yet he was
immensely popular with the wits, and continually
urged to write again. In 1675 Rochester addressed
him—

> Now Apollo had got gentle George in his eye,
> And frankly confessed that, of all men that writ,
> There's none had more fancy, sense, judgment, and wit,
> But, i' the crying sin, idleness, he was so hardened
> That his long seven years' silence was not to be pardoned.

Ten years later Lord Middleton wrote to Etherege
at Ratisbon: "Every week there are plays at
Court. The last time *Sir Fopling* appeared with
the usual applause, and the King was pleased to
tell me that he expected you should put on your
socks." But Etherege knew, better than his
critics, that to force his muse would be fatal.
It throve upon idleness. To do easily was to
do well. It was fundamental in the comic
dramatists that they should be amateurs, affecting
that their plays were to be numbered as among
their more frivolous escapades. Moreover they
had a sense of proportion, only very thinly disguised in the general interchange of eulogy that
marks the period. They were coxcombs of life,
and knew it was in their character to be so; but
they were not literary coxcombs. They had too
severe a literary conscience and too fine an ear
for the ring of an English phrase. At the time
Middleton was writing to Etherege that the King
desired of him a successor to *Sir Fopling,* Etherege
was writing to Dryden: " Though I have not been

able formerly to forbear playing the fool in verse
and prose, I have now judgment enough to know
how much I ventured, and am rather amazed at my
good fortune than vain upon a little success; and
did I not see my own error, the commendation you
give me would be enough to persuade me of it."

The slender output of Sir George Etherege and
his affected indifference to the glories of authorship
are entirely in character with the time. Cursed,
or gifted, with that noble laziness of the mind which
forbade him to take life seriously, he had, at any
rate, a sufficiently clear sense of style and proportion,
not to attach to his artificial reflexion of life the
importance which he refused to life itself.

Etherege seldom writes of religion; but, when
he does so, his references wonderfully illumine the
indifference of the time to fundamental questions.
We begin to understand why Charles II. was the
friend of Penn—almost ready to sacrifice his security
for a declaration of indulgence. " I have ever enjoyed a liberty of opinion in matters of religion,"
writes Etherege in December, 1667. "'Tis indifferent to me whether there be any other man in the
world who thinks as I do. This makes me have
no temptation to talk of the business; but quietly
follow the light within me. I leave that to them
who were born with the ambition of becoming
prophets or legislators." " The light within "
Sir George Etherege was the unassisted flesh.
His was the temperament that would never per-
secute. To make of the world a proselyte would
be entirely repugnant to his indifference or aphasia
of the spirit. In the same year Etherege wrote

of the battle between the Hind and the Panther :
" Let them go and turn the churches into what
beasts they please, I shall never turn my religion
which teaches me to be always obedient and faithful
to the King my master." It is curious to notice
how the friends of Charles II. bore the ascendency
of his brother. James II.'s "principles," religious
and political, were one of the death blows of the
opportune, single-hearted Erastianism in which the
comedies of Etherege and the philosophy of Hobbes
had flourished. In a letter of February, 1687,
which Dryden wrote to Etherege at Ratisbon,
we are able to measure the dismay with which
this revolution of attitude at Court was received.
Dryden was writing from virtual retirement ; but
he is keenly conscious of the change. " I cannot
help hearing," he writes, "that white sticks change
their masters, and that officers of the army are
not immutable in their places because the King
finds they will not vote for him in the next session.
Oh, that our monarch would encourage noble
idleness by his example, as he of blessed memory
did before him ; for my mind misgives me he will
not much advance his affairs by stirring."

Upon the "easiness" of Etherege and his contemporaries in affairs of sex it is scarcely necessary
to insist. Accepting the apologies of Mr. Boyle
in May, 1687, for a long silence, Etherege writes :
"I need not tell you I am good-natured. I who
forgive so many mistresses who have been false
to me can well forgive a friend who has only been
negligent." What, indeed, was there for Etherege
to forgive in these so many mistresses ? The

society in which he moved had no horror of promiscuous exogamy.   The jealous husband is
ridiculous in the plays of the earlier comic dramatists
not so much because he is a husband as because
he is jealous. Jealousy is the necessary product
of a society in which monogamy is a moral standard ;
but at this time the monogamous instinct was in
abeyance.   Restoration literature—had it taken
a publicist or philosophic turn—would have
abounded in the distinction, of which we hear so
much to-day, between the impersonal needs and
instincts of sex, and the personal relations of
friendship. Charles II. was the very good friend
of Mrs. Palmer. He made her a Duchess, because
he liked her. Incidentally Mrs. Palmer was also
his mistress.   But so much less important were her
relations with Charles from this point of view that
he winked with complete indifference at her
notorious infidelities. Men and women of the
Restoration saw nothing sacred or romantic in the
act of sex, and this has been taken to imply that
friendship and the bonds of honour did not exist
among them.   The assumption is impertinent.
Those who cannot for Elia's dreamwhile forget that
sexual pleasure is abominable, unless it be tem-
pered with exalted sentiments and a keen spiritual
delight of the parties in each other's society, will of
course be too profoundly disgusted with the morality
reflected in the plays we are about to discuss liberally
to enjoy them. But to understand the morality of our
comic writers we must discard this habit of approach.
We must entirely be rid of the idea that the comic
dramatists were susceptible to the sentiments proper

to a well-conducted monogamous society. When
Etherege "falls in love," he is not necessarily
contemplating a union of hearts, an exchange of
sentiments, a comparison of ideas, a lifetime of
social and intellectual conversation ; but something
very much simpler, and, for him, entirely dissociated. Nor does he require any of the monopolies or sanctities inherent in the Victorian idea
of marriage as an exalted ceremony of conveyance.
He makes no proprietary claims upon his mistress.
His doctrine is the doctrine of tenancy or possession.
This doctrine may be less commendable absolutely
than that by which Collier and Macaulay have
measured it. But the detached historian must be
rid of prejudice. For him the doctrine of Etherege
is neither better nor worse. It is simply different.
Charles II. kept his regard and affection for Mrs.
Palmer as a friend quite distinct from his "love"
for her as a mistress. This does not necessarily
mean that Charles was a brutal sensualist incapable
of loyalty. Charles had some very fine sentiments
indeed ; but he did not take them to bed.

Etherege at Ratisbon accepted his duties as
Resident in the true spirit of a gentleman of the
Restoration—precisely as he accepted his religion
and his morality. The opportunist temper that
looked no further than obvious, insistent things
immediately plunged him into international politics,
and gave him a craftsman's interest in his despatches. He encountered his duties as a matter
of course—in the same spirit with which his friends
had packed aboard to fight De Ruyter though they
were unable to tell the jib from the main sheet.

Once in the business, they carried it through in the style of a dashing amateur—as they wrote their plays, or caballed against the Parliament. Etherege despised the people who took their politics seriously, just as he would have despised his friends had they taken seriously their feats of gallantry in the war or in Mulberry Garden. "The business of the diet," he writes home from Ratisbon, " is only fit to entertain those insects in politics who crawl under the trees in St. James' Park";—and in October, 1687, he fears he "may return into England well enough accomplished to be admitted to walk with Mr. Spicer and Mr. Vandebendy and the rest of that wise company who never talk of any affairs but such as do not concern them."

But just as Etherege need not exaggerate his literary importance in order to write good plays ; so his contempt of busy-bodies did not preclude his writing very excellent despatches. His are the sentiments of the perfect amateur. "This was a fine place," he writes to Sunderland in May, 1687, "to correct the laziness of my nature. But yet you have not quite lost your aim. The sense I have of your benefits has so spurred me up that I have twice a week given the best account I have been able to do of what has passed in the Empire, which begins to beget in me such a relish of business that I should be more vain of making a good despatch than of writing a witty letter." A good despatch or a witty letter—it is immaterial. This sudden bracketing as things of equal value, the small with the great, is an open window upon the period. They *were* of equal value. The important thing is the present and the urgent thing which fills the hour; and should be well undertaken as a matter of personal honour. "Nature no more intended me for a politician," Etherege writes to Dryden in a letter already quoted, "than she did you for a courtier. But since I am embarked, I will endeavour not to be wanting in my duty."

A little further in the same letter we read: "The conversation I have here with ministers improves me more in philosophy than in policy, and shows me that the more necessary part of it is better to be learned in the wide world than in the Gardens of Epicurus." Alas, for Etherege at Ratisbon! Life in the London he frequented was entirely in the Garden of Epicurus. Though we have so little direct evidence as to the pursuits and manner of the life of Etherege in England, we are able clearly to picture it from his letters of exile. Etherege at a blow was transferred from a society which he knew and understood to a town where all was antipodes. The life of Etherege among the earnest, religious, well-conducted, ceremonious, plain-dealing citizens of Ratisbon is a comedy of manners ready-made for an author that had the gift to use it. His friends scarcely knew to what they had condemned him. Middleton writes in November, 1685, "I hope in a little time we may hear of your diversions as well as your business, which would be much pleasanter and perhaps as instructive. I can tell you for your comfort that this place is as dull as your diet. The young fellows you left here are so unlike you that they have neither had vigour enough to afford scandal nor wit enough to invent any."

Meantime, Etherege, the life and soul of the wits of
the Mulberry Garden, was freezing to death, body
and mind, among the offended, sullen burghers of
Ratisbon, who wondered what sort of King's envoy
was this that had come among them.   In an early
letter to Sunderland, December, 1685, he has already
measured his misfortunes.   "Is it not enough to
breed an ill habit of body in a man who was used
to sit up till morning, to be forced, for want of
knowing what to do with himself, to go to bed
in the evening ?   One who has been used to see
his friends with all freedom never to approach anybody but with ceremony ; instead of rattling about
the streets to seek variety of company, to sit at
home and entertain himself with solitude and
silence ?   If I do well after all this, you must
allow me to be a great philosopher ; and I dare
affirm Cato left not the world with more firmness of
soul than I did England."

    The persistent nostalgia of Etherege's letters
home is a sustained note of this correspondence.   He lives again the life with Rochester
and Sedley.   "There is not a day," he writes to
Corbet in April, 1687, "but my thoughts dog
you from the coffee house to the play. . . .
Some of the ancients have imagined that the
greatest possible torment of the dead was an impatient longing after what they delighted most
in while they were living, and I can swear by my
damnation in Germany this hell is no jesting
matter."   Later in the same year he writes to Mr.
Cooke, his home-thoughts quicker for the approach
of Christmas : "You can do no less than pity me

A BIRD'S-EYE VIEW OF COVENT GARDEN IN 1720.

Engraved by Sutton Nichols.

who have been forced from the shores of delightful
Thames to be confined to live on the banks of the
unwholesome Danube, where we have been this
month choked with fogs, and cannot now set foot
out of doors without being up to the knees in snow.
. . . It is not much out of season to wish you a
merry Christmas and as good a stomach to the plum
broth as an old servant of my grandfather had,
whose only grace all the good time was, God love
me as I love plumpottage."

So far we have quoted entirely from Etherege's
despatches copied into the MS. letter-book of his
secretary. Before parting with this valuable collection of documents we have yet to tell the story
of Julia, the beautiful German comédienne who
came to Ratisbon in 1686, and furiously embroiled
Etherege with the town. The fullest account of
this adventure is given, not by Etherege himself,
but by his secretary. It seems that when Etherege
fled to France in 1688, he neglected to pay his
secretary the full sum to which he was entitled.
Seeing that Etherege absconded in such haste
that even his precious books were abandoned, it
was probably his extreme necessity that left the
account uncleared. The secretary, at any rate,
set about getting the money from the Government
at home. He wrote home an ill-feeling report of
his master's doings in Ratisbon, intended to show
how scandalously Etherege had used him, also calculated to please ministers anxious to hear the worst
of a Jacobite. What the precise facts are as to Julia
is not entirely clear. Mr. Edmund Gosse hopes that
Etherege's relations with her were entirely correct.

Is the problem of her perfect chastity important? Quite conceivably Julia was melted. "The best adventure I have had here," Etherege himself writes in February, 1688, "has been with a comédienne no less handsome and no less kind in Deutschland than Mrs. Johnson in England." And a month later Etherege tells Mr. Jepson: "I am just now going to a ball where there will be a great many and some pretty young women, though to tell you the truth, I have of late lived as chaste as my Lady Etherege. The best fortune I have had here has been a player something handsomer and as much a jilt as Mrs. Barry." This is distinctly ominous. Tradition has obstinately presented Mrs. Barry with a child by Etherege.

But the point is trivial. The offence of Etherege in the eyes of Ratisbon was his open entertainment, innocent or otherwise, of a player; his obvious good-fellowship and delight in her company. He was already unpopular. Etherege was not a very successful drinker, whereas the burghers of Ratisbon were the finest topers in the world. Etherege was unable to keep the pace. His secretary tells us how he spent a night dead drunk in the streets of the Hague, disgraceful in the King's envoy no doubt. But, as always, the secretary has missed the point. Etherege was despised not for his drinking or for being drunk; but for his incapacity to hold an honourable quantity of liquor. Another cause of his unpopularity was his partiality for the French. As King's envoy he should undoubtedly have distributed his favours equally between the embassies. But Etherege

disliked the Germans (it was a mutual antipathy);
he loved the French. In 1687 he wrote home
as to these same charges of the Secretary: "I
am taxed," he said, "for being of the French
faction. . . . All the accounts I have given of
affairs unto England . . . show that I have behaved
myself according to my instructions, with all the
impartiality imaginable. If I have visited the Count
de Crecy more than the Emperor's ministers, it is
because I was admitted without ceremony, which
is the plague of this place, there being scarce any
other house here where I could enjoy my freedom
and find any diversion." For Etherege French was
his native idiom. His perfect knowledge of French
manners, the French books of his library, his minute
acquaintance with contemporary public characters
of Paris, show that much of his early life had been
spent in France. Probably in 1664 when he came
into our literary history with the production of
Love in a Tub he was fresh from Paris. In Ratisbon,
at any rate, his friends were of the French embassy;
and the Germans resented it.

Their opportunity came in 1686 with the arrival
of Julia. Etherege was used to the society of the
Bettertons, friends of the King, polite and esteemed
companions. He did not realise that players in
Germany were entirely on another level in public
estimation. Ratisbon incredulously heard that the
English envoy had called upon Julia in his coach,
and was dining her at the official residence. The
secretary's bitter story of this affair, as his account
of Sir George's riotous and wicked life generally, is
full of amusing detail; but the task of picking his

evident falsehood from the truth, and of correcting
his bias, would lead us too far for the purposes of
this chapter.

Here, however, is the tale of her first arrival :
" Amongst a company of strawlers," the secretary
writes, "lately come hither from Nuremberg (under
the name of comedians), there happened to be one
woman who seemed to have something of grace in
her face, though none in her manners.   She had not
been here many days before his Excellency, Sir G. E.,
intending to forestall the rest of the ministers in
paying the honour due to her character (of an arrant
whore), was civilly pleased to send his steward to
make her a compliment and to desire audience
(which is the only kind he has hitherto had). . . .
He gently proposed that without any cavil or con-
testation they should presently proceed to name a
place—*ad designandos limites* (as France and the
Empire had done some days before).   'The Whale-
fish' (a petty little alehouse) where she lodged was
pitched upon for one, and his Excellency's house for
another.   They lost no time in this negotiation ; for
either he sent his coach to fetch her, or went himself to her lodgings, where he would make his coach
wait on her for whole nights, and most of the day, for
fear (as it were), that the town should not come to
the knowledge of the scandal.   She was so bare in
clothes as his Excellency was in money and credit
at that time, which made him pawn his watch to
buy her a new suit.   The Jew who had it was afraid
of the bargain, and, therefore, showed it in many
places, till at last the whole town come to ring of
it.   But he was so far from being concerned with

what any one said that sometimes, after the play was ended, he has put her into his coach before all the company, notwithstanding all the giggling and hissing of the Austrian ladies and of the Minister's wives and daughters, himself humbly walking home on foot."

Several closely written pages of the letter-book continue the story. The secretary, without being in the least aware of it, gives any one who cares to disentangle the truth, a vivid picture of the Restoration gentleman in difficulties. Etherege stuck to his comrade, though the town literally roared for her extrusion. Once, while she was dining with Etherege at his home, an unmannerly crowd, in a rage of propriety, surrounded the house and bellowed for her to be thrown out. Etherege armed his servants ; beat off the rioters ; and took home the comédienne in his coach with flambeaux and musketoon : " So they continued on," says the secretary (who kept out of the battle), "some crying one thing, and some another ; but all with one voice agreed in this : *that great was the Diana of the English Envoy.*"

Henceforth Etherege was snubbed and insulted wherever he went. The secretary, as an instance of the contempt in which he was held, describes a public dinner to which Sir George had been invited : " One person being left to keep Sir George in discourse, the rest of the company sat down at table, and reserved only a place for one. Sir George approaching and thinking to sit down, the other without ceremony seized the place leaving Sir George noun substantive. To expose him the more the Anhalt Minister, whom he had abused,

asked him faintly to sit down ; but without any
further care of him they fell to it, all strutting and
stretching to kept him out, when otherwise they
could have made place enough for half a dozen
more."

Sir George, in spite of his secretary's assertion
that he told the people " upbraidingly " that he
could find a supper at home, kept his temper and
his manners in almost impossible circumstances.
This is clearly shown in a letter to the Baron de
Sensheim, a leader of the attack upon his house.

" MONSIEUR,
        " J'estois surpris d'apprendre que ce jolli
gentilhomme travesti en Italien hier au soir estoit
Le Baron de Sensheim.   Je ne savois pas que les
honnêtes gens se mêloint avec des lacquays
ramassés pour faire les fanfarons et les batteurs
des pavés.   Si vous avez quelque chose à me dire
faites la moy (scavoir) comme vous devez, et ne vous
amusez plus à venir insulter mes domestiques ni
ma maison.   Soyez content que vous l'avez échappé
belle, et ne retournez plus chercher les récompenses
de cettes follies.   Pour vos beaux compagnons j'ay
des autres mesures à garder avec eux.
                        " GEO. ETHEREGE."

Julia was privately warned by the magistrates of
Ratisbon to leave the town.   She went to Nuremberg.   If we may believe the secretary, a town
council was immediately called to deal with this
serious domestic crisis, and Julia was decreed to the
Zuchthaus.   Etherege was furious, setting out at

once for Nuremberg. Whereupon the frightened
elders of the city released Julia. Etherege, who
seems at this point only to have cared for asserting
his dignity and Julia's privilege, first thought of
coaching her triumphantly back into Ratisbon by
way of establishing a principle. Probably Julia
objected. Etherege saw her safely lodged in the
suburb of Bayrischenhoff, and, as a matter of
courtesy, paid her one or two formal visits (even
the secretary admits they were merely " out of
formality and for fashion's sake "). It was a public
assertion of victory.

Only in a life of Etherege, yet to be written in
English, would it be possible to do perfect justice
to the wealth of material in the MS. letter-book.
Apart from the letters of Sir George, rich in politics
as in character, the secretary's account of his master,
as a model .essay in misunderstanding, would, in
itself, justify a printed transcription by a careful
editor. But the letter-book must here be left to
repose among the archives of the British Museum
till an editor be found to introduce it to the public
with its store of literary and historical matter
cursively explained. We close it upon two short
letters which can scarcely be omitted in a study of
Etherege, however brief.

It seems that my Lady Etherege heard of the
comédienne, and wrote in anger to Sir George.
The letter drew from her husband the following reply:

" MY LADY,
          " I beg your pardon for undertaking to
advise you. I am so well satisfied by your last

letter of your prudence and judgment that I shall
never more commit the same error. I wish there
were copies of it in London, that it might serve as a
pattern to modest wives to write to their husbands ;
you shall find me so careful hereafter how I offend
you that I will no more subscribe myself your
loving, since you take it ill, but—madame, y^r most
dutiful husband,

"G. E."

Polite anger could scarcely have to it a finer
edge.

Our second letter was written to Betterton, the
actor—an excellent foil to the scenes in Ratisbon.
Etherege writes to the Bettertons as to the polite
friends of his leisure :

" To Betterton (the player). A poor man, who
has lost the enjoyment of his friends and the
pleasures of London, ought to have all the means
he can to divert his chagrin and pass away the
time as easy as is possible ; in order to [do] this I am
often forced to trouble my acquaintance in England,
and I do not doubt but you will forgive me making
bold with you among the rest. I have three in
my family who now and then give me a little music ;
they play very well and at sight, and we have all
the operas, and I have a correspondent at Paris,
who sends me what is new there. If you could do
me the favour to procure me some of the best com-
positions with the several parts, and let them be
given to Dr. Wynne at my Lord Middleton's office,
he will take care to send them to me. I shall

esteem myself much obliged to you for this courtesy, and your kindness will be greater if now and then you give me an account of the stage, and of other matters which (you shall judge) I will be glad to hear of. You will not mistake if you have the same opinion you had of me formerly, for I assure you I am not changed in my inclination, and can never be otherwise than, etc. *My humble service to Mrs. Betterton.*"

Closing the letter-book, we turn to a source almost as inaccessible to the general reader. Dryden wrote to Etherege in 1687 : " I will never enter the lists in prose with the undoubted best author of it which our nation has produced." We have had little opportunity from the scraps already cited to test this apparently extravagant opinion. Happily Oldys has preserved for us in the *Biographia Britannica* two long letters of Etherege written from Ratisbon to the Duke of Buckingham. From their perfection of manner and their accurate reflexion of the time they are worth fully as much to a modern reader as the plays. They explain, better than reams of critical discourse, the society of the Restoration and the comedy of Congreve. Undoubtedly these letters should have been included in the excellent edition of the works of Etherege introduced by Mr. A. W. Verity in 1888. They cannot here be transcribed without disastrous abridgment ; for they would prolong this chapter as far again. But to omit a transcription of their livelier passages would be neglecting our most precious opportunity.

The first letter was written to the Duke of

Buckingham at the time of his retirement into
Yorkshire. Etherege hearing the news is re-
minded of the Emperor Charles V. who " amidst
all his African laurels and Gallic triumphs freely
divested himself of the Empire of Europe." He
continues : " Is it possible that your Grace, who
has seen ten times more luxury than that Emperor
ever knew, conversed with finer women, kept
politer company, possessed as much too of the
true real greatness of the world as ever he enjoyed,
should in an age still capable of pleasure, and
under a fortune whose very ruins would make a comfortable Electorate here in Germany ; is it possible,
I say, that your Grace should leave the play at the
beginning of the fourth act, when all the spectators
are in pain to know what will become of the hero,
and what mighty matters he is reserved for, that
set out so advantageously at first ? That a person
of your exquisite taste, who has breathed the air
of Courts even from your infancy, should be content,
in that part of your life which is most difficult to
be pleased, and most easy to be disgusted, to take
up with the conversation of country parsons, a sort
of people whom to my knowledge, your Grace
never much admired ; and do penance in the
nauseous company of lawyers, whom I am certain
you abominate !

   " To raise our astonishment higher, who could
ever have prophesied, though he had a double gift
of Nostradamus spirit, that the Duke of Buckingham,
who never vouchsafed his embraces to any ordinary
beauty, would ever condescend to sigh and languish
for the heiress apparent of a thatched cottage, in

a straw hat, flannel petticoat, stocking of as gross
a thrum as the blue-coat boys' caps at the hospital,
and a smock (the Lord defend me from the wicked
idea of it!) of as coarse a canvas as ever served
an apprenticeship to a mackerel-boat? Who could
have believed, till matter of fact had confirmed the
belief of it (and your Grace knows that matter of
fact is not to be disputed), that the most polished
refined epicure of the age, that had regaled himself
in the most exquisite wines of Italy, Greece, and
Spain, would in the last scene of his life, debauch
his constitution in execrable Yorkshire ale? and
that he, who all his lifetime had either seen princes
his stay-fellows or companions, would submit to
the nonsensical chat and barbarous language of
farmers and higglers."

Etherege continues the vein; but later, turns
to his position in Ratisbon: he is not yet as
uncomfortable as he will be; but already he has
learned to his cost that the Germans "make good
the observation that Tacitus made of their ancestors
—that they debate their weightiest negotiations
over their cups." The letter proceeds: "Ten
years ago I as little thought that my stars designed
to make a politician of me, and that it would come
to my share to debate in public assemblies, and
regulate the affairs of Christendom, as the Grand
Signior dreamed of losing Hungary; but my royal
master having the charity to believe me master
of some qualities of which I never suspected myself,
I find that the zeal and alacrity I discover in myself
to support a dignity which he has thought fit to
confer upon me has supplied all other defects, and

given me a talent for which, till now, I justly fancied
myself incapable.

"They are indeed a free-hearted, open sort of
gentlemen that compose the diet, without reserve,
affectation, and artifice ; but they are such unmerciful plyers of the bottle, so wholly given up to what
our sots call good fellowship, that 'tis as great a
constraint upon my nature to sit out a night's entertainment with them as it would be to hear half
a score long-winded Presbyterian divines cant
successively one after another."

There follows an extremely enlightening discourse, in Epicurus' vein, of the true use and abuse
of strong liquors.   Etherege writes :

"To unbosom myself frankly and freely to your
Grace, I always looked upon drunkenness to be an
unpardonable crime in a young fellow who without
any of these foreign helps has fire enough in his
veins to enable him to do justice to Caelia, whenever she demands a tribute of him.   In a middle-
aged man I consider the bottle only as subservient
to the nobler pleasure of love. . . . In old age,
indeed, I am of opinion that a little drunkenness
discreetly used may as well contribute to our health
of body as tranquillity of soul.

"Thus have I given your Grace a short system
of my morals and belief in these affairs.   But the
gentlemen of this country go upon quite a different
scheme of pleasure.   The best furniture of their
parlours instead of innocent china are tall over-
grown runners ; and they take more care to enlarge
their cellars than their patrimonial estates.   In
short, drinking is the hereditary sin of this country,

and that hero of a deputy that can demolish at one sitting the rest of his brother envoys is mentioned with as much applause as the Duke of Lorrain for his noble exploits against the Turk, and may claim a statue erected at the public expense in any town in Germany.

"Judge then, my Lord, whether a person of sober principles, and one that only uses wine as the wiser sort of Roman Catholics do images, to raise up my imagination to something more exalted, and not to terminate my worship upon it, must not be reduced to very mortifying circumstances in this place, where I cannot pretend to enjoy conversation without practising that vice which directly ruins it."

This passage by no means exhausts all that Etherege has to say upon the subject. But lest these citations should grow unduly long, we must pass to the second letter. Between them, Oldys has inserted a note which sufficiently justifies their reproduction. Here, indeed, we have not only the most lively images of Sir George's sentiments upon Buckingham's retirement, and of his own political employment in Ratisbon ; but what is more directly to the purpose in this place, a "faithful and perspicuous portrait of his own humour and genius."

Etherege in the second letter has realised the full extent of his misfortunes as an exile. But we will pass over his eloquent complaints as to the manners and customs of Ratisbon and suffer him to tell some part of his story of Frau Hoffman. Frau Hoffman was the unhappy widow of one of Etherege's few German friends, who died untimely

by the upsetting of a boat upon the Danube.
Etherege writes :

"I was sensibly afflicted at the death of my
worthy friend ; and so indeed were all who had the
honour of knowing him.   But his wife took on so
extravagantly that she in a short time was the only
talk both of city and country.   She refused to
admit any visits from her nearest relations ; her
chamber, her ante-chamber, and pro-ante-chamber
were hung with black ; nay, the very candles, her
fans, and tea table wore the livery of grief.   She
refused all manner of sustenance and was so averse
at the thoughts of living that she talked of nothing
but death.   In short you may tell your ingenious
friend, Monsieur de Saint Evremonde, that Petronius
his Ephesian matron, to whose story he has done
so much justice in his noble translation, was only a
type of our more obstinate, as well as unhappy,
German widow.

"About a fortnight after this cruel loss . . . I
presumed so much upon the friendship her late
husband had always expressed for me, not to
mention the particular civilities I had received from
herself, as to think I should be admitted to have a
sight of her.   Accordingly I came to her house,
sent up my name, and word was immediately
brought me that if I pleased I might go up
to her.

"When I came into the room I fancied myself
in the territories of death : everything looked so
gloomy, so dismal, so melancholy.   There was a
grave Lutheran minister with her who omitted
no arguments to bring her to a more composed

disposition of mind. 'Madam,' says he, '. . . this is downright impiety; what would you say now, if heaven should punish it with some exemplary visitation?' 'That is impossible,' replies the lady, sighing, 'and since it has robbed me of the only delight I had in the world, the only favour it can do me is to level a thunderbolt at my head, and put an end to my sufferings.' The parson, seeing her in this extravagant strain, and seeing no likelihood of persuading her to come to a better temper, got up from his seat, and took his leave of her.

" It came to my turn now to try whether I was not capable of comforting her ; and, being convinced by so late an instance that arguments brought from religion were not likely to work any extraordinary effects upon her, I resolved to attack her ladyship in a more sensible part, and represent to her the great inconveniences, not which her soul, but her body, received from this inordinate sorrow.

" ' Madam,' says I to her, 'next to my concern for your worthy husband's untimely death, I am grieved to see what an alteration the bemoaning of his loss has occasioned in you.' These words raising her curiosity to know what this alteration was I thus continued my discourse. 'By endeavouring, madam, to extinguish, or at least to alleviate, your grief, than which nothing can be more prejudicial to a beautiful woman, I intend a public benefit; for if the public is interested, as most certainly it is, in the preserving of a beautiful face, that man does the public no little service who contributes most to its preservation.'

" This odd beginning operated so wonderfully

upon her that she desired me to 'leave this general
road of compliments, and explain myself more
particularly.' Upon this, delivering myself with an
unusual air of gravity . . . I told her that 'grief
ruins the finest faces sooner than anything else
whatsoever ; . . . that I had heard an eminent
physician at Leyden say that tears, having abundance of saline particles in them, not only spoiled
the complexion, but hastened wrinkles. But,
madam,' I concluded, 'why should I give myself
the trouble to confirm this by foreign instances, and
by the testimony of our most knowing doctors, when,
alas ! your own face so fully justifies the truth of
what I have said to you.'

   " ' How ? ' replied our disconsolate widow with
a sigh that came from the bottom of her heart,
'and is it possible that my just concern for my dear
husband has wrought so cruel an effect upon me
in so short a time ? ' With that she ordered her
gentlewoman to bring the looking-glass to her ;
and, having surveyed herself a few minutes in it,
she told me she was perfectly convinced my notions
were true. ' But,' cries she, ' what would you have
us poor women do in these cases ? ' . . . ' Why,
madam,' says I, ' in the first place forget the
defunct ; and, in order to bring that about, relieve
nature, to which you have been so long unmerciful,
with the most exquisite meats and the most generous
wines.' ' Upon condition you will sup with me,'
cries our afflicted lady, ' I will submit to your
prescriptions.' . . .

   " In short, we had a noble regale that evening
in her bedchamber ; and our good widow pushed

the glass so strenuously about that her comforter, meaning myself, could hardly find the way to his coach. To conclude this farce, this phœnix of her sex, this pattern of conjugal fidelity two mornings ago was married to a smooth-chinned ensign . . . that had not a farthing in the world but his pay to depend upon. I assisted at the ceremony, though I little imagined the lady would take the matrimonial prescription so soon."

From these transcripts we may judge for ourselves of Etherege's quality as a writer of prose; and find that the opinion of Dryden is not far short of justified. The delicate urbanity, smoothness, felicity, and balance of these letters survives the mutilation they have necessarily suffered to be in part included here. But it is even more important for our own immediate purpose to capture the writer's spirit, with which they are so vitally informed. In Etherege's story of the widow there is a worldly simplicity, captivating from its entire absence of self-consciousness. For the reader critically alive to the minute touches of character in which they so happily abound these letters are a perfect introduction to our subject — the best possible preparation for a critical consideration of the plays.

CHAPTER III

THE PLAYS OF SIR GEORGE ETHEREGE

WAS Etherege aware that *Love in a Tub* was to open a new period in English dramatic literature? The prologue suggests he was consciously breaking with tradition. Pointedly he challenges no comparison with "Fletcher's nature or the art of Ben;" but asks to be compared with his immediate contemporaries—

> Our author therefore begs you would forget,
> Most reverend judges, the records of wit;
> And only think upon the modern way
> Of writing, whilst you're censuring his play.

Whether Sir George knew or not how original he was, his contemporaries realised it beyond question. They had not yet seen a comedy upon the English stage in the least resembling *Love in a Tub*; and immediately they saw it they recognised it for an expression of themselves and their period for which they had unconsciously been waiting. Up to the production of *Love in a Tub*, the London theatre was the theatre of Charles I. Its comedy was the Elizabethan comedy of humours, pale, withered and exhausted. But Etherege changed all that. It is necessary to be quite clear—first, as to the relation between the comedy of Etherege and the comedy

of Jonson; second, as to the relation of the comedy
of Etherege and the comedy of Molière.

Mr. Edmund Gosse has written by far the best
critical estimate of the importance of Etherege in
English dramatic literature. But while he recog-
nises, what is most important of all, that Restoration comedy begins with *Love in a Tub*, and insists
that the break in English dramatic literature was
rather a revolution than a development, he urges a
little too heavily the connexion between Etherege
and Molière. It is true that Etherege had Molière
by heart; and extremely probable that in 1664 he
was newly arrived in London from Paris, where he
had seen the first productions of the comedies of
Molière at Versailles, 1660–1663. It is also true that
echoes of Molière are distinctly heard in his comedies
of 1667 and 1676. But there is no real kinship
between the French and the English playwright.
The historical facts are in contradiction with the
critical. The comedy of Molière is in spirit and
character nearer to the comedy of Jonson, which
Etherege displaced, than to the Restoration comedy,
which Etherege introduced. Only one of our
comic dramatists was touched with the comic spirit
of France. There is a real identity of purpose
and spirit between Wycherley and Molière. But
Wycherley, as we shall see, has for this very reason
to be considered from rather a different point of
view from Etherege and Congreve.

Much learned nonsense has been written about
the comedy of "humours." It would here be
impertinent to go into the Elizabethan system of
psychology founded upon the use and misuse

of this word-of-all-work. The practical result for us to-day is that in the personages of the comedies of Jonson and his school, this "humour" or that predominated, and fixed the type. The characters were not personal studies; but generalisations upon a quality or an attribute. Here the analogy is obvious between the comedy of "humours" and the comedy of *Tartuffe* or *Le Misanthrope*. But just as there is little kinship between the types of Jonson, set forth as studies in good and evil, and the persons of Etherege's theatre, so the analogy fails completely for Etherege and Molière. To put the distinction for a moment quite superficially, the persons of Jonson and Molière are types. The persons of Etherege are not. The importance of the persons of Etherege is that they are not general, but particular. Molière and Jonson write the comedy of morals; Etherege the comedy of manners. Mr. Gosse in one or two passages seems sensible of the need to distinguish; but the need is extreme. Restoration comedy owed almost as little to France as to the English school it displaced. It was an independent growth springing spontaneously from the impulse of English Restoration Society to view itself in reflexion upon the stage.

The stage history of *Love in a Tub* was brilliant. History is silent as to Etherege till its production; but immediately he became an important figure of the town and the court. "I could not have wished myself more fortunate than I have been in the success of this poem," Etherege writes in his dedication of the first edition to Lord Dorset.

" The writing of it was a means to make me known to your lordship ; the acting of it has lost me no reputation ; and the printing of it has now given me an opportunity to show how much I honour you." Oldys writes of *Love in a Tub* that " the fame of this play with his lively humour, engaging conversation and refined taste in the fashionable gallantries of the town soon established him in the societies and rendered him the delight of those leading wits among the quality and gentry of chief rank and distinction, who made their pleasure the chief business of their lives in that reign." The play ran through four editions in twenty years. Pepys found it " very merry "; Evelyn thought it " facetious "; and Langbaine wrote of it, " Has succeeded admirably on the stage, it having always been acted with general applause." It seems to have been extremely well presented. Mr. and Mrs. Betterton, Harris, and Mrs. Davies were in the caste. In a word, Sir George Etherege had the good fortune of his merits.

Love in a Tub is a prose comedy, variegated with passages of verse in heroic couplets. The important point as to the versified section is that it conflicts in spirit and in style with the prose, and that the experiment was not again repeated until Vanbrugh's *The Relapse* prepared the decline of English comedy. The idyllic loves of Aurelia and Graciana, told in smooth numbers in the intervals of Sir Frederick Frollick's escapades, are obviously out of the picture. Artistically they are as clearly false to the period—as clearly immoral—as the sentiments expressed are impeccably virtuous. Written in 1850

for presentation on speech-day at Mr. Pinkerton's
Academy, they would have suited admirably the
time and the occasion.   Fortunately the literary
consciences of the comic dramatists were too robust
to repeat this palpable falsehood.   It is the special
credit and glory of the early Restoration stage that
it is continuously in touch with the life it reflects ;
and we have exhausted the significance of the
aberration of Etherege's first comedy into romantic
love when we have pointed out that it never happened again till the comedy of his successors was
ripening for a fall.

The prose section is a first flavour of that exquisite style hereafter to draw repeated eulogy from
readers of Congreve in all ages.   But at the outset
two important concessions must be made to a
modern reader.   The first is a point of manners.
Every play with which we are in these pages to
deal is freely blotted with words that have long disappeared from the vocabulary of polite conversation.
This, of course, quite justly condemns the unexpurgated plays as family reading in an age which
is even more afraid of brutal words than of brutal
facts.   Precisely the same demerit advises a discreet
handling of Shakespeare and his contemporaries.
The just critic simply has to overlook the offensive-
ness of words which to-day are æsthetically—we are
not now upon a question of morals—offensive.
Words which jar the ear of a modern reader, and
spoil his pleasure, passed unnoticed in the Theatres
of Fletcher and of Congreve.   The just critic must
simply ignore them.   Indeed, to recover the true
flavour of passages where they occur, they must

to-day be omitted.   This is not, it must be insisted,
a question of morality, but of literary taste.   The
habits of speech we are discussing affect us to-day
not as wicked or sinful habits, but as offences against
style.   The language of Congreve's fine gentlemen
affects us precisely as would the table-manners and
chamber-manners of his fine ladies.   It is mere
weakness of the critical flesh that these comparatively
unimportant details should have such power to disturb appreciation ; but it is a weakness that must be
taken into serious account.   It is merely common
justice to the comic dramatists of the Restoration to
overlook such manners of their conversation as were
entirely due to contemporary fashion, especially as
to-day we have outgrown the fashion without by
any means outgrowing the facts.   To condemn the
comic dramatists for their use of words no longer
current in polite conversation is precisely the offence
of an uneducated crowd that would hoot a pedestrian
who elected to appear publicly in Fleet Street in
Elizabethan costume.

Our second concession to the school of critics
that finds these plays unprintable to-day, pierces
deeper than the superficies of fashion.   The subject is unpleasant ; but, once encountered, it need
not again be mentioned.   In Etherege, as in
Shakespeare, sexual disease is a common topic of
the jester.   Here, we are faced with nothing less
than a social revolution.   Really, it is a revolution in medical science.   In the seventeenth
century people neither knew nor worried about
disease ; it was not a social, but a personal matter.
Dufoy of *Love in a Tub*—the subject meets us

at the threshold of our inquiry—is for his contemporaries a legitimate object of merriment. His
affliction is a personal misfortune, analogous to the
physical misfortune of a drunkard—one of the stock
figures of simple farce. To-day the scenes in which
the plight of Dufoy is for comic purposes exploited
are wholly disgusting. The point of view has
completely changed. We are so fully awake to
the consequences in our midst of a tragic scourge
that it is entirely impossible to recover the light-
hearted, irresponsible attitude of Etherege and his
contemporaries. The revolution here is not merely
new fashions for old; nor, definitely, is it a moral
development. It is a change of attitude due to an
increase of knowledge and a clearer appreciation of
consequences. Sexual disease can never more be
matter for jesting; for we have lost touch with the
mental attitude that made it possible, as completely
as we have lost touch with the mental attitude of
Socrates towards the loves of Harmodius and
Aristogeiton. These facts must continually be
remembered as we read the comic dramatists. To
credit them with the modern view, and thereafter
to find them playing with a subject from which
to-day we reflexively shrink, is to see them, quite
unjustly, as the malignant devils of Macaulay.

These difficulties cleared, the way is open.
Passing into the comic world of Etherege we are
immediately naturalised. The two questions of
taste and attitude which we have discussed, inevitably intrude, because they are to a large extent
æsthetic questions. Words that by lapse of
fashion strike disagreeably upon the ear; ideas that

by a fundamental change of attitude are, in their
discovered nature, horrible to the fancy—these are
blemishes that the critic has consciously to dis-
count as they force themselves upon him. But
the life itself of the period—in other words, its
morality—may be accepted imaginatively without
demur as we enter. Every imaginative writer
assumes that the laws of his kingdom will be
recognised and admitted by those who choose it
for their excursion, just as, in playing a game, it
is understood that the players will observe the
rules. If we set out to be amused by the escapades
of Sir Frederick Frollick, and then in the height
of the fun, object to his moral character on the
plea that he is not behaving as we should ourselves
behave in a like situation, we are acting as would a
card-player, who, at the end of a round, objected to
pay his losses, not on the justifiable ground that the
accepted rules of the game had been infringed, but
on the irrelevant ground that he had a moral or
metaphysical objection to an ace ranking higher
than a knave.

The hero of *Love in a Tub* is the first of a
line that culminated in Congreve's Mirabell. Almost
as the curtain rose the audience must have felt that
here was something new—no straw-splitting of
"humours," but a gentleman that had walked into
comedy from their midst, the image of their time
and manner. He seized the immediate occasion,
turning it to epigram. Each moment sufficed him,
so long as it might be gracefully encountered. His
first apology to Jenny for his conduct over-night
sounded a new note in English comedy. "Men are

now and then subject to those infirmities in drink
which women have when they're sober." Here was
an epigram of fine life, with fine life itself for
company. "Pray tell the consequence, how you
marched bravely at the rear of an army of link-
boys; upon the sudden how you gave defiance, and
then waged a bloody war on the constable; and
having vanquished that dreadful enemy, how you
committed a general massacre upon the glass
windows."

The characters that fill the prose sections of
Love in a Tub fall into two groups—fine gentlemen
and plain rogues. How the plots thicken and cross
is not critically to the purpose. It would be as
futile to illustrate the effect of a Restoration comedy
by summarising the plot or describing the characters
as to convey the quality of *Hamlet* in a scenario.
Direct citation is the only method of dealing critically with the comic dramatists.

From *Love in a Tub* it were best to choose ex-
clusively from the passages between Sir Frederick
and Widow Rich. Sir Frederick's impudent courtship sends us forward irresistibly to the loves of
Mirabell and Millamant—to a vein only exhausted
in Farquhar's *Sir Harry Wildair*.

Sir Fred. Whither, whither, do ye draw me,
widow? What's your design?

Wid. To take a turn in the garden, and then
repose in a cool arbour.

Sir Fred. Widow, I dare not venture myself
in those amorous shades; you have a mind to be
talking of love, I perceive, and my heart's too
tender to be trusted with such conversation.

Wid. I did not imagine you were so foolishly conceited; is it your wit or your person, sir, that is so taking?

Sir Fred. Truly, you are much mistaken. I have no such great thoughts of the young man you see. Who ever knew a woman have so much reason to build her love upon merit? Have we not daily experience of Great Fortunes that fling themselves into the arms of vain idle fellows? Can you blame me then for standing upon my guard. . . .

Later the fencing continues with parts neatly reversed:

Sir Fred. By those lips—

Wid. Nay, pray forbear, Sir.

Sir Fred. Who is conceited now, widow? Could you imagine I was so fond to kiss them.

Wid. You cannot blame me for standing on my guard so near an enemy. . . .

In pursuit of the widow Sir Frederick serenades her at midnight, and is admitted with his fiddlers.

Widow (after the masque). These are men of skill.

Sir Fred. I disguised 'em for your entertainment.

Wid. Well, sir, now I hope you'll leave me to my rest.

Sir Fred. Can you in conscience turn a young man out of doors at this time o' the night, widow? Fie, fie, the very thought on't will keep you waking.

Wid. So pretty, so well-favoured a young man; one that loves me.

Sir Fred. Ay, one that loves you.

Wid. Truly 'tis a very hard-hearted thing.
　　　　　　　　　　[She sighs.]

Sir Fred. Come, come, be mollified. You may go, gentlemen [*to the masquers*], and leave me here; you may go.

Wid. You may stay, gentlemen; you may stay, and take your captain along with you.

Sir Fred. Go, go to bed, and lie idle, widow; that's worse than any misfortune I can meet with.

The lightness and ease of these passages is for the successors of Etherege a model of comic style. The friends of Etherege, hearing these scenes between Sir Frederick and the widow of *Love in a Tub* could not, without conscious reaction, go back to the Jonson models they had so pitifully exhausted. Beside the brilliant pages of Congreve the passages here cited ring but thinly upon the ear; but we must read them, not with Congreve for their importance in 1664, but with Wilson, and Browne.

She would if She could followed, as we have seen, in 1667. Pepys assisted at the première, and has touched the occasion in unusual detail: "My wife, being gone before, I to the Duke of York's Playhouse, where a new play of Etherege's called *She would if She could*, and though I was there by two o'clock, there were one thousand people put back that could not have room in the pit; and I, at last, because my wife was there, made shift to get into the eighteen-pence box, and thus saw; but Lord! how full was the house." A brilliant house, too, it seems; for the King was in his box, and Buckingham was there with my Lord Buckhurst and Sedley, and Etherege the poet—"the last of

THE DUKE'S THEATRE, DORSET GARDENS.

Built by Sir Christopher Wren. Opened 1671. Demolished 1709.

From an old print.

whom I did hear mightily find fault with the actors, that they were out of humour, and had not their parts perfect."

The play, badly acted as it was, was recognised for the best comedy written since *Love in a Tub.* Shadwell wrote of it in his preface to *The Humourists:* "*She would if She could,* I think, and have the authority of some of the best judges for it, is the best comedy that has been written since the reformation of the stage. And even that, for the imperfect representation of it, at first received such prejudice that, had it not been for the favour of the Court, in all probability it had never got up again ; and it suffers for it, in great measure to this day." Langbaine wishes, apropos of *She would if She could,* that the author "would oblige the world with more of his performances, which would put a stop to the crude and indigested plays, which, for want of better, cumber the stage."

Oldys fully appreciated the importance of Etherege. Quoting the eulogies of Shadwell and Langbaine upon *She would if She could,* he writes of its reception generally: "These applauses arose from our author's changing the study after old copies, and chimerical draughts from unguarded speculation, which is but painting with dead colours, for those taken directly from the freshest practice and experience in original life. He drew his characters from what they called the beau monde ; from the manners and modes then prevailing with the gay and voluptuous part of the world."

She would if She could was the first finished example of the new comedy of manners. Looking

back towards its production in 1668 Shadwell and
Oldys were able clearly to see that Etherege had
now definitely arrived whither he had pointed the
way for his contemporaries with *Love in a Tub* in
1664. It is significant that Steele, in *Spectator* 51,
lights upon this play as a supreme example of
the meretricious comedy he deplored.   Speaking
generally of comic authors he writes : " I know but
one who has professedly writ a play upon the basis
of the desire of multiplying our species, and that is
the polite Sir George Etherege ; if I understand
what the lady would be at in *She would if She
could*.   Other poets have here and there given
an intimation that there is this design under all
the disguises and affectations which a lady may put
on ; but no other author, except this, has made
sure work of it, and put imaginations of the audience
upon this one purpose from the beginning to the
end of his comedy.   It has always fared accordingly ;
for whether it be that all who go to this piece would
if they could, or that the innocents go to it to guess
only what she would if she could, the play has
always been well received."

The lady who in Etherege's comedy undoubtedly
would if she could is Lady Cockwood, the first of a
long series of studies in fashionable virtue coquetting
with fashionable vice.   Mr. Edmund Gosse sees
in the Lady Cockwood a study in the manner of *Le
Tartuffe*, a play which Etherege had very probably
seen presented at Paris in the summer of 1667.
Here it is difficult to agree.   Etherege in his
second comedy is even further from Molière, if it
be possible, than in his first.   The Lady Cockwood

is not a study of the female devout hypocrite.
The scenes in which she plays a part are of the
common Restoration type—scenes in which the
author depends for his comedy on a conflict,
necessarily so familiar to Mr. Courtal and Mr.
Freeman of the period, between the pride of their
mistresses—delicate, or merely affected—and an
urgent necessity to be "kind." "And swearing
she would ne'er consent, consented" is the comic
theme which Etherege and his successors varied
interminably; and Etherege has already written
upon it a favourite variation of the period—a
variation where the lady would if she could, but
is ever ready to feign that she could not if she
would.

The Lady Cockwood scenes are a leitmotiv of
Restoration comedy. Another, equally remote
from anything to be borrowed from Molière, is
the fun of the chase when the resourceful witty
gallant of the time is in pursuit of the no less
resourceful and witty maiden. It was a claim of
the period, or its disgrace—at any rate it was a
necessary postulate of its comedy—that in affairs of
sex men and women met equally equipped for the
encounter. Meredith has said, profoundly, that
refined comedy is only possible in a society where
men and women meet upon an intellectual equality,
and here we have one of the first axioms of Restoration comedy. Here, too, is a further explanation
of the horror with which the comic dramatists have
been regarded, through the poker-work period of
our social history. Nineteenth-century moralists
have seen in the Restoration gallant, as Macaulay

has it, a scoundrel that abused the trusting confidence of Mrs. Pinchwife. The attitude is entirely foolish. The Restoration gallant saw in Mrs. Pinchwife—or to confine ourselves to the comedy in hand—in Ariana or Gatty, an antagonist armed at all points, meeting him on a basis of intellectual equality, where it was give or get no more than he bargained for. This was the attitude, charming or disgraceful, that culminated in the most delightful scenes in comedy of any language—the duello passages between Congreve's Mirabell and Millamant.

Etherege was working towards these passages in the scenes between Sir Frederick and his widow. *She would if She could* continues and improves the model.

Courtal. Your true lover, madam, when he misses his mistress, is as restless as a spaniel that has lost his master; he ranges up and down the plays, the Park, and all the gardens, and never stays long but where he has the happiness to see her.

Gatty. I suppose your mistress, Mr. Courtal, is always the last woman you are acquainted with.

Courtal. Do not think, madam, I have that false measure of my acquaintance which poets have of their verses, always to think the last best—though I esteem you so, in justice to your merit.

Gatty. Or if you do not love her best, you always love to talk of her most; as a barren coxcomb that wants discourse is ever entertaining company out of the last book he read in.

To abuse the confiding tenderness of Mistress

Gatty—the ingénue of Restoration comedy—does not lie within the wit of man—not even of Restoration man.

" Ranges up and down the plays, the Park, and all the gardens," this was the intimate, familiar touch that went directly home to the contemporaries of Etherege. It was something entirely new; and it helped to awaken the playwrights of the time to the novelty of his method and to its real direction. Their comedy was henceforth to be a reflexion of manners, set in the world they knew— Spring Garden, Gray's Inn Walk, S. James' Street and Park, the New Exchange, Pall Mall, the play-houses, and the ordinaries or clubs—the London Charles II. had himself helped to fashion. Etherege's scenes are all laid in the walks and meeting places immediately associated in the minds of his audience with recreation and adventure. The " Rose " and the " Bear " of *She would if She could* were ordinaries where Etherege and Pepys dined within elbow reach. They are among the places longingly remembered by Etherege in his exile. " Remember me," he writes from Ratisbon, " to all my friends at the ' Rose,' and do not forget the lily at the ' Bear.' " The familiar touches that enable us in this comedy even now to recover the air and aspect of the town as it lay to the west of the city in 1668 are one of the pleasantest features. For a contemporary audience they were not easily resisted.

Etherege's style in dialogue has improved in 1668. Almost it is too smooth, There is too little resistance for the ear. *She would if She could*

flows evenly from scene to scene, only occasionally arresting us with a touch or a phrase which
with more than ordinary vivacity fits the life and
temper of its people. " Eat well," says Mr.
Freeman as he comes into the play, " and prepare
ourselves with a bottle or two of good Burgundy
that our old acquaintance may look lovely in our
eyes. For, for ought as I see, there is no hopes of
new." This is as far as a man of the Restoration
got with a philosophy or rule of life. Gatty tells us
how the days were spent, " from one playhouse to
the other playhouse, and, if they like neither the
play nor the women, they seldom stay any longer
than the combing of their periwigs, or a whisper or
two with a friend ; and then they cock their caps
and out they start again." " Truly," says Gatty in
another place to Mr. Courtal and Mr. Freeman, " you
seem to be men of great employment, that are
every moment rattling from the eating-houses to
the playhouses, from the playhouses to the Mulberry
Garden." These are their habits ; and their
manners are consonant—" I find it a mere folly to
swear anything "—says Mr. Courtal—" it does but
make the devil more earnest in his temptation."
And later he says of constancy, " A single intrigue in
love is as dull as a single plot in a play, and will
tire a lover worse than t'other does an audience."
As it is tedious to be constant, so is it absurd to be
jealous. Gatty and Ariana, requiring Mr. Freeman
and Mr. Courtal to be constant and see no other
women for a few hours, ask for an oath—" Not that
we are jealous, but because we would not have you
tired with the impertinent conversation of our sex,

and come to us dull and out of humour." Such is
the comic gallantry of Etherege.

The Man of Mode, or Sir Fopling Flutter,
followed as the third and last comedy of Etherege
in 1676. "The play met with extraordinary
success upon the stage," says Oldys; and Langbaine, with Gildon's approval, writes of it: "It is
written with great art and judgment; and is
acknowledged by all to be as true comedy, and
the characters as well drawn to the life, as any
play that has been acted since the restoration of
the English stage." Upon the other side Steele
has again raised his voice of the *Spectator*:
"This whole celebrated piece is a perfect contradiction of good manners, good sense, and common
honesty."

The immediate contemporary success of *Sir
Fopling* was due, first to its excellent presentation;
second, to the zeal with which every one set out to
track the originals of its comic people. Betterton,
Harris, and Mrs. Berry were in the caste; Dryden
wrote the epilogue; Sir Car Scroope contributed the
prologue; and the Duchess of York accepted the
dedication. Etherege remembered the comparative
failure of *She would if She could* where he had asked
help neither of fine acting nor fashionable patronage.
As to the identifications made at the time between
characters of the comedy and characters of the
Court, their authenticity is best measured by their
confusion. Dean Lockier is reported by Spence to
have said: "Sir George Etherege was as thorough
a fop as ever I saw; he was exactly his own Sir
Fopling Flutter, and yet he designed Dorimant the

genteel rake of wit for his own picture." Oldys
finds the Earl of Rochester in Dorimant, Beau
Hewitt in Sir Fopling, Etherege himself in Medley.
This is the most probable intention. Sir Fopling
is despised by the real wits of the play as Hewitt
was despised by Rochester and Dryden; whereas
Medley is almost certainly the gentleman who, if
ever he lacked the vigour to afford scandal, never
lacked the wit to invent it. "I love to hear him
talk o' the intrigues," says Emilia, "let 'em be never
so dull of themselves, he'll make 'em pleasant i' the
relation." Others found Etherege in Bellair; and
in Medley discovered Sir Charles Sedley. These
efforts, unimportant in themselves, are excellent
evidence how the comedy was accepted for a model
of the time.

Sir Car Scroope introduces Sir Fopling thus:

> Of foreign wares why should we fetch the scum,
> When we can be so richly served at home?
> For, heaven be thanked, 'tis not so wise an age,
> But your own follies may supply the stage.

Here there is actual insistence that Etherege must
not be referred to the French for his models; and
Sir Car Scroope closes with an indication of the
true source of his comedy:

> Then for your own sakes be not too severe,
> Nor what you all admire at home, damn here;
> Since each is fond of his own ugly face,
> Why should you, when we hold it, break the glass?

Dryden writes the epilogue in a similar vein of
insistence that the work of Etherege must be

referred to no foreign or ancient model, but judged
as an artistic reflexion of the London world :

> Most modern wits such monstrous fools have shown,
> They seemd not of heaven's making, but their own.
> Those nauseous harlequins in farce may pass ;
> But there goes more to a substantial ass ;
> Something of man must be exposed to view,
> That, gallants, they may more resemble you.

Sir Fopling is essentially a comedy of manners.
Restoration society, viewed in Etherege's comic art,
moves in our fancy as we read. We accept the
laws of this strangely distant world ; and fall,
imaginatively, into the attitudes of its people. The
spirit of the early Restoration—the spirit that lived
only for adventure, but accepted it, when it came,
with indifference—is well put in the declaration of
Dorimant, the finished amateur of intrigue. "We
are not masters of our affections," he tells Loveit in
one of his most impudently written scenes, "our
inclinations daily alter ; now, we love pleasure, and
anon we shall dote on business : human frailty will
have it so, and who can help it ? "

Perhaps we most rarely savour the atmosphere of
this court and town when some stray breath of the
country blows into the comedy to be immediately
detected and expelled. " The Country Gentlewoman
I told you of (Lord! they have the oddest diversions !)
would never let me rest," Belinda tells Loveit in
considerable astonishment, "till I promised to go
with them to the markets this morning to eat
fruit and buy nosegays." "Are they so fond
of a filthy nosegay ? " disgustedly answers Loveit,
suggesting that Belinda should in complaisance

have had a nosegay too. "Do you think, my dear," says Belinda, "I could be so loathsome to trick myself up with carnations and stock gilly-flowers? I begged their pardon and told them I never wore anything but orange flowers and tuberose." For a companion touch as to country matters we must turn to where Harriet, threatened with exile from town, pictures herself as confined "to a great rambling lone house that looks as it were not inhabited, the family's so small ; there you'll find my mother, an old lame aunt, and myself, sir, perched up on chairs at a distance in a large parlour, sitting, moping like three or four melancholy birds in a spacious volery."

Etherege places some scenes of his play at the house of my Lady Townley—a typical salon of the day.

Dorimant. The town has been very favourable to you this afternoon, my Lady Townley ; you use to have an *embarras* of chairs and coaches at your door, an uproar of footmen in your hall, and a noise of fools above here.

Lady Townley. Indeed, my house is the general rendezvous, and, next to the playhouse, is the common refuge of all the young idle people.

Emilia. Company is a very good thing, madam, but I wonder you do not love it a little more chosen.

Lady Townley. 'Tis good to have an universal taste ; we should love wit, but for variety be able to divert ourselves with the extravagances of those who want it.

Medley. Fools will make you laugh.

Emilia. For once or twice, but the repetition of

their folly after a visit or two grows tedious and insufferable.

Lady Townley. You are a little too delicate, Emily.

"A little too delicate"—it is the key of the whole composition. Harriet and Young Bellair, pretending to talk and to behave as though they were falling in love, are an exquisite study in artifice. They are observed, and know they are observed, by their parents, who have bidden them to a marriage that neither of them desires. To deceive them and "for the dear pleasure of dissembling," they agree to blind their parents with a pretence of courtship. Etherege uses the scene, as nearly every scene of the play, to exhibit the manners and attitude of the society he frequented.

Harriet. Peace! Here they come. I will lean against this wall, and look bashfully down upon my fan, while you, like an amorous spark, modishly entertain me. . . .

Young Bellair. Now for a look and gestures that may persuade 'em I am saying all the passionate things imaginable.

Harriet. Your head a little more on one side, ease yourself on your left leg, and play with your right hand.

Young Bellair. Thus, is it not?

Harriet. Now set your right leg firm on the ground, adjust your belt, then look about you.

Young Bellair. A little exercising will make me perfect.

Harriet. Smile, and turn to me again very sparkish.

Young Bellair. Will you take your turn to be instructed ?

Harriet. With all my heart.

Young Bellair. At one motion, play your fan, roll your eyes, and then settle a kind look on me.

Harriet. So.

Young Bellair. Now spread your fan, look down upon it, and tell the sticks with a finger.

Harriet. Very modish !

Etherege brings the affectation of the period to a full close in his figure of Sir Fopling. Dryden has described him in famous lines :—

> Sir Fopling is a fool so nicely writ,
> That ladies would mistake him for a wit . . .
> So brisk, so gay, so travelled, so refined,
> As he took pains to graft upon his kind.
> True fops help nature's work, and go to school
> To file and finish God Almighty's fool.

In the juxtaposition of Dorimant, the man of true wit and perfect fashion, with the fool or half-wit, who merely apes the smartness of the time, Etherege was setting a model for Congreve, whose *The Way of the World* almost entirely rests upon the subtle opposition of Mirabell and Witwoud.

Sir Fopling is valuable not only as a piece of literary history, but in himself. He is one of the few perfect fops of literature. He is first introduced in a conversation between Dorimant and his friends.

Dorimant. That a man's excellency should lie in neatly tying a ribbon or a cravat ! How careful is nature in furnishing the world with necessary coxcombs ?

Bellair. That's a mighty pretty suit of yours, Dorimant.

Dorimant. I am glad it has your approbation.

Bellair. No man in town has a better fancy in his clothes than you have.

Dorimant. You will make me have an opinion of my genius.

Medley. There is a great critic, I hear, in these matters lately arrived piping hot from Paris.

Bellair. Sir Fopling Flutter, you mean.

Medley. The same.

Bellair. He thinks himself the pattern of modern gallantry.

Dorimant. He is indeed the pattern of modern foppery.

Medley. He was yesterday at the play, with a pair of gloves up to his elbows, and a periwig more exactly curled than a lady's head newly dressed for a ball. . . . His head stands for the most part on one side, and his looks are more languishing than a lady's when she lolls at stretch in her coach, or leans her head carelessly against the side of a box in the playhouse.

Sir Fopling arrives in the third act, his entrance most carefully prepared. Lady Townley presents him to Emilia, and the conversation is pure foppery :

Lady Townley. Wit, I perceive, has more power over you than beauty, Sir Fopling, else you would not have let this lady stand so long neglected.

Sir Fopling (to Emilia). A thousand pardons, madam. . . . The *éclat* of so much beauty, I confess, ought to have charmed me sooner.

Emilia. The *brilliant* of so much good language, sir, has much more power than the little beauty I can boast.

Sir Fopling. I never saw anything prettier than this high work on your *point d'Espagne.*

Emilia. 'Tis not so rich as *point de Venise.*

Sir Fopling. Not altogether, but looks cooler, and is more proper for the season.   Dorimant, is not that Medley?

Dorimant. The same, sir.

Sir Fopling. Forgive me, sir, in this *embarras* of civilities I could not come to have you in my arms sooner.   You understand an equipage the best of any man in town, I hear.

Medley. By my own you would not guess it. . . .

Sir Fopling. Have you taken notice of the *calèche* I brought over?

Medley. Oh yes!   It has quite another air than the English makes.

Sir Fopling. 'Tis as easily known from an English tumbril as an Inns of Court man is from one of us.

Dorimant. Truly, there is a *bel-air* in *calèches* as well as men.

Medley. But there are few so delicate to discern it.

Sir Fopling. The world is generally very *grossier* here, indeed.

Lady Townley. He's very fine.

Emilia. Extreme proper.

Sir Fopling. A slight suit I made to appear in at my first arrival, not counting your consideration, ladies.

Dorimant. The pantaloon is very well mounted.

Sir Fopling. The tassels are new and pretty.

Medley. I never saw a coat better cut. . . .

Lady Townley. His gloves are well-fringed, large and graceful.

Sir Fopling. I was always eminent for being *bien-ganté.*

Emilia. He wears nothing but what are originals of the most famous hands in Paris.

Sir Fopling. You are in the right, madam.

Lady Townley. The suit?

Sir Fopling. Barroy.

Emilia. The garniture?

Sir Fopling. Le gras.

Medley. The shoes?

Sir Fopling. Piccat.

Dorimant. The periwig?

Sir Fopling. Chedieux.

Scenes like these, of exquisite foppery, are the background of the threefold intrigue of Dorimant, carried forward with that impudent cynicism which is the conspicuous virtue of these studies in Restoration gallantry. The period had the courage of its convictions—or, perhaps we should say—of their agreeable absence. " I am not one of those troublesome coxcombs," says Dorimant, playing for a fall with Loveit, "who because they were once well received take the privilege to plague a woman with their love ever after." Stripped of disguise sexual passion stands nakedly apart, horrid spectacle for an after-age which insisted that even an abduction should be entirely respectable. Dorimant in nineteenth-century phrase " breaks the heart " of Mistress Loveit as follows:

Dorimant. Constancy at my years! 'Tis not a virtue in season; you might as well expect the fruit the autumn ripens in the spring.

Loveit. Monstrous principle!

Dorimant. Youth has a long journey to go, madam: should I have set up my rest at the first inn I lodged at, I should never have arrived at the happiness I now enjoy.

Loveit. Now you begin to show yourself.

Dorimant. Love gilds us over, and makes us show fine things to one another for a time, but soon the gold wears off, and then again the native brass appears.

Loveit. Think on your oaths, your vows and protestations, perjured man.

Dorimant. I made 'em when I was in love.

Loveit. And therefore ought they not to bind?

Dorimant. What we swear at such a time may be a certain proof of a present passion; but, to say truth, in love there is no security to be given for the future.

Upon this note of honest knavery we will for the moment leave the comedy of Sir George Etherege. We shall be more in a position to determine his place and stature among the comic dramatists when we have dealt with his successors. But already we may very precisely assert that he is as little of the kindred of Molière whom he so clearly admired, as of Jonson whom he so clearly displaced. There is nowhere the corrective laugh of the intellectual satirist. Etherege, in fact, rarely falls within the stimulating definition of laughter which Henri Bergson bases so inevitably upon the comedy of his countrymen. Laughter, as a social gesture—critical, weighted with ethical and social persuasion—is not to be won from the figures of Etherege's comedy. There is nowhere the grave purpose and intentness of mind, which we find in comedies of the pattern of Molière. The comedies of Etherege are the natural product of an age for which life was an accepted pageant, incuriously observed, uncritically accepted, stuff for a finished epigram. Etherege accepted life for the purposes of his comedy in precisely the same spirit in which he accepted it for his serious pilgrimage. He intercepted without effort for his immediate purpose the things that came to him, and gracefully encountered the one problem which his generation acutely recognised. Whether it were fighting the Dutch, defeating the policy of Achitophel, tying a riband, or writing a play—style was the man. There was form ; and there was bad form. The whole duty of man was to find the one, and to eschew the other. Etherege found a form for the spirit of his age ; wherein, as we shall see, lies his unquestionable merit.

CHAPTER IV

WILLIAM WYCHERLEY

FROM Easy Etherege to Manly Wycherley is a remarkable transition. Etherege was the expression of his period. His plays were an agreeable transcription of the life he knew. The imperturbable elegance with which his contemporaries held life, as it were, at arm's length, and gracefully postured through the seven ages, is in the plays of Etherege an unrippled reflexion. But in the plays of Wycherley there is a critical current of satire. Alone of the comic dramatists he shares in the comic spirit, though to a less extent than is commonly maintained, of Molière. In the plays of Wycherley we are frequently startled into a consciousness of moral fury, which, because it is unpremeditated, is only the more disturbing.

Wycherley's contemporaries were naturally more sensible of this than we who have outlived some part of the particular folly he so rigorously chastised. Evelyn has boldly declared :—

> As long as men are false and women vain,
> Whilst gold continues to be virtue's bane,
> In pointed satire Wycherley shall reign.

Nevertheless many a later critic has failed sufficiently to emphasise this quality of Wycherley which distinguishes him from every other one of our

selected authors. Macaulay, whose critical reflexions upon Wycherley are as grotesque as his
biographical memoir is ill-natured, entirely missed it.
He speaks of Wycherley as a "worse Congreve."
If Macaulay had read his authorities with an open
mind, he must clearly have perceived that Wycherley
stands quite apart from Congreve in the opinion of
his contemporaries. As a literary figure they distinguish him equally from Congreve and from
Etherege. He was not, as were these, the supreme
stylist. "Satire, wit and strength" are the qualities Dryden bestows upon "Manly Wycherley."
"Brawny" was Rochester's epithet. "To lash this
crying age" was his mortal office, as described by
Congreve. These phrases and epithets would ring
falsely in the ears of a reader of Etherege or Congreve. Pointed at Wycherley they ring remarkably
true.

Wycherley's plays should be read, as we read
them here, immediately upon leaving Etherege.
Fled are the airiness, delicacy, and absolute reliance
upon the finer values of style. Wycherley's phrases
are less pleasing to the ear; but they bite into their
topic. Here is a writer whose matter is sometimes of
equal importance with his manner—here, in fact, we
are not dealing with a typical figure of the time, as was
Etherege. Wycherley seems a man to whom life,
had he flourished in another period, would immensely
have mattered—a man who, fundamentally, had an
instinct to look quite through the shows of men.
Fundamentally he was a Puritan. Superficially, in
his life and writing, he accepted the pageant and
portrayed it; but frequently the moral fury of a

satirist breaks violently through the fine gentleman.
The plays of Wycherley and his life—the little we
may know of it—equally leave us with the impression of a Restoration gentleman, not born, but made.
They are a fascinating complementary study to the
life and plays of Etherege.

Wycherley was by birth a country gentleman
of Shropshire. He was born in 1640; and at
fifteen was sent out of the country for his education to France, where his royalist father might
esteem him safe from the teaching of Round-
heads. There he was accepted into the brilliant
society that surrounded the Duchess of Mentausier
—a circumstance which explains the success with
which he burst upon the town in 1671. After the
Restoration Wycherley went to Queen's College,
Oxford ; left the University without taking a degree ;
and entered at the Temple. Like Etherege he seems
to have been quite unknown to the Court and the
town until after the production of his first play.

Wycherley's plays were all produced between
1671 and 1674. The age of their authorship is
a problem. Spence says in his ancedotes that
Pope had informed him: " the chronology of
Wycherley's plays I am well acquainted with, for
he told it me over and over. *Love in a Wood* he
wrote when he was but nineteen ; *The Gentleman
Dancing Master* at twenty-one ; *The Plain Dealer* at
twenty-five ; and *The Country Wife* at one or two and
thirty." Macaulay, whose method with Wycherley
is to run through the main incidents of his life,
putting upon each in turn the worst possible construction, rejoices to detect in the plays clear evidence

that Wycherley was deceiving Pope. Wycherley, writing *Love in a Wood* at nineteen, would fix the year 1659 for its composition. Macaulay discovers many allusions in the play that would put the writing of it at least after 1669 ; and there is little doubt that Macaulay is right as to the main fact— namely, that all the plays were written at least after the great fire. But his incidental sneer, " Nothing that we know of Wycherley leads us to think him incapable of sacrificing truth to vanity," is quite unwarrantable. An impartial critic, instead of leaping at the opportunity of putting Wycherley in the wrong, would have pointed out (1) that Spence might very well have misreported or misunderstood Pope, (2) that Pope's account of his dealings with Wycherley is itself entirely untrustworthy, (3) that, even if the witness of Pope and Spence were flaw- less, Wycherley's memory at the time he was acquainted with Pope was unable to carry him from the evening of any one particular day to the morning of the next. Pope, as reported by Spence, tells us himself that Wycherley lost his memory (forty years before he died) by a fever, and would "repeat the same thought, sometimes in the com- pass of ten lines, and did not dream of its being inserted but just before : when you pointed it out to him, he would say, 'Gads-so, so it is! I thank you very much : pray blot it out.'" These reflexions leave it open as to whether Wycherley lied either in fact or intention.

Wycherley was—shall we say ?—intentionally careless. He entered with zest into all those affecta- tions of the period which we have observed in

Etherege as fundamental in the Restoration temperament. "I'd have you to know I scorn writing," says Wycherley's Mr. Sparkish, who would be taken by his friends for a wit; and Etherege's Sir Fopling Flutter holds that "writing is a mechanic part of wit; a gentleman should never go beyond a song or a billet." It was probably much in this spirit of deprecation that Wycherley met the boyish enthusiasm of young Pope. "These plays you admire? wild oats, my dear little infallible." It was perfectly natural that Wycherley should affect to have written his comedies as Charles II. governed England—his best efforts but mere lapses of the amateur. "Many gentlemen do things that are below 'em," as Sir Fopling says; "damn your authors." Congreve fell into precisely this attitude when Voltaire came to do him reverence. Voltaire visited the great author; Congreve insisted upon being the simple gentleman. Macaulay, who can always appreciate a good thing when it is uttered upon his own part, himself reminds us of Congreve's characteristic attitude towards his work in the encounter with Collier. Congreve, answering Collier, described *The Old Bachelor* as a trifle of no importance, much as Wycherley must have spoken to Pope of *Love in a Wood*. "I wrote it," he said, "to amuse myself in a slow recovery from a bit of sickness." "What his disease was," retorted Collier, "I am not to inquire, but it must be a very ill one to be worse than the remedy." Suppose that the worst is true of Wycherley, as Macaulay hoped and believed. Suppose he deliberately lied about his age of authorship. The lie was, at any rate, in character—one of the small sacrifices to fashion upon which polite society is founded. The problem may be left to the charity or malevolence of whoso will undertake a definitive life of Wycherley.

Whenever Wycherley wrote his plays, it is certain that none was performed till *Love in a Wood* in 1671. Like Etherege's *Love in a Tub*, the play at once made him free of the town and the Court. The Duchess of Cleveland was his first important friend. The tale of this acquaintance is an illuminating piece of social history. Charles II. was far too lazy to insist upon keeping a mistress entirely to himself; and the Duchess of Cleveland, in addition to the many successful gallants who boasted discreetly of her favours, had an unsuccessful suitor in the Duke of Buckingham. Just at the time when Buckingham wooed in vain, Wycherley came within view of the Duchess and immediately pleased her. By all the rules of gallantry in any period but the one we are trying to understand, Charles II. should have quarrelled with Buckingham, and Buckingham with Wycherley. But it was Buckingham who introduced Wycherley to the Court, who procured him the King's friendship, and obtained for him military honours. It is too strange a story to be anything but true.

For the account of how Wycherley came by the acquaintance of the Duchess of Cleveland we are indebted to John Dennis. In 1728 a certain Major Pack published an assortment of prose and verse as Wycherley's posthumous works. We may forgive the disservice to Wycherley's memory (a

true friend would have burned the MS.); for
Major Pack's prefatory memoir drew from Dennis
an *Original Letter* which is perhaps the most valuable of the small surviving pieces of Wycherley's
biography. Dennis tells us in his letter to Major
Pack the whole story of Charles, Wycherley,
Buckingham, and his cousin Barbara.

The tale begins with the production in 1671 of
Wycherley's *Love in a Wood.* "The writing of
this play," says Dennis, "was the occasion of his
becoming acquainted with one of King Charles'
mistresses after a very particular manner." Wycherley was going through Pall Mall to St. James' in
his chariot when the Duchess met him in hers.
"Thrusting half her body out of the chariot," she
roundly suggested, in terms no longer polite, that
Wycherley had come irregularly into the world.
The point of her delicate raillery lay in a song
from Wycherley's play, heard overnight, to the
effect that "great wits and great braves," like
Shakespeare's Edmund, take "more composition and
fierce quality" than usually go to the making of a
lawful gentleman born. Dennis continues : "As,
during Mr. Wycherley's surprise, the chariots drove
different ways, they were soon at a considerable
distance from each other, when Mr. Wycherley,
recovering from his surprise, ordered his coachman
to drive back, and to overtake the lady. As soon
as he got over-against her, he said to her, ' Madam,
you have been pleased to bestow a title on me
which generally belongs to the fortunate. Will
your Ladyship be at the play to-night?' 'Well,'
she replied, 'what if I am there?' 'Why, then

I will be there to wait on your Ladyship, though I disappoint a very fine woman who has made me an assignation.' 'So,' said she, 'you are sure to disappoint a woman who has favoured you for one who has not.' 'Yes,' replied he, 'if she who has not favoured me is the finer woman of the two. But he who will be constant to your Ladyship, till he can find a finer woman, is sure to die your captive.' The lady blushed, and bade her coachman drive away. . . . In short, she was that night in the first row of the King's box in 'Drury Lane,' and Mr. Wycherley in the pit under her, where he entertained her during the whole play."

Thus started an acquaintance of which Voltaire writes in his *Letters concerning the English Nation*, that henceforth Wycherley was known publicly to be happy in the good graces of the most celebrated mistress of King Charles II. When, a few months later, the play was published, he wrote the Duchess an impudent witty dedication lest the town might be ignorant of his conquest. The passage, here presented, shows *inter alia*, that Wycherley was already reading the maxims of La Rochefoucauld. "Poets," he says, "let them pass in the world ever so much for modest, honest men, but begin praise to others which concludes in themselves; and are like rooks, who lend people money but to win it back again, and so leave them in debt to 'em for nothing; they offer laurel and incense to their heroes, but wear it themselves, and perfume themselves. This is true, Madam, upon the honest word of an author who never yet writ dedication. Yet though I cannot lie like them, I am as vain as they; and cannot but publicly give your Grace my humble acknowledgments for the favours I have received from you :—this, I say, is the poet's gratitude, which, in plain English, is only pride and ambition; and that the world might know your Grace did me the honour to see my play twice together.   Yet, perhaps, my enviers of your favour will suggest 'twas in Lent, and therefore for your mortification.   Then, as a jealous author, I am concerned not to have your Grace's favours lessened, or rather my reputation; and to let them know you were pleased, after that, to command a copy from me of this play; the only way without beauty and wit, to win a poor poet's heart."

From the *Original Letter* of Dennis it would seem that Buckingham was at first sore at Wycherley's success with a lady who so stubbornly resisted himself.   But Sedley and Rochester, who saw in Wycherley a man who would considerably add to the pleasure of life, arranged that they should meet.   The result followed quite naturally from the manners of the time.   Beautiful mistresses were not so rare as wits of the quality of William Wycherley.   Buckingham took the wit and let his cousin go, as a woman that at any rate had an excellent taste in gallants.   The Duke was charmed to that degree, says Dennis, that he cried out in a transport, "*By* G——, *my cousin is in the right of it;* and from that very moment made a friend of a man whom he believed to be his happy rival."

Every good thing was immediately taken to King Charles.   Wycherley was at once accepted as an *objet d'art et de vertu*.   His career at Court was brilliant as it was brief. "As King Charles was extremely fond of him upon account of his wit," says Major Pack, "some of the royal mistresses, I have been credibly informed, set no less value upon those parts in him of which they were more proper judges." That Charles cherished Wycherley's acquaintance is shown by the story, true or false, that in 1678, when the dramatist fell ill of a fever, the King visited him at his lodging in Bow Street; recommended him to try Montpelier, and gave him £500 towards the expenses of a holiday. It is at any rate fairly certain that when Wycherley returned in 1679, better for the journey, the King proposed he should accept the charge of his son Richmond's education. Dennis says the King urged Wycherley to accept this position of royal tutor with a promise "that when the time came that his office was to cease he would take care to make such a provision for him as should set him above the malice of the world."

But Wycherley's fortunes at this point disastrously turned. Going down to Tunbridge, possibly to finish his cure begun at Montpelier, he came upon the Countess of Drogheda inquiring for *The Plain Dealer* at a bookstall. "Since you are for the Plain Dealer," said Wycherley's companion of the walk, "there he is for you." Some polite gallantry ensued, ending in a secret marriage.

Wycherley's father was his evil counsellor. The old man, none too rich for a country gentleman, feared that Wycherley might lose the King's favour did he confess to the marriage at a moment when he was expected to keep himself free to wait upon the Duke of Richmond. Perhaps Wycherley himself would not be excessively eager to come suddenly upon the town as a married man. In the event everything went wrong. The Countess appears to have been extravagant and imperious of temper. Undoubtedly she was jealous. Wycherley is pictured as meeting his friends in a tavern opposite his house with the windows open for his wife to keep a watch upon their proceedings.

The King was offended at his breach of manners; and his Countess seems to have kept him from appearing at Court in his justification. Moreover this was the period of the opposition and imprisonment of Buckingham, of whom " Manly " Wycherley had written :

> Your late disgrace was but the Court's disgrace.

This, with a vengeance, was plain dealing. It might well cool the royal favour, for Charles was at this time annoyed with the political situation. Wycherley, at any rate, had no more kindness of King Charles. Shortly after his marriage the Countess died; her relatives captured the fortune she had intended to leave her husband ; and Wycherley disappeared for seven years into the Fleet, a prisoner for debt.

Wycherley's career pointedly illustrates Sir Walter Scott's description of the Stuart Kings— " The needy Charles who loved literary merit without rewarding it ; the saturnine James who rewarded without loving it ; the phlegmatic William who neither loved it nor rewarded it." Wycherley had been the friend of Charles ; but it was James who released him from the Fleet. Seeing a performance of *The Plain Dealer*, the story runs, James remembered his brother's friend, was touched, and sent to relieve him. Macaulay enters here with a malicious and utterly ungrounded insinuation that Wycherley paid for his release with his religion. "We cannot help suspecting," says Macaulay, "that it was at this time that Wycherley returned to the Communion of the Church of Rome." Macaulay writes, quite unintentionally, with an ingenuous sincerity. It is literally true, that Macaulay "cannot help suspecting" the worst of his victims, even when there is not a shred of evidence to justify him.

Macaulay has suggested for Wycherley a horrible old age with an equal disregard of the witnesses. We will leave aside for the moment the story of Wycherley's friendship with Pope; and pass to events of his second marriage and death. First let us see how artfully Macaulay builds a totally false impression. "Pope," he writes apropos of the friendship he hereafter describes, "though at no time scrupulously delicate in his writings or fastidious as to the morals of his associates, was shocked by the indecency of a rake, who at seventy, was still the representative of the monstrous profligacy of the Restoration." This is pure invention. We shall discover that Pope, far from being shocked at Wycherley's indecency, is the liveliest witness of his excellent qualities. The confederate suggestion as to Wycherley's horrible old age is entirely ungrounded.

Macaulay thus passes to Wycherley's second marriage. "The last scene of his life was perhaps the most scandalous. Ten days before his death he married a young girl merely in order to injure his nephew, an act which proves that neither years nor adversity, nor either of the religions which he had at different times professed, had taught him the rudiments of morality." The picture is now complete of a lecherous and spiteful old man, dying as shamefully as he had lived.

The circumstances of Wycherley's second marriage are not sufficiently clear for posterity to form any definite opinion as to its merits. We have to rely upon the impression it made upon Wycherley's friends and contemporaries. Happily Pope, Macaulay's chosen witness to the indecency of Wycherley's last years, has left for our reading a letter upon this very subject written in January, 1715-6, to his friend Blount. From this, and from the anecdotes of Spence, we learn that Wycherley had suffered some ill-usage at the hands of his nephew. We also know that Wycherley was heavily in debt ; but that the estate was entailed. Apparently his nephew and heir would not in any way accommodate him. Wycherley's device was to marry a young woman who brought him enough money to pay his debts ; and in return for her portion to settle upon her a jointure charged upon the estate. This had the effect of securing the interest of Wycherley's creditors upon his nephew's inheritance—by no means a discreditable intention. Pope, at any rate, tells the story to Blount in approbation of his friend : " I know of nothing that will be so interesting to you at present," he writes, " as some circumstances of the last act of that eminent comic poet, and our friend, Wycherley. He had often told me, as I doubt

not he did all his acquaintance, that he would marry
as soon as his life was despaired of. Accordingly,
a few days before his death, he underwent the
ceremony: and joined together those two sacra-
ments, which, wise men say, should be the last we
receive: for, if you observe, matrimony is placed
after extreme unction in our catechism, as a kind of
hint of the order of time in which they are to be
taken. The old man then lay down, satisfied in his
conscience of having by this one act paid his just
debts, obliged a woman, who, he was told, had merit,
and shown an heroic resentment of the ill-usage of
his next heir. Some hundred pounds, which he
had with the lady, discharged those debts: a
jointure of four hundred a year made her a recom-
pense; and the nephew he left to comfort himself
as well as he could, with the miserable remains of
a mortgaged estate. I saw our friend twice after
this was done, less peevish in his sickness than he
used to be in his health; neither much afraid of
dying, nor (which in him had been more likely)
much ashamed of marrying. . . .

" So trivial as these circumstances are, I should
not be displeased myself to know such trifles, when
they concern or characterise any eminent person.
The wisest and wittiest of men are seldom wiser
or wittier than others in these sober moments. At
least, our friend ended much in the character he
had lived in : and Horace's rule for a play may as
well be applied to him as a play-wright

——————————*Servetur ad imum*
Qualis ab incepto processerit, et sibi constet.

" I am, etc."

Spence's anecdote enables us a little more precisely to understand the financial difficulty. He is more explicit as to the nephew's part in the affair. " Wycherley's nephew," he tells us, " on whom his estate was entailed (but with power to settle a widow's jointure) would not consent to his selling any part of it; which he wanted much to do, to pay his debts, about a thousand pounds. He had therefore long resolved to marry, in order to make a settlement from the estate, to pay off his debts with his wife's fortune, and 'to plague his damned nephew,' as he used to express it." This is the best and worst that we know of the scene in Wycherley's life which Macaulay determines as the most scandalous of his career.

Wycherley's friendship with Pope was fortunate for his biographers. It has enabled them to recover from oblivion the circumstances of his later years. Wycherley was a gentleman of the Restoration who occasionally descended into authorship. Pope was of the next generation, that surrendered even its private letters to the publisher. In 1735 Pope edited and published the correspondence that had passed between himself and Wycherley; which remains to this day one of the principal sources of our information.

Wycherley was already an old man when Pope in his sixteenth year first made his acquaintance. *Quantum mutatus ab illo !* was the burden of his years. Illness, it seems (probably the illness of 1678, for which he had visited Montpelier and Tunbridge), had almost destroyed his memory. But *The Plain Dealer* and *The Country Wife* kept

WILLIAM WYCHERLEY.

From a mezzotint by J. Smith, after a painting by Peter Lely.

green his reputation; and it is clear that despite his infirmities he was held in great respect by the younger men—Lansdowne, Dennis, and Pope. Macaulay, whose memoir is for Wycherley a convenient text for contradiction, would have us believe that Wycherley died in contemptible obscurity; and that Pope, of necessity, parted from him in impatient anger.

The correspondence published in 1735 by Pope turns upon a very curious fragment of literary history. Wycherley was amongst the first to perceive in Pope the young poet who would one day write perfectly in the manner at which the gentlemen scribblers of his time had unsuccessfully aimed. He had very little illusion about himself as a poet; but he was eager to be in the fashion; and he proposed to publish a "damn'd miscellany" of verses. At this point it occurred to him to ask his young friend to look through his papers, and, when it was possible, to suggest improvements. Pope, highly flattered, accepted this very delicate and difficult commission. When we reflect upon what happened to Gil Blas when he so unfortunately acted upon the instructions of the Archbishop of Toledo, it would seem that little short of a miracle could save this enterprise from disaster; and it is immensely to the credit of the parties, respectively liable to the infirmities of age and youth, that their friendship survived it.

Macaulay's version of the story is in the spirit of his introduction. Wycherley, he falsely says, "though blinded by self-love to the imperfections of what he called his poetry, could not but see that there was an immense difference between his young companion's rhymes and his own. He was divided between two feelings. He wished to have the assistance of so skilful a hand to polish his lines; and yet he shrank from the humiliation of being beholden for literary assistance to a lad who might have been his grandson."

These lines were written by Macaulay with Wycherley's letters actually before him. He not only refers to the letters; but quotes from them such passages as best colour his analysis of Wycherley's motives. It is only fair to judge Macaulay from the evidence at his command. We shall afterwards discover that even this evidence had been edited by Pope to his own advantage; but this Macaulay could not possibly have known. Judging, however, from what he undoubtedly did know, the malignancy of his bias is quite sufficiently clear.

Macaulay formed his opinion from the correspondence published by Pope himself in 1735— Pope's own story of the vexed verses. According to this, Wycherley first wrote of them to Pope on 22 March, 1705–6: "I must lay a penance upon you," he writes, "which is to desire you to look over the damned miscellany of madrigals of mine [Wycherley is referring to the 1704 collection], to pick out, if possible, some that may be so altered that they may yet appear in print again, I hope with better success than they hitherto have done." "I doubted your meaning in this," Pope answered about three weeks later, "whether it was to pick out the best of those verses . . . to make the method and numbers more exact; for though I believe they might receive such an alteration with advantage, yet they would not be changed so much but any one would know them for the same at first sight. Or if you mean to improve the worst pieces, which are such, as, to render them very good, would require a great addition and almost the entire new writing of them." Pope included a sample of his work: "Some," he said, "I have contracted as we do sunbeams to improve their energy and force; some I have taken quite away, as we take branches from a tree to add to the fruit; others I have entirely new expressed and turned more into poetry."

This was plain-speaking with a vengeance. Had Wycherley been the vain old man of Macaulay's invention, this letter had ended all between them. But Wycherley writes in the following November: "As to the damned verses I entrusted you with, I hope you will let them undergo your purgatory to save them from other people's damning them. . . . I beg you to peruse my papers and select what you think best and most tolerable and look over them again; for I resolve suddenly to print some of them, as a hardened old gamester will, in spite of all former ill-usage by fortune, push on an ill hand with no expectation of recovering himself, especially since I have such a *croupier* or second to stand by me as Mr. Pope."

In his next letter Pope tells Wycherley that though he has made the *Poem on Dulness* "as short again as at first," yet there is "not one thought omitted," and that there are some thoughts "new expressed or added." "The versification," he

continues, "is such as nobody could be shocked at.
The repeated permissions you give me of dealing
freely with you, will, I hope, excuse what I have
done : for if I have not spared you when I thought
severity would do you a kindness, I have not
mangled you where I thought there was no absolute
need of amputation."

Wycherley acknowledges this "extreme kind
and obliging letter" two days after it was written ;
thanks Pope for the pains he has taken and
promises him—"it will be as hard for you to get
quit of my mercenary kindness for you as it would
be for me to deserve or return yours." The correspondence continues in the same strain, even after
Pope has suggested (13 May, 1708) that if
Wycherley is not prepared drastically to "metho-
dise" his verses, he had better destroy the whole
frame, and reduce them into single thoughts in
prose like those of La Rochefoucauld.

Finally, in April, 1710, came what Macaulay has
treated as a breach between the friends. Pope
having again been carefully through some of the
"damned verses," writes to Wycherley a detailed
account of his work. He is uncertain as to how
much he ought to deface Wycherley's MSS., and
he asks for more particular instructions. " I am at
once," he writes, " equally fearful of spoiling you,
and of offending you by too impudent a correction."

Wycherley on getting back his papers was
appalled. Clearly he had not realised how bad his
memory had become. In his answer to Pope,
where Macaulay has found offended vanity and
petulance, a fair critic will discover a sincere regret

that he should have put his young friend to so much trouble, and not a little pathetic astonishment at the extent of his own infirmity. " You give me an account in your letter," he writes, " of the trouble you have undergone for me. . . . You say you find numerous repetitions of the same thoughts and subjects, all which, I must confess, my want of memory has prevented me from imagining. Of all figures, that of tautology is the last I would use, or least forgive myself for. But seeing is believing; wherefore I will take some pains to examine and compare those papers in your hands with one another, as well as with the former printed copies, or books of my damned miscellanies; all which, as bad a memory as I have, with a little more pains and care, I think I can remedy. Therefore I would not have you give yourself more trouble about them, which may prevent the pleasure you have, and may give the world, in writing upon new subjects of your own, whereby you will much better entertain yourself and others." There follow some fresh instructions, and as a conclusion of the episode an assurance that " as to what you call freedom with me, which you desire me to forgive, you may be assured I would not forgive you unless you did use it : for I am so far from thinking your plainness a fault or an offence to me, that I think it a charity and an obligation, which I shall always acknowledge with all sort of gratitude." Pope's ensuing return of the MSS. with advice reiterated that the verses should be transcribed into single maxims and reflexions in prose brings this correspondence abruptly to an end.

It would be fortunate if all authors of Wycherley's fame had no more of the natural infirmities of a literary temperament than is here disclosed. If we must find in these letters matter for censure, it should be directed not so much against Wycherley as against Pope. The autograph MSS. of Wycherley's letters, preserved at Longleat and printed as an appendix to Courthope's *Life of Pope*, when compared with the 1735 edition are an illuminating evidence of the petty insincerities into which an author's vanity may lead him. Pope was precocious enough in simple truth ; but he was ambitious in middle life to be thought even more a prodigy of infancy than he really was. He has systematically misdated the correspondence between himself and Wycherley ; omitted paragraphs ; and run letters of a different date into one. Indeed, he has so obviously edited the correspondence to give his readers of 1735 a profound impression of his youthful precocity that Mr. Courthope, his learned and careful editor, is compelled to conclude that no letter published by Pope as coming from Wycherley is to be trusted unless it is confirmed from the Longleat MSS. The point rather concerns a biographer of Pope than of Wycherley, except for a general impression obtained from reading the two versions in favour of the dramatist. In Wycherley's MS. letters we more clearly recover the mood of the writer—the lively interest and affection of a celebrated author far in years, for a talented young prodigy of wisdom and learning, so assiduous with his homage and attention. " My Great Little Friend, My Dear Little Infallible "—

these are the expressions which coloured the first
intercourse of the writers. Pope does not care
to insist upon this affectionate raillery. It takes
from his dignity as a youthful genius.

It is quite clear that Wycherley intended no
suppression of the fact that his "damned miscellany" had been thoroughly revised by Pope.
Wycherley, in fact, almost immediately began to
publish the enterprise abroad. Doubtless, he
thought he was doing his young friend, whose
laurels were yet to win, an excellent turn in allowing it to be known that he thought him so much
a better poet than himself. Pope did not see
the matter quite in that light. Pope, in his heart,
knew that Wycherley's verses were doggerel, and
was even then quite sure that he preferred his name
to be kept from all connexion with the contemplated volume. As soon as he heard that Wycherley had been informing the town of his share in the
enterprise he wrote to him in panic : " No man
alive shall ever know any such thing from me ; and
I give you this warning besides, that, though yourself should say I had any way assisted you, I am,
notwithstanding, resolved to deny it." Wycherley
thought this was modesty of his young friend.
The situation is not empty of humour. We can
faintly imagine of Pope, how amazed and baffled
he was when he received Wycherley's answer.
"As for owning your assistance to me," Wycherley writes, "in overlooking my unmusical numbers
and harsher sense, and correcting them both with
your genius in judgment, I must tell you I always
own it in spite of your importunate modesty, who

would do with your friendship as your charity—conceal your bounty to magnify the obligation. But that shall not serve your turn. I will always own it is my infallible Pope has, or would, redeem me from a poet's damning."

Wycherley's friendship with Pope persisted to the time of his death. The letters we have already examined ended on 2 May, 1710, and in the preceding year there is a big gap in the correspondence. This lacuna of 1709 is happily explained in a letter of Pope to Cromwell dated October, 1711. Cromwell had written to Pope of Wycherley's recovery from a dangerous illness. Pope answers him : "You have delivered me from more anxiety than he imagines me capable of on his account. . . . I am surprised at the danger you tell me he has been in, and must agree with you that our nation would have lost in him as much wit and probity, as would have remained (for aught I know) in the rest of it. My concern for his friendship will excuse me (since I know you honour him so much, and since you know I love him above all men) if I vent a part of my uneasiness to you, and tell you that there has not been wanting one to insinuate malicious untruths of me to Mr. Wycherley, which, I fear, may have had some effect on him."

This letter sufficiently explains what might appear as a temporary estrangement. As to the period between Pope's returning of the MSS. and Wycherley's death, Macaulay's brief statement, "thus terminated (in 1710) this strange friendship," is clearly disproved if we may trust to the words of Pope himself as conveyed to us by Spence.

Spence's report of their last relations bears every
mark of veracity. It is so precisely what we should
have imagined them to be. " In after years, speaking of Wycherley," runs Spence's anecdote, " Pope
said : 'We were pretty well together to the last :
only his memory was so totally bad, that he did not
remember a kindness done to him, even from minute
to minute. He was peevish, too, latterly ; so that
sometimes we were out a little, and sometimes in.
He never did an unjust thing to me in his whole
life ; and I went to see him on his death-bed.' "

This anecdote is supported by a short passage
from one of Cromwell's letters in the autumn of
1711—after the correspondence had been broken
off. Cromwell writes : " Mr. Wycherley came to
town on Sunday last and surprised me with a visit
on Monday morning. We dined and drank together ;
and I saying, 'To our loves,' he replied, 'It is
Mr. Pope's health.' " These testimonies, taken with
the letter to Blount describing the second marriage
and death, which we have already cited, are evidence
enough that despite his infirmities the man who of
all others had most to bear with him was his friend
to the last.

We now perceive that Wycherley was not the
satyr of Macaulay's invention. Contemporaries dwell
particularly upon two traits of his character—his
virility and his kindliness. " Manly," in the contemporary view, describes the author as well as his plays.
His championship of the disgraced Buckingham,
and of the poet Butler for whom he endeavoured to
obtain the patronage of the Court, are some justification of the sobriquet. Even more particularly

Wycherley's friends insist upon his kindliness. They liked to contrast the severity of the author with the gentleness of the man. In a letter of Lansdowne written during Wycherley's lifetime we read : " To judge by the sharpness and spirit of his satires you might . . . imagine him an ill-natured man ; but what my Lord Rochester said of my Lord Dorset is applicable to him—the most good-natured man with the worst-natured muse. As pointed and severe as he is in his writings, in his temper he has all the softness of the tenderest disposition ; gentle and inoffensive to every man in his particular character, he only attacks vice as a public enemy, compassionating the wound he is under a necessity to probe, or grieving like a good-natured conqueror at the occasions which provoke him to make such havoc."

Major Pack writes of Wycherley in the same sense : " He is justly celebrated," says Pack, " among the best of our English comic poets. His plays are an excellent satire upon the vices and follies of the age in which he lived. His style is masculine and his wit is pointed. And yet, with all that severity and sharpness with which he appears on the stage, they who were of his familiar acquaintance applauded him for the generosity and gentleness of his manners. He was certainly a good-natured man ; and I reckon it as one great mark of such a disposition that he was as impatient to hear his friends calumniated as some other people would be to find themselves defamed. I have more than once been a witness of that honourable tenderness in his temper."

Wycherley could be famous without drawing to himself the envy of his rivals. "Your writings," says Dennis, "are as bold as your conversation is modest. . . . That you are esteemed at this high rate you owe to your wit and your penetration ; but that you are esteemed without envy, that you are with joy and gladness esteemed, you owe to this, that while the force of your fancy and judgment makes all the world admire you, you remain yourself unmoved by it." To which Wycherley very suitably returned : "Your praise rather humbles me than makes me (though a damned poet) more vain. For it is so great that it rather seems the raillery of a witty man than the sincerity of a friend."

Clearly Wycherley was esteemed by the men of his generation. "Congreve," writes Lord Lansdowne to his correspondent in a letter already quoted, "is your familiar acquaintance ; you may judge of Wycherley by him : they have the same manly way of thinking and writing, the same candour, modesty, humanity, and integrity of manners. It is impossible not to love them for their own sakes, abstracted from the merit of their works."

What is the merit of the works of Wycherley ? Estimating Wycherley's place in English letters, not the most scrupulous biographer is tempted beyond the four comedies—*Love in a Wood*, *The Gentleman Dancing Master*, *The Country Wife*, and *The Plain Dealer*. Wycherley himself wrote in a preface to his "damned miscellany" : "My pretensions are but small in the province of poetry and the title of poet is the least of my ambitions "—

with which self-judgment we may leave the poet out of consideration.

Let us recall two points of the contemporary verdict as to the plays of Wycherley, one of which has already met us at the start of our inquiry. First, Wycherley in seventeenth-century eyes was undoubtedly, astonishing as it may seem, a moral force. " *The Country Wife* and *The Plain Dealer*," Dennis writes to Wycherley in 1694, "are stores of delight which you have laid up by a noble charity to supply the poor in spirit through all ages." The plays of Wycherley as food for spiritual humility is an idea to stagger posterity. But a finer critic than Dennis also regarded Wycherley as a fountain of moral energy and regeneration. " Satire," says Dryden in his *State of Innocence*, "lashes vice into reformation, and humour represents folly so as to render it ridiculous. Many of our present writers are eminent in both these kinds ; and particularly the author of *The Plain Dealer*, whom I am proud to call my friend, has obliged all honest and virtuous men by one of the most bold, most general and most useful satires which has ever been presented in the English theatre."

Second, there is a tradition that Wycherley was a slow and a laborious writer.

> Hasty Shadwell and slow Wycherley

is Rochester's line ; also the couplet :

> But Wycherley earns hard whate'er he gains,
> He lacks no judgment and he spares no pains.

Upon Rochester's evidence Macaulay has concluded that Wycherley's mind was "naturally a very meagre soil and was forced only by great labour to bear fruit which after all was not of the highest flavour." A careful reading of Wycherley's plays gives no such impression—in fact, we miss in them that evidence of care and repeated finishing which appears upon every page of Congreve. Many passages of Wycherley are a bout of intellectual high spirits. To be tolerable they would have to be played at full speed. His dialogue is breezily rapid, boisterous, and full-winded. He seldom approaches the anxiously balanced, antithetical excellence of his predecessor Etherege or of Congreve, his successor. It is therefore not altogether surprising that Rochester's criticism, never very accurate or wise, is directly contradicted both by Lansdowne and Pope. Pope says of Wycherley that "he was far from being slow in general, and, in particular, wrote *The Plain Dealer* in three weeks." And Lansdowne says of him, what would certainly be true of almost any writer of the period, that, "if it had been a trouble to him to write, I am much mistaken if he would not have spared himself that trouble." These testimonials do not necessarily mean that Wycherley was a slovenly or a lazy writer. "That among these fellows is called easy writing which any one may easily write" is an epigram attributed to Wycherley by Dick Steele, writing in *The Tatler* upon "insects called easy writers." But the balance of the evidence is clearly against assuming that Wycherley wrote at enormous expense of energy.

It is tolerably clear from circumstantial evidence —putting aside the personal witness of the author—

that *Love in a Wood* was Wycherley's first play ;
that it was produced at Drury Lane early in 1671 ;
and that it was tolerably successful.   Hart, Mohun,
Lacy, and Kinaston were in the caste ; and Mrs.
Knipp, Pepys' "Merry Jade," took the part of my
Lady Flippant.   The play has been little noticed
by contemporary or later critics.   The author of
The Country Wife and *The Plain Dealer* has eclipsed
the author of *Love in a Wood*.

"Have I not constantly kept Covent Garden
Church, St. Martin's, the playhouses, Hyde Park,
Mulberry Gardens and all the other public marts
where widows and maids are exposed ? " asks my
Lady Flippant in the opening duologue of Wycherley's first play.   The contrast between Wycherley
and Etherege must not blind us to a fundamental
similarity.   We are in the same world of ordinaries,
theatres, and walks.   We are looking into the same
mirror of contemporary life.   Manners are observed
with eyes equally alert, and are presented comically
in terms of realism.   We are equally far, as with
Etherege, from any deliberate naturalising of
French comedy upon English soil, or from any
connexion with the satirical categories of Jonson.
Wycherley comes more nearly in contact with these
men than any other dramatist of the period ; but,
even so, the distance between them is still greater
than the distance between any two authors of the
Restoration.

Wycherley's "noble and useful satire" is not the
product of an untroubled view of life—the view of
a man who thinks in universal types of humanity.
Wycherley's main business is still with manners,

not with morals ; and where his moral fury intrudes
it spoils rather than uplifts his comedy. Ordinarily
he accepted life. But suddenly he sees clean
through the spectacle that has served his turn, and
breaks into a furious, confused passion of disgust.
Only in this way can we explain the alternating of
scenes handled in a spirit purely laughter-loving
with scenes of violent rage against humanity. It
is precisely this moral fury of Wycherley which is
accountable for passages that have persistently disgusted the critics. There are passages in any one
of the four plays which, independently of any
change of attitude or manners, are revolting.
Laughter is extinguished ; the jester bursts irrecog-
nisably upon us, a ferocious prophet, dredging into
the filth of human nature with precisely the sombre
satisfaction with which certain devout people relish
the possibilities of hell. The spirit of these scenes
is as far from the easy nonchalance of Etherege as
from the sunshine satire of Molière. But it puts
Wycherley quite definitely in touch with the French
satirical school of comedy, despite the distance that
is between them. More especially there are scenes
where Wycherley's shrewd good humour and passing pleasure in the life of his time combine with
his fundamental puritanism to produce scenes of a
faintly subacid quality which agreeably suggest the
manner of French comedy at its best.

The darker side of the comedy of Wycherley
appears even as we scan the dramatis personæ of
his first play. Alderman Gripe, even before his
appearance, is obviously well-hated by the author
of his being. "Seemingly precise, but a covetous,

lecherous old usurer of the City" is disquieting.
Soon the scorpions are loosed. Alderman Gripe,
betrayed by Miss Lucy into the hands of Mrs.
Crossbite and her confederates, is flatly hideous.
Wycherley is doing his moral worst to show vice
its own image.

Love in a Wood is, for its faults, an excellent
introduction to a reading of Wycherley's plays.
It is prentice work. There is no unity of style;
and it is therefore possible, from page to page, to
run along the whole scale of Wycherley's literary
moods. The scene to which we have already
alluded, in its inequitable disgust with the devil,
is a prototype of *The Plain Dealer*, where, as we
shall see, Wycherley's moral fervour precipitated
him into one of the most unpleasant extant pieces
of English literature. Thence we may gradually
ascend till we arrive at scenes almost in the vein
of Etherege and Congreve. As an instance of
the intermediate scene, where satire is softened
with humanity and seasoned with laughter—a passage in Act I. between Alderman Gripe and Mrs.
Joyner may be noted; and, with an irony less
bitter, the symmetrical backbiting passages between
Dapperwit, Ranger, and Vincent; also the scenes
where the prudery of my Lady Flippant is exposed.

At the opposite extreme from Alderman Gripe
are the scenes which definitely place Wycherley
in the same school with Etherege and Congreve.
Dapperwit is the successor of Sir Fopling; the
predecessor of Witwoud. He is the half-wit, dear
to his author as a foil to the fine gentlemen of his
comedy. "Wit" is his occupation. He teems

with pleasantry. He is continually athroe with sonnets and lampoons. But he is far from being the Restoration idea of a perfect companion. The art of conversation was very highly studied in the late seventeenth century. Wycherley and Congreve asked of true wit that it should inform a gentleman's conversation without effort ; that it should spring naturally from the thing he had to say. They abhorred the man who collected after-dinner stories, related the newest jests from the coffee house, or conscientiously cudgelled his invention for an epigram or a trope. Such a man, though he might amuse one so long as his repertory lasted, or his invention held, was recognised for the worst enemy of good conversation. The type is perennial ; and in periods of social depression passes triumphantly for the real thing. A comedy of manners, resting for much of its point upon an antithesis between Mirabell and Witwoud, is to-day impossible. It too often happens that Witwoud takes the head of a table, where Mirabell, if he happened to be present, would be ignored.

Dapperwit and Witwoud, though they are not the Restoration idea of social perfection, are nevertheless amusing ; and in the intervals of the story the gallants upon whom they conscientiously model their behaviour put them through their paces much as Shakespeare's heroes test the mettle of his fools. In one of the liveliest passages of *Love in a Wood* Lydia is thus engaged with Dapperwit. It is excellently typical of Wycherley's lighter style of writing. The talk is of wits and their several qualities :

Lyd. If you are for proving your wit, why do not you write a play?

Dap. Because 'tis now no more reputation to write a play, than it is honour to be a knight. Your true wit despises the title of poet, as much as your true gentleman the title of knight; for as a man may be a knight and no gentleman, so a man may be a poet and no wit, let me perish!

Lyd. Pray, sir, how are you dignified or distinguished amongst the rates of wits? and how many rates are there?

Dap. There are as many degrees of wits as of lawyers. . . . There is first your court-wit, your coffee-wit, your poll-wit, or politic-wit, your chamber-wit, or scribble-wit, and last of all, your judge-wit, or critic.

Lyd. But are there as many wits as lawyers? Lord, what will become of us!—What employment can they have? how are they known?

Dap. First, your court-wit is a fashionable, insinuating, flattering, cringing, grimacing fellow— and has wit enough to solicit a suit of love; and if he fail, he has malice enough to ruin the woman with a dull lampoon :—but he rails still at the man that is absent, for you must know all wits rail; and his wit properly lies in combing perukes, matching ribbons, and being severe, as they call it, upon other people's clothes.

Lyd. Now, what is the coffee-wit?

Dap. He is a lying, censorious, gossiping, quibbling wretch, and sets people together by the ears over that sober drink, coffee : he is a wit, as he is a commentator, upon the Gazette ; and he rails at the pirates of Algier, the Grand Signior of Constantinople, and the Christian Grand Signior.

Lyd. What kind of man is your poll-wit?

Dap. He is a fidgetting, busy, dogmatical, hot-headed fop, that speaks always in sentences and proverbs, (as other in similitudes,) and he rails perpetually against the present government. His wit lies in projects and monopolies, and penning speeches for young parliament men.

Lyd. But what is your chamber-wit, or scribble-wit?

Dap. He is a poring, melancholy, modest sot. . . . He employs his railing against the ignorance of the age, and all that have more money than he.

Lyd. Now your last.

Dap. Your judge-wit, or critic, is all these together, and yet has the wit to be none of them : he can think, speak, write, as well as the rest, but scorns (himself a judge) to be judged by posterity : he rails at all the other classes of wits, and his wit lies in damning all but himself :—he is your true wit.

Wycherley omits the finer values of style. His plays should be read rapidly, so that we may fully appreciate the quick flow of his ideas ; the liveliness of their expression ; the happy surprise of his best effects. Much of his laughter is simple high spirits. There is rough-and-tumble in his best comic scenes. Lightheartedness blows as a steady, purifying, and persistent wind.

Wycherley appears at his lightest in *The Gentleman Dancing Master*. This play was produced— or, as Professor Ward conjectures, revived—at the New Theatre in Dorset Gardens in 1671. " It was not much liked," says Genest, "and was acted only six times." Wycherley in the prologue of his next play describes himself as "the late so-baffled scribbler," and he published *The Gentleman Dancing Master* without dedication or comment of any kind.

Yet it is the merriest of Wycherley's comedies. More than any other it should be swiftly read. It is a bottle of high spirits. Once opened, it must not be allowed to go flat. Quotation is perhaps the worst method of conveying its peculiar quality, always excepting an analysis of the plot, which no play of the comic dramatists could for a moment survive. With this prefatory warning, we will here transcribe possibly the one passage that can be lifted from its context without grievous bodily harm.

The characters of the ensuing dialogue are Monsieur, the Gallicised wittol of the play, and Flirt, a daughter of Paphos. Wycherley and his friends had already discovered—it is the theme of a celebrated modern comedy—that an exacting mistress is infinitely worse than an exacting wife. Monsieur and Flirt, making their compact, fantastically present the consequences of marriage outside the law :

Mons. Come, come, I am thine ; let us strike up the bargain : thine, according to the honourable institution of keeping.—Come.

Flirt. Nay, hold, sir ; two words to the bargain ; first, I have ne'er a lawyer here to draw articles and settlements.

Mons. How ! is the world come to that ? A

man cannot keep a wench without articles and settlements! Nay, then 'tis e'en as bad as marriage, indeed, and there's no difference betwixt a wife and a wench.

Flirt. Only in cohabitation ; for the first article shall be against cohabitation—we mistresses suffer no co-habitation.

Mons. Nor wives neither now.

Flirt. Then separate maintenance, in case you should take a wife, or I a new friend.

Mons. How! that too! then you are every whit as bad as a wife.

Flirt. Then my house in town and yours in the country, if you will.

Mons. A mere wife!

Flirt. Then my coach apart, as well as my bed apart.

Mons. As bad as a wife still!

Flirt. But take notice, I will have no little, dirty, second-hand chariot new furnished, but a large, sociable, well-painted coach ; nor will I keep it till it be as well known as myself, and it come to be called Flirt-coach ; nor will I have such pitiful horses as cannot carry me every night to the Park ; for I will not miss a night in the park, I'd have you to know. . . .

Mons. Is this all?

Flirt. No.—Then, that when you come to my house, you never presume to touch a key, lift up a latch, or thrust a door, without knocking beforehand. . . .

Mons. But what allowance? let's come to the main business : the money.

Flirt. Stay, let me think : first for advance money, five hundred pounds for pins.

Mons. A very wife !

Flirt. Then you must take the lease of my house, and furnish it as becomes one of my quality. Then for housekeeping, servants' wages, clothes, and the rest, I'll be contented with a thousand pounds a year present maintenance, and but three hundred pounds a year separate maintenance for my life, when your love grows cold.

From *The Gentleman Dancing Master* we pass in due succession to *The Country Wife. The Country Wife* was produced some time between 1672 and 1674 ; and seems to have been extremely successful. In Garrick's bowdlerised version it survived to the days of Mrs. Jordan, whose Mrs. Pinchwife is eloquently approved by Leigh Hunt. It is the most brilliant of Wycherley's plays, and the most perfect farce in English dramatic literature —a whirlwind of inspired buffoonery. It lifts the reader from solid ground, and bears him to a region where laughter alone administers the law and the constitution. All questions of motive and moral value disappear. It is true that Wycherley keeps to the realistic method of his school. Mr. Horner, as Macaulay contends, is intimately modelled upon the fine gentlemen of Covent Garden. But the naturalistic method of Mr. Horner's presentation does not in the least affect Elia's fundamentally right contention that he is a native of Cloud-Cuckooland. His famous project, upon which every situation of the play so brilliantly hangs, at once puts him beyond the cool estimates of morality; and it would be absurd in a critical reader to feel towards Mr. Horner as he would feel towards an actual twentieth-century social figure of Mr. Horner's character and habits. But it must not be forgotten that Mr. Horner is an imaginative reflexion of a society that really existed, and that *The Country Wife* was written from the point of view of an actual and definite code of morality.

The husband, or jealous cuckold of the play, is typical of everything in sexual morality that Restoration society disliked. Critics who have urged that the comic dramatists systematically ridicule the marriage tie have surely missed the point of Mr. Pinchwife. The comic dramatists' attitude towards Mr. Pinchwife was precisely the attitude urged to-day with every symptom of moral fervour and righteousness by an energetic group of contemporary authors towards the husband who regards the marriage tie as dissolving all rights and decencies of personal relationship between the parties. The Restoration was a period of intellectual equality between the sexes. Sex equality, then as now, subjected the commonly accepted morality of married life to vigorous and pertinacious criticism. "So you only married to keep a whore to yourself," retorts Mr. Horner upon Pinchwife. "Let me go back to my own freehold," says Pinchwife in a later scene. Granted that Restoration society was coarsely regulated, it is, at any rate, fairly clear that the idea of marriage as conferring upon a husband the rights of a proprietor was one which moralists of the time of Charles II. could not easily digest. The anxieties of the ridiculous husbands in the plays of Wycherley and his contemporaries are not the anxieties of men of honour. They are the anxieties of men of property—surely a legitimate subject for ridicule.

The career of Mr. Sparkish, Dapperwit of *The Country Wife*, clearly illustrates this very definite social feeling of the time. Sparkish, living up to his character of a wit, perpetually refuses to condescend to the vulgar passion of jealousy. Sparkish says contemptuously of Horner: "Your stingy country coxcomb keeps his wife from his friends, as he does his little firkin of ale for his own drinking." His own attitude is merrily set forth in a dialogue with Alithea. She warns him that he has a rival. But Sparkish refuses to be told:

Spark. That's a good one! I hate a man for loving you! If he did love you, 'tis but what he can't help; and 'tis your fault, not his, if he admires you. I hate a man for being of my opinion! I'll n'er do't, by the world.

Alith. Is it for your honour, or mine, to suffer a man to make love to me, who am to marry you to-morrow?

Spark. Is it for your honour, or mine, to have me jealous? That he makes love to you, is a sign you are handsome; and that I am not jealous, is a sign you are virtuous. That I think is for your honour.

Later he says of Alithea: "I have that noble value for her that I cannot be jealous of her"; and, speaking generally, he declares: "I love to be envied, and would not marry a wife that I alone could love; loving alone is as dull as eating alone.

Is it not a frank age? and I am a frank person;
and, to tell you the truth, I love to have rivals in
a wife."

It is necessary, for reasons that will shortly
appear, here to transcribe a short passage from
The Country Wife, introducing us to the celebrated china of Mr. Horner. It is the most
indecent passage of the most indecent play by the
most indecent author of the most indecent period
of English literature—so much has been emphatically
settled by a powerful majority.

The passage is closely associated with the
impudent project of Mr. Horner; so that a word
may here perhaps be necessary to indicate what the
impudent project of Mr. Horner really was. Mr.
Horner is an extremely dry and an entirely
passionless embodiment of adventurous gallantry.
Sensuously presented, with every meretricious accom-
paniment that a febrile imagination and a full stomach
can suggest, Mr. Horner is the popular hero of the
vast number of plays and romances upon which the
British public persistently feeds without the least
notion of harm taken. Seen in the dry light of
Wycherley's classical farce, Mr. Horner is morally
intolerable. Wycherley has dared to emphasize a
fact invariably avoided in the modern theatre—
namely, that adultery is not entirely a matter of fine
phrases and exalted frenzy. Adultery is a physical
fact. Like most physical facts, it may for artistic
purposes be regarded comically or tragically; and,
so long as all the facts are present in their due
proportion, no moral harm, either way, can ensue.
Mr. Horner is an active and indefatigable gallant

who fulfils the artistic purpose of his being with energy and resource. In order that this purpose may the more easily be effected, he causes a report to be spread through the town that suddenly he has become as bad as an eunuch. This immensely pleases the husbands. They confide their wives into his keeping. The intricate positions that ensue, the double-dealing, innuendo, and misunderstanding to the fifth degree, will be supplied by the ingenious reader. Suffice it that Lady Fidget, when she comes into the scene we are on the point of transcribing, has been for some time locked away in Mr. Horner's room ; and that she has there received an entirely satisfactory proof that Mr. Horner was misreported. Lady Fidget is supposed by her friend—samong them Mrs. Squeamish, who also has a private understanding with Mr. Horner—to be acquiring a piece of Mr. Horner's celebrated china :

Re-enter LADY FIDGET *with a piece of china in her hand and* HORNER *following.*

L. Fid. I have been toiling and moiling for the prettiest piece of china, my dear.

Horn. Nay, she has been too hard for me, do what I could.

Mrs. Squeam. Oh, lord, I'll have some china too. Good Mr. Horner, don't think to give other people china, and me none ; come in with me too.

Horn. Upon my honour, I have none left now.

Mrs. Squeam. Nay, nay, I have known you deny your china before now, but you shan't put me off so. Come.

Horn. This lady had the last there.

L. Fid. Yes indeed, madam, to my certain knowledge, he has no more left.

Mrs. Squeam. O, but it may be he may have some you could not find.

L. Fid. What, d'ye think if he had had any left, I would not have had it too? for we women of quality never think we have china enough.

Innuendo deservedly has an evil name in English ears, because most of the innuendo with which we are familiar in the English theatre has been of a particularly dishonest character. The comic possibilities of adultery are exploited to-day as thoroughly as in the time of Wycherley; but social hypocrisy has hitherto steadily insisted that physical facts shall as far as possible be slurred. By this door the talents of English dramatic authors for innuendo have mainly entered, especially when they are adapting plays from the French. Wycherley's procedure by innuendo is entirely different. The innuendo of the above passage does not slur any fact of the situation so far as the audience is concerned. It is Wycherley's ingenious device for presenting the facts to the audience without presenting them to such persons of the play as must remain persistently ignorant.

There is a passage of *The Country Wife* which excellently prepares us for *The Plain Dealer*. Mr. Horner, admitted to the bosoms of our ladies of quality and reputation, has many opportunities to observe them at their ease. Passing the guard of their fair appearances he enables Wycherley to break into a really hideous indictment. The scene where Horner drinks with my Lady Fidget,

Mrs. Dainty Fidget, and Mrs. Squeamish, and receives their confidences of the boudoir, is in Wycherley's most malignant vein.   It is a serious blot upon the play; for, where we have hitherto enjoyed the dry, impersonal quality of our author's delivery, we are now conscious of a furious disgust with the world, chaotically expressed, governed by no very clear artistic purpose.   It is a passage in the vein of *The Plain Dealer*, intruded into *The Country Wife.*

Wycherley's *The Plain Dealer*, the last and in his own period the most celebrated of his plays, was produced not later than the spring of 1674. This was the "noble and useful satire" which, more than any of his plays, determined Wycherley's reputation in contemporary eyes.   Plain-dealer was Wycherley's complimentary sobriquet.   Manly was accepted at the time as the embodiment of an honourable misanthropy.   Virtually he was Wycherley's opportunity freely to indulge the moral ferocity which had already spoiled many scenes of his earlier plays. There are a few passages in Wycherley's best manner—notably the scenes in the second act between Olivia, Lord Plausible, and Mr. Novel. But for the most part *The Plain Dealer* is inferior work; and its indecency must frankly be admitted.

What is the precise nature of this indecency? *The Plain Dealer* is not indecent in the sense that was urged by Jeremy Collier and Lord Macaulay. *The Plain Dealer* is exactly the reverse of any attempt to administer an aphrodisiac.   It is nowhere sensuous.   It is far from being a call to the pleasures of Venusberg.   On the contrary, it is the deliberate attempt of a ferocious moralist to expose the vices of nature for our disgust. It is the unhappy protest against life of a man who lived semi-consciously against the grain of his nature. It is indecent in the sense that any protest against life is indecent— in the sense that any deliberate tendency to turn the seamy side without and to ignore the equitable balance of nature is indecent.

The Plain Dealer urges us to face the question of Wycherley's indebtedness to Molière and other authors. Manly corresponds with Alceste of Molière's *Le Misanthrope*, and here, if anywhere, we should expect the approach of the two comic writers to be nearest. "The surliness of Molière's hero is copied and caricatured; but the most nauseous libertinism and the most dastardly fraud are substituted for the purity and integrity of the original," says Macaulay. On the other hand, Professor Ward, Wycherley's latest editor, asserts that in *The Plain Dealer* we are conscious of a fertility of invention, a richness of wit and satire, which make even *Le Misanthrope* seem tame. Are not these comparisons otiose? Molière helped Wycherley with his plots in the sense that Holinshed and North helped Shakespeare; and in the sense that the French Revolution helped Carlyle. Wycherley borrowed his themes; but the final result is not less his own. *The Country Wife* is in part based upon the *Ecole des Femmes*. Scenes from *The Plain Dealer* are grounded upon *Twelfth Night*. An idea or so of *The Gentleman Dancing Master* is taken from Calderon's *Maestro de Danzar*. But in every case there is so complete a transmutation of material that plagiarism is not suggested. There is not very much in common between Wycherley and Molière; there is nothing in common between Wycherley and Shakespeare. Wycherley no more borrowed Fidelia from *Twelfth Night* than Shakespeare borrowed *Twelfth Night* from *Apollonius and Silla* of Barnabe Rich.

It remains to justify our indecorous inclusion in this chapter of Mr. Horner's "prettiest piece of china." It seems that the town was divided in opinion as to the propriety of *The Country Wife*. Wycherley in *The Plain Dealer* has inserted a scene where Olivia (Wycherley's ludicrously malignant study in female depravity) reprobates the play as unfit to be seen, whereas Eliza, honest girl, undertakes to defend it. The passage occurs in the scene we have already noted as the best of the play—the backbiting scene between Olivia, Lord Plausible, and Mr. Novel, with Eliza as occasional chorus. Plausible is an admirably imagined type —a soft-spoken gossip whose defence of his friends invariably injures them from the clumsy half-heartedness of its expression:

Oliv. (TO LORD PLAUSIBLE: *spitefully discussing an absent friend*). Then for her conduct, she was seen at *The Country Wife* after the first day. There's for you, my Lord.

L. Plausible. But, madam, she was not seen to use her fan all the play long, turn aside her head, or by a conscious blush discover more guilt than modesty.

Oliv. Very fine! Then you think a woman modest that sees the hideous *Country Wife* without blushing or publishing her detestation of it ? D'ye hear him, cousin ?

Eliza. Yes, and am, I must confess, something of his opinion. . . . For all those grimaces of honour and artificial modesty disparage a woman's real virtue, as much as the use of white and red does the natural complexion : and you must use very, very little, if you would have it thought your own.

Oliv. Then you would have a woman of honour with passive looks, ears, and tongue, undergo all the hideous obscenity she hears at nasty plays.

Eliza. Truly, I think a woman betrays her want of modesty, by showing it publicly in a playhouse, as much as a man does his want of courage by a quarrel there; for the truly modest and stout say least, and are least exceptious, especially in public.

Oliv. O hideous, cousin ! this cannot be your opinion. But you are one of those who have the confidence to pardon the filthy play.

Eliza. Why, what is there of ill in't, say you ?

Oliv. O fy! fy! fy! would you put me to the blush anew ? call all the blood into my face again ? But to satisfy you then; first, the clandestine obscenity in the very name of Horner.

Eliza. Truly, 'tis so hidden, I cannot find it out, I confess.

Oliv. O horrid! Does it not give you the rank conception or image of a goat, or town-bull, or a satyr ?

Eliza. What then ? I can think of a goat, a bull or a satyr, without any hurt.

Oliv. Ay : but cousin, one cannot stop there.

Eliza. Nay, no farther, cousin. We have enough of your comment on the play, which will make me more ashamed than the play itself.

Oliv. O, believe me, 'tis a filthy play! and you may take my word for a filthy play as soon as another's. But the filthiest thing in that play, or any other play, is—

Eliza. Pray keep it to yourself, if it be so.

Oliv. No, faith, you shall know it ; I'm resolved to make you out of love with the play. I say, the lewdest, filthest thing is his china ; nay, I will never forgive the beastly author his china. He has quite taken away the reputation of poor china itself, and sullied the most innocent and pretty furniture of a lady's chamber ; insomuch that I was fain to break all my defiled vessels. You see I have none left ; nor you, I hope.

Eliza. You'll pardon me, I cannot think the worse of my china for that of the playhouse.

Oliv. Why, you will not keep any now, sure ! 'Tis now as unfit an ornament for a lady's chamber as the pictures that come from Italy and other hot countries ; as appears by their nudities, which I always cover, or scratch out, whereso'er I find 'em. But china ! out upon't, filthy china ! nasty debauched china !

Eliza. All this will not put me out of conceit with china, nor the play, which is acted to-day, or another of the same beastly author's, as you call him, which I'll go see. . . .

Oliv. Well—but my Lord, though you justify everybody, you cannot in earnest uphold so beastly a writer, whose ink is so smutty as one may say.

L. Plausible. Faith, I dare swear the poor man did not think to disoblige the ladies, by any amorous, soft, passionate, luscious saying in his play.

How unfortunate that Wycherley, when Jeremy Collier fell upon him in after years, did not follow up the line of defence here suggested! It is the final answer. The comic drama of the Restoration rested upon a comic treatment of sex. It depended for its effect upon the elimination of passion. Comic treatment is treatment in a dry light. The heart of the matter lies in the epigram of Walpole that life is a comedy to the man who thinks, a tragedy to the man who feels. The swelling of human passion and the clash of emotion may for the spectators at a play be either comic or tragic. If the author has presented them so that the audience is invited to look upon them at a distance, if he makes his appeal to the intelligence rather than to the sympathy of his hearers, he is making the comic appeal. Thus employed he must avoid all that Lord Plausible has described as "passionate" or "luscious." So soon as the comedy of sex becomes in any degree impassionate then it must pass either into tragedy or into pornographic excitement. To take an extreme instance, it is perfectly true that rape and adultery are part of the action of the majority of the plays of our comic dramatists. But the treatment being purely comic, these actions cease to be morally significant. The sexual emotion of the spectator is not involved. Intercepting his laughter he will find that it is an entirely wholesome hilarity. This holds true only so long as the author is writing purely in the comic manner. We are hereafter to discover that English comedy, after Jeremy Collier, drooped, withered, and passed finally away precisely in the proportion that the " amorous, soft, passionate, luscious saying " persistently tended to intrude.

CHAPTER V

WILLIAM CONGREVE

DRYDEN in 1692 addressed to his friend Southerne a rhymed epistle :

> The standard of thy style let Etherege be ;
> For wit the immortal spring of Wycherley ;
> Learn after both to draw some just design,
> And the next age will learn to copy thine.

In less than two years from the delivery of this invitation Dryden was congratulating a younger than Southerne upon having lived up to it.

Congreve's contemporaries estimated his achievements justly. They referred him back to Etherege for the style of his delivery, to Wycherley for the severity and chastity of his portraiture. Congreve was for them the natural and perfect heir of these earlier men. " Finis coronat " was the mood of their appreciation.

To critics who with Macaulay see in the Restoration drama of Charles II. a tempest of licentious reaction against Commonwealth severity, this contemporary attitude would seem to require some explanation. Congreve does not belong to Macaulay's hypothetical period of licentious reaction. When Congreve first appears Wycherley has already retired for twelve years. Congreve is

the friend and contemporary of Addison, Steele
and Pope ; the junior of Swift; the literary executor
of Dryden.   Accordingly, all those critics who
approach the literature of the Restoration as a
violent reaction against Fifth Monarchy are compelled when they come to Congrev₃ to sigh with
relief of their tender consciences, and emphatically
to assert that the worst is over, that the height of
Restoration licentiousness is past, that the plays of
the friend of Dick Steele are less wickedly of the
1660–1685 model than their predecessors.   But
mark how the plain contemporary tale has set
them down!   So far from seeing in Congreve a
turn of the moral tide, or finding in him any such
post-reformation of manners as Macaulay and his
followers have alleged, the kitcat critics welcomed
in the plays of Congreve a happy union of the gifts
of his predecessors.   They, at any rate, perceived
no reaction in Congreve against the characteristic
enormities of Etherege and Wycherley.   Their
formula for Congreve was to combine the qualities of Etherege with the qualities of Wycherley,
and raise them to a higher power.   Such was the
verdict of Dryden—a very clear-thinking critic—
who had lived to welcome all three men in turn to
the English stage.

If Congreve's position is to be rightly measured
it will be wise to assume that Dryden was right.
If Etherege, in the vocabulary of our nineteenth
century authorities, is wicked, indecent, and licentious ; we must be prepared to find that Congreve
is still more wicked, indecent, and licentious.   Congreve's contemporaries saw the period that included

these three men as a whole, with Congreve as its most complete expression. Congreve's comedies, as in the popular idea of them, should rather be associated with King Charles and his spaniels than with Queen Anne and her dish of tea. The popular idea is right and wrong. It is right in assuming that Congreve is King Charles and his spaniels at their highest expression. It is wrong in not having realised that King Charles and his spaniels at their highest expression is Queen Anne and her dish of tea. Pope is the perfection of Etherege. The *Essay on Man* is the polished expression of Rochester's attitude towards life. Etherege and Rochester were amateurs of paganism; Pope played with it, like a virtuoso, in heroic couplets.

We are therefore invited to study the career of Congreve as that of a Restoration gentleman, in the sense that he lived in the world of Etherege not the less definitely for his living in the world of Pope. If this should seem too tall an assumption, it may here be serviceable to add that the greatest critic of English literature has already seemed to suggest it. Congreve morally less fit to be read than Wycherley? Certainly it sounds a little strange. Is not Congreve almost clean enough to be admitted for family reading in an unexpurgated edition? Who would venture to say as much of Wycherley? Yet, obviously, if Congreve's contemporaries were right, he must needs be morally the less—the more finished fruit and example of a wicked and profligate period. But it may be objected that contemporaries are always wrong: that we cannot accept so extravagant a

supposition on the word of a contemporary.   But
a greater critic than Dryden supports it.   Coleridge
writes of the comedy of Congreve: "Wickedness is
no subject for comedy.   This was Congreve's great
error and peculiar to him.   The dramatic personages of Dryden and Wycherley and others are often
viciously indecent, but not like Congreve's, wicked."
    William Congreve was born at Bardsley in
Yorkshire in 1670.   Like Wycherley he was
of gentle and vehemently-royalist blood ; like
Wycherley he was educated out of England ; like
Wycherley he was entered at the Middle Temple ;
and like Wycherley he has been joyfully suspected
of lying as to the facts of his biography.   Congreve
went to school at Kilkenny, and afterwards to
Dublin.   At Kilkenny he was the schoolfellow of
Swift, three years his senior.   At Dublin he was,
still with Swift, the pupil of St. George Ashe.
Congreve's worst lie was his personal statement
that he was an Englishman.   For Southerne told
Giles Jacob, the biographer, that Congreve was
born in Ireland.   Dr. Johnson, without casting his
vote, does not omit to damn him with a moral
reflexion : " To doubt whether a man of eminence
has told the truth about his own birth is, in appearance, to be very deficient in candour ; yet nobody
can live long without knowing that falsehoods of
convenience or vanity, falsehoods from which no
evil immediately visible ensues except the general
degradation of human testimony, are very lightly
uttered and once uttered are sullenly supported."
Dr. Johnson's taxing like a wild-goose flies, so far
as Congreve is concerned.   The register of Bardsley

proves indubitably that Congreve's worst lie was the simple truth.

Congreve did not burst upon the town with a comedy in the sudden fashion of Etherege and Wycherley. Already, as an undergraduate, he had published the novel *Incognita*, of which Dr. Johnson said he would rather praise it than read it. There is one really notable thing about *Incognita*. Congreve's first venture into literature is in form a novel; but really it is a play—or, at any rate, a scenario. Nor is this surprising when we encounter in the preface a passage which very definitely promises that the author already sees the stage at the end of his ambition. " Since all traditions," he writes, "must indisputably give place to the drama; and since there is no possibility of giving that life to the writing or repetition of a story which it has in the action, I resolved in another beauty to imitate dramatic writing, namely, in the design, contexture and result of the plot."

Congreve seems to have arrived in London with introductions. The world as yet knew nothing of *The Old Bachelor;* but, when the *Juvenal and Persius* of 1692 was prepared, Congreve was allowed to contribute a translation; and to prefix to *Persius* a complimentary poem to Dryden—the editor and principal author. Congreve had evidently commended himself in some way to the wits, and been admitted to the freedom of Will's coffee-house. Probably he had waited upon Southerne, also an alumnus of Dublin University; and through Southerne had secured opportunities of making himself agreeable to the established authors.

Congreve finally emerged upon the stage in January, 1693, with Dryden, Southerne, and Maynwaring for sponsors. Southerne tells us that, having read *The Old Bachelor*, he showed the MS. to Dryden, who said, "he had never seen such a first play in his life, and that, the author not being acquainted with the stage or the town, it would be a pity to have it miscarry for want of a little assistance." Accordingly, they gave it the "fashionable cut"; and secured a production at the Theatre Royal, in which Betterton, Mrs. Mountfort and Mrs. Bracegirdle took parts. It was a brilliant début.

Congreve's five plays, *The Old Bachelor*, *The Double Dealer*, *Love for Love*, *The Mourning Bride*, *The Way of the World*, were all produced within the period 1693 to 1700. Congreve, like Wycherley, had a brief and brilliant career as a dramatic author. He virtually retired from the stage at thirty; living to the end of his life upon the fame of his seven years' activity. Like Wycherley, again, Congreve spent the period of his retirement in a desultory pursuit of the Muses. In 1701, he wrote *The Judgment of Paris* (music by Daniel Purcell). Later in the same year, to be in the fashion, he wrote an *Ode for S. Cecilia's Day* (music by John Eccles). In 1704 he collaborated with Vanbrugh and Walsh to adapt *Monsieur de Pourceaugnac*—a lost version. He wrote the usual epilogues and occasional poems, of which a Pindaric Ode to Queen Mary is remarkable for a critical introduction upon true and false Pindarics, and for an excellently intended model of the real thing. These various publications are interesting biography. Congreve retiring from the work

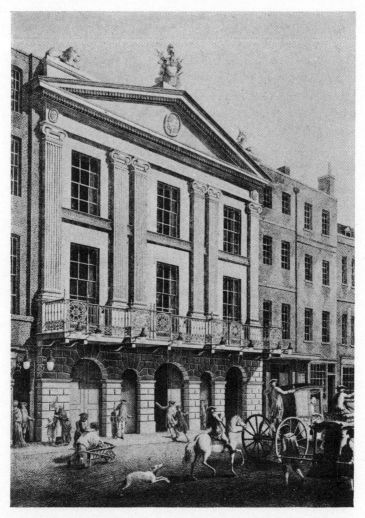

VIEW OF THE NEW FRONT OF THE THEATRE ROYAL, DRURY LANE.

that places him permanently in English literature, continued to please his contemporaries with small incursions into publicity. They kept his memory green at the coffee-houses; but, so far as posterity is concerned, his memory can safely dispense with anything of his writing that followed his last and best comedy.

Congreve was never a wealthy man—nor, till the end, was he even as comfortable as he could wish. His first patron was Charles Montague, afterwards Lord Halifax; and Congreve held in turn from first to last three small sinecures. His first post was Commissioner for licensing hackney-coaches; then came that place in the pipe office which Thackeray found so incredible; finally, but not till 1705, he became an officer of the Customs at £600 a year. Swift's lines are an exaggeration.

> Thus Congreve spent in writing plays,
> And one poor office, half his days;
> While Montague, who claimed the station
> To be Mæcenas to the nation,
> For poets open table kept,
> But ne'er considered where they slept;
> Himself as rich as fifty Jews,
> Was easy, though they wanted shoes,
> And crazy Congreve scarce could spare
> A shilling to discharge his chair.

But Congreve was at no time free of financial worry. In February, 1703, he wrote to his friend Keally: "I forgot to thank you for the hint you gave me concerning a commissioner's place in your former letter, which you have repeated in your last. You may imagine I would not omit such an advantage if it were practicable; but I know it is vain,

notwithstanding all the fair promises I have had ;
for I have not obtained a less matter that I asked
for.   I must have patience, and I think I have.   Of
my philosophy I make some use, but, before God, the
greatest trial of it is that I know not how to have
the few people that I love as near me as I want."
The feeling of this last passage is unmistakable.
Even when Congreve was at his fullest prosperity
he must have felt continually uneasy at any prospect
of a change of Government.   Halifax went out of
office in 1711.   Swift writes to Stella in June of
that year :

" I saw Will Congreve attending at the Treasury,
by order, with his brethren, the Commissioners of
the Wine Licences.   I had often mentioned him
with kindness to my Lord Treasurer ; and Congreve told me, that after they had answered to what
they were sent for, my Lord called him privately,
and spoke to him with great kindness, promising
his protection, etc.   The poor man said he had been
used so ill of late years, that he was quite astonished
at my Lord's goodness, etc., and desired me to tell
my Lord so ; which I did this evening and recommended him heartily.   My Lord assured me he
esteemed him very much and would be always kind
to him ; that what he said was to make Congreve
easy, because he knew people talked as if his
Lordship designed to turn everybody out, and
particularly Congreve ; which indeed was true,
for the poor man told me he apprehended it.   As
I left my Lord Treasurer, I called on Congreve
(knowing where he dined), and told him what
had passed between my Lord and me ; so I have

made a worthy man easy and that is a good day's work."

Thereafter Congreve had little to fear. In 1714 he exchanged his Commissionership of Wine Licences for a better post—also in the Customs ; and in 1715 he obtained yet another sinecure. Eighteen years after Swift had made a worthy man easy Congreve died with £10,000 to his credit.

The little we are able in glimpses to recover of Congreve's life reveals a succession of unbroken friendships ; a battle royal with the critics of his day ; an anthology of golden opinions. He seems to have lived a life profoundly uneventful and entirely decorous. Curll in 1730 issued a fragmentary volume entitled *Memoirs of the Life, Writings, and Amours of William Congreve, Esq.* —a loose collection of papers, most of which survive quite independently for our reading. Obviously *Amours* was slipped into the title to tickle purchasers ; for the volume is implicitly a proof that Congreve afforded his contemporaries no opportunity for scandal. One "love-letter" is inserted— to Arabella Hunt, a lady whom Congreve has neatly celebrated in verse for her vocal accomplishment. The letter is entirely correct in phrase and feeling ; and the editor's comment is illuminating. "Upon this article of *Amours*," he writes, "I am sensible the ill-natured would expect much scandal, though they will find nothing but the most elegant and polite conversation."

Upon this article of *Amours* Congreve's name is associated with two celebrated women of his time ; and in neither case is there the least necessity to assume the worst.   The best parts of his comedy—including incomparable Millamant—were written for Mrs. Bracegirdle.   It is as certain that the whole town was in love with Mrs. Bracegirdle as that Mrs. Bracegirdle was successfully out of love with the whole town.   There was a life-long friendship between Mrs. Bracegirdle and Congreve—and scandal asserted no more.   Cibber's description is famous : " Mrs. Bracegirdle was now [1690 or 1691] but just blooming to her maturity; her reputation as an actress gradually rising with that of her person ; never any woman was in such general favour of her spectators, which, to the last scene of her dramatic life, she maintained by not being unguarded in her private character.   This discretion contributed not a little to make her the *Cara*, the darling of the theatre ; for it will be no extravagant thing to say, scarce an audience saw her that were less than half of them lovers, without a suspected favourite among them ; and though she might be said to have been the universal passion, and under the strongest temptations, her constancy in resisting them served but to increase the number of her admirers. . . . Her youth and lively aspect threw out such a glow of health and cheerfulness that on the stage few spectators, that were not past it, could behold her without desire.   It was even a fashion among the gay and young to have a taste or *tendre* for Mrs. Bracegirdle."   It is possibly best left to the charity or malice of the reader to infer whether her unspotted reputation was the result of calculating discretion, or unusual virtue.

As to the Duchess of Marlborough, only the

malice of her dreadful mother has dared to suggest
that she received more pleasure than honour in
Congreve's society.   This was the friendship of
Congreve's retired years.   It was the full blossom
of his career as a social figure of the time, whereas
the Bracegirdle friendship was the fruit of his
activities as a dramatic author.   This seems to
explain why Congreve chose the Duchess for his
heir, and made a testament as worldings do.   To
Mrs. Bracegirdle he left but £100 ; to the Duchess
he left his fortune.   It was his last assertion
as a man of mode that his career as a wit and a
gentleman was of more importance than his career
as an author.

What indignation has been spent upon this
affectation of Congreve!   We have already discussed the attitude it typifies in the lives of
Etherege and Wycherley.   In Congreve, as we
have seen, it reached its highest expression.   It is
scarcely surprising that Voltaire, the voluble young
littérateur, full of books, was disappointed.   "He
was infirm," says Voltaire, "and come to the verge
of life when I knew him.   Mr. Congreve had one
defect, which was his entertaining too mean an
idea of his own first profession, that of a writer,
though it was to this he owed his fame and fortune.
He spoke of his works as trifles that were beneath
him, and hinted to me in our first conversation
that I should visit him upon no other footing
than that of a gentleman, who lived a life of plainness and simplicity.   I answered that had he been
so unfortunate as to be a mere gentleman, I should
never have come to see him, and I was very much

disgusted at so unseasonable a piece of vanity."
Dr. Johnson is even more severe. "He treated the
Muses with ingratitude," says the Lexicographer;
"for, having long conversed familiarly with the great,
he wished to be considered rather as a man of
fashion than of art." Charles Lamb thought "the
impertinent Frenchman was properly answered";
Horace Walpole that "Voltaire has been charm-
ingly absurd." Our own view was determined in a
previous chapter.

What Dr. Johnson has called this "strange
affectation in authors, of appearing to have done
everything by chance," must be again invoked to
explain the early retirement of Congreve upon his
laurels. In Congreve's case, besides that "noble
laziness of the mind" which determined so much
of what were otherwise unaccountable in the
careers of Etherege and Wycherley, there were
qualities intellectual and personal that strengthened
the appeal of leisure and a dignified independence.
Without forestalling our account of Congreve's
several plays more than is strictly necessary, it
is well to deal immediately with the various
encounters of Congreve with his critics. Jeremy
Collier, of course, claims a chapter for himself
apart; but Congreve had other critics to contend
with who met him upon different issues.

Congreve's battle with the critics dates from
the production of *The Double Dealer*. Previously
there was no ground of dispute. His first comedy
was too completely a popular success for him to find
in its reception any ground for dissatisfaction. In
his dedication of *The Old Bachelor* to Montague,

we find a honied satisfaction, a little loftily expressed, perhaps, but entirely peaceable and correct. " I must declare myself sensible," said Congreve, " of the good nature of the town in receiving this play so kindly, with all its faults, which I must own were, for the most part, very industriously covered by the care of the players ; for I think scarce a character but received all the advantage it would admit of from the justness of the action.

" As for the critics, my Lord, I have nothing to say to or against any of them of any kind ; from those who make just exceptions, to those who find fault in the wrong place. I will only make this general answer in behalf of my play (an answer which Epictetus advises every man to make for himself to his censurers), viz.—'That if they who find some faults in it were as intimate with it as I am, they would find a great many more.' This is a confession which I needed not to have made ; but however I can draw this use from it, to my own advantage, that I think there are no faults in it but what I do know ; which, as I take it, is the first step to an amendment."

But *The Double Dealer* was not so well received ; and the friends of Congreve seem but hardly to have persuaded the town of the play's superlative merit. Congreve was disappointed. As we are about to discover, he was himself an excellent critic, and an exceptionally sound judge of his own work. He knew better than his advisers wherein it lacked, and much of their comment seemed irrelevant or mistaken. In these circumstances the best thing for an author to do is to hold his tongue.

Once he embarks upon a justification, the heat of his argument, however sincerely impersonal it may be, will usually be interpreted as the rage of vanity.

In the first heat of his disappointment Congreve severely rebuked the critics in his dedication of the published play—again to Charles Montague. "And give me leave," he addresses Montague, "without any flattery to you, or vanity in myself, to tell my illiterate critics, as an answer to their impotent objections, that they have found fault with that which has been pleasing to you. This play, in relation to my concern for its reputation, succeeded before it was acted, for through your early patronage, it had an audience of several persons of the first rank both in wit and quality ; and their allowance of it was a consequence of your approbation. Therefore, if I really wish it might have had a more popular reception, it is not at all in consideration of myself, but because I wish well, and would gladly contribute to the benefit of the stage and the diversion of the town. They were not long since so kind to a very imperfect comedy of mine, that I thought myself justly indebted to them in all my endeavours for an entertainment that might merit some little of that applause which they were so lavish of when I thought I had no title to it. But I find they are to be treated cheaply, and I have been at an unnecessary expense." In later editions Congreve omitted these angry passages, retaining all those parts of the dedication which were necessary to his argument.

Congreve in *The Double Dealer* makes free use of soliloquy—a technical device which, to say the least,

is as legitimate as the "aside," so skilfully elaborated
in Restoration Comedy.   But the critics pedantically
objected to soliloquy—it was not in fashion.   Where
Congreve was hoping for reasonable advice and
possibly some explanation as to why his second
venture had not succeeded so well with the public
as his first, he received instead a few grandmotherly
strictures of the type with which we are to-day
so dreadfully familiar.   Congreve's critics were of
the school which imagines that Ibsen's most notable
contribution to the theatre is his discovery of a
fourth wall.

Congreve meets them in his dedication.   " I
have since the acting of this play," he says,
" hearkened after the objections which have been
made to it ; for I was conscious where a true critic
might have put me upon my defence.   I was prepared for the attack ; and am pretty confident I
could have vindicated some parts, and excused
others ;   and where there were any plain mis-
carriages, I would most ingenuously have confessed
them.   But I have not heard anything said sufficient
to provoke an answer.   That which looks most like
an objection, does not relate in particular to this
play, but to all or most that ever have been written ;
and that is, soliloquy.   Therefore I will answer it,
not only for my own sake, but to save others the
trouble, to whom it may hereafter be objected. . . .
When a man in soliloquy reasons with himself,
and *pro's* and *con's*, and weighs all his designs, we
ought not to imagine that this man either talks to
us or to himself ; he is only thinking, and thinking
such matter as were inexcusable folly in him to

speak. But because we are concealed spectators
of the plot in agitation, and the poet finds it
necessary to let us know the whole mystery of
his contrivance, he is willing to inform us of this
person's thoughts; and to that end is forced to
make use of the expedient of speech, no other
better way being yet invented for the communica-
tion of thought." This is sound, practical criticism
of the technician who works after a model of his
own making.

We may perhaps note in passing that *The Double
Dealer* was resented by women of the time as a
cruel satire upon their sex. So, at any rate, it
was suggested to Congreve in explanation of its
ill success. The explanation is not very convincing.
Congreve has little of Wycherley's offensive zeal
to tax humanity. The quality of his satire will
in due time be considered. But there is a passage
of the dedication to *The Double Dealer* which, apart
from any critical appreciation of Congreve's satiric
comedy, excellently shows us the attitude—disdain-
ful, delicately superior, touched with a light, fastidious
irony—which marks him in most of his recorded
dealings with the world. " But there is one thing," he
writes, turning aside in an admirably feigned contempt
of his detractors, "at which I am more concerned than
all the false criticisms that are made upon me; and
that is, some of the ladies are offended. I am heartily
sorry for it, for I declare I would rather disoblige
all the critics in the world, than one of the fair sex.
They are concerned that I have represented some
women vicious and affected : how can I help it ?
It is the business of a comic poet to paint the vices

and follies of humankind; and there are but two sexes, male and female, men and women, which have a title to humanity : and if I leave one half of them out, the work will be imperfect. I should be very glad of an opportunity to make my compliment to those ladies who are offended ; but they can no more expect it in a comedy, than to be tickled by a surgeon when he is letting them blood. They who are virtuous or discreet should not be offended ; for such characters as these distinguish *them*, and make their beauties more shining and observed : and they who are of the other kind, may nevertheless pass for such, by seeming not to be displeased, or touched with the satire of this comedy. Thus they have also wrongfully accused me of doing them a prejudice, when I have in reality done them a service."

It was in his dedication of *The Way of the World*—yet again to Montague—that Congreve thrust most deeply at his critics. *Love for Love* had been accepted with universal applause. *The Way of the World* was accepted with faint praise. Congreve knew it was his masterpiece ; it was as obvious to him as it is to us after 200 years of English criticism. Congreve's critics, on this occasion, gave themselves completely away. In *The Way of the World* Congreve reached the highest expression of that antithesis we have noted in the plays of Etherege and Wycherley between the true wit and the false. It seems that not a few of the critics of *The Way of the World* blundered into an opinion of the play's merit before they had grasped even this elementary distinction. The real reason of the play's dubious success was clear. It was too delicately written; its merit lay in an exposition of social values too subtle to be measured by the vulgar.

Congreve thus diagnoses the reception of his play :

" That it succeeded on the stage, was almost beyond my expectation; for but little of it was prepared for that general taste which seems now to be predominant in the palates of our audience.

" Those characters which are meant to be ridiculed in most of our comedies, are fools so gross, that, in my humble opinion, they should rather disturb than divert the well-natured and reflecting part of an audience; they are rather objects of charity than contempt; and instead of moving our mirth, they ought very often to excite our compassion.

" This reflexion moved me to design some characters which should appear ridiculous, not so much through a natural folly (which is incorrigible, and therefore not proper for the stage) as through an affected wit; a wit, which at the same time that it is affected, is also false. As there is some difficulty in the formation of a character of this nature, so there is some hazard which attends the progress of its success upon the stage; for many come to a play so overcharged with criticism, that they very often let fly their censure, when through their rashness they have mistaken their aim. This I had occasion lately to observe; for this play had been acted two or three days, before some of these hasty judges could find the leisure to distinguish betwixt the character of a Witwoud and Truewit."

Congreve continues his dedication asking Montague to receive the comedy into his protection. "It is only by the countenance of your Lordship," he declares, "and the *few* so qualified that such who wrote with care and pains can hope to be distinguished; for the prostituted name of *poet* promiscuously levels all that bear it." Do we not here find at any rate an auxiliary reason why Congreve so early abandoned the ungrateful stage?

Congreve's attack upon his critics finds its best excuse in the circumstance already noted, that he was right and they were wrong. Like Dryden, Congreve was a really able critic. The *Essay upon Humour in Comedy*, contained in a letter written to John Dennis in 1695, can scarcely be neglected in a history of English criticism. Modern readers must be careful not to misinterpret the purport of this letter. The "humour" of which Congreve writes is "a singular and unavoidable manner of doing or saying anything, peculiar and natural to one man only, by which his speech and actions are distinguished from other men." Congreve, in fact, is discussing humour in the paulo-post-Elizabethan sense. His analysis is admirably clear and consistent, evidence of deep thought upon the principles of his art.

There is in this essay a passage which clearly shows that Congreve in retorting upon his critics was moved more with a poet's indignation in behalf of his muse than with a merely personal spleen. As we have seen in the dedication of *The*

Way of the World Congreve wrote in some contempt of " fools so gross—that they should rather disturb than divert the well-meaning and reflecting part of an audience." In the *Essay on Humour*, written as a private letter with no thought of self-justification, we read :

" For my part, I am as willing to laugh as anybody, and as easily diverted with an object truly ridiculous ; but, at the same time, I never care for seeing things that force me to entertain low thoughts of my nature. I don't know how it is with you, but I confess freely to you, I could never look long upon a monkey without very mortifying reflexions. . . . I think the follies [with which we are diverted] should be only such as men's humour may incline them to, and not follies entirely abstracted from both humour and nature."

Two other passages of the Essay may be quoted for their penetration and their admirable expression. " Talking of the ladies," says Congreve, " methinks something should be observed of the honour of the fair sex, since they are sometimes so kind as to furnish out a character for comedy. But I confess I had never made any observation of what I apprehend to be true humour in women. Perhaps passions are too powerful in that sex to let humour have its course ; or may be by reason of their natural coldness humour cannot exert itself to that extravagant degree which it does in the male sex. For if anything does appear comical or ridiculous in a woman, I think it is little more than an acquired folly or an affectation. We may call them

the weaker sex, but I think the true reason is
because our follies are stronger and our faults are
more prevailing." Observe in this passage the
penetrating veracity of that seeming contradiction
between passions "too powerful in the sex" and
"their natural coldness."   ·

The passage upon humour and the English national
character should certainly be more familiar than it
is. "There is more of humour in our English
comic writers," says Congreve, "than in any other.
I do not at all wonder at it, for I look upon humour
to be almost of English growth; at least, it does
not seem to have found such increase on any other
soil. And what appears to me to be the reason of
it is the great freedom, privilege, and liberty which
the common people of England enjoy. Any man
that has a humour is under no restraint or fear of
giving it vent; they have a proverb among them
which, may be, will show the bent and genius of the
people as well as a longer discourse, 'He that will
have a Maypole, shall have a Maypole.' This is
a maxim with them, and their practise is agreeable
to it. I believe something considerable, too, may
be ascribed to their feeding so much on flesh, and
the grossness of their diet in general. But let the
physicians agree [about] that."

Congreve was good enough critic to be justi-
fiably disgusted with the public and their bear-
leaders. Also he was by temperament a man that
shunned much company. So far as we are able to
perceive him, he was ever agreeable, imperturbably
courteous, outwardly tolerant of fools. Men of
all opinions liked him, and regarded him as apart

from their sects and schisms. But the affable exterior only the more perfectly masked his fastidious, difficult temperament. The few glimpses we are allowed of his private sentiments are of a man who, beneath a manner socially accessible, admitted but few men to his affection or esteem. One of the most brilliant social figures of any time, he was nevertheless by nature an eremite. Here, again, we are helped to understand his virtual retirement at thirty from dramatic authorship.

Congreve, the social figure, is perhaps best described for us in the sentence of Curll : " I find Mr. Congreve was the universal peace - maker amongst the poets." He was supreme arbiter at Will's coffee house. The smoothness of his tongue and temper are indicated in the tradition that he succeeded in reconciling Dennis, who had more than the usual venom of an eighteenth-century pamphleteer, with Pope, who had more than the usual vanity of an eighteenth-century author.

Congreve's conversation succeeded in being brilliant without being ill-natured. " But were the company better or worse, I would have you expect no characters from me," he writes to Dennis in 1695 ; "for I profess myself an enemy to detraction." Congreve undoubtedly struck his contemporaries as a peaceable man. " An agreeable companion," is Swift's description. We can hardly ascribe this to any exceptional disposition to agree with his kind. We detect in Congreve's social attitude the perfection of temper that comes of an inward security of opinion. He did not readily quarrel, because he

was content with the private knowledge that he was
right, and that his opponents were wrong. He had
no impulse to convert the world. He was too
polished a gentleman to endeavour after a proselyte.
It is true that he rebuked his critics. But he was
young at the time, and the rebuke was administered
upon the assumption that his critics were not so much
his opponents as men who might conceivably consent
to receive from him some necessary instruction.
We must be careful, of course, not to misunderstand
this cool urbanity. Congreve was not the superior
person. The superior person is the least respectable of social types. Congreve's attitude was a
sublimation of *tot homines.* His delicate disdain
would in conversation include himself with his
friends, the world, heaven, and earth. Of the perfection of his social manner perhaps our best witness
is the celebrated Lady Mary Wortley Montagu.
"It was my fate to be much with the wits ; my
father was acquainted with all of them. Addison
was the best company in the world. I never knew
anybody that had so much wit as Congreve."

Happily we are able to see below this smooth
exterior. Congreve had an intimate friend in Joseph
Keally. Letters passed frequently between them
in the period between 1700 and 1712. They are
not the letters of an author. They do not place
him as a literary figure. They are personal.
"There is no news," Congreve writes 20 June
1704 ; "the town is extreme thin; rather thinner
than usual at this time of year ; good wine scarcer
than ever, and lemons very dear ; but I hope that
these things will mend by the time I get abroad."

Such is the tenour of this intimate correspondence. But how does Congreve address a friend—one of the few for whom he has a real affection? In June, 1706, he writes: "I am sure you know me well enough to know I feel very sensibly and silently for those whom I love." Here is light indeed upon the impenetrable polish of Congreve's social manner. In July, 1700, Congreve had informed his friend of some people who very much regretted his absence. "I need not tell you," he continues, "that *I* do; who am not apt to care for many acquaintances, and never intend to make any friendship. You know I need not be very much alone; but I choose it."

In November, 1710, we get a glimpse into the temper of Congreve's retirement. "Dear Keally," he writes, "Si vales bene est, ego quidem valeo. And what else can a man write in these latter times. . . . I write to you because I will write to you, and always must desire to hear from you. I live entirely at home, see nobody, nor converse in any manner."

Congreve, in outward character a round man, had an appearance in keeping. "I have a multitude of affairs," he writes to Keally in October, 1704, "having just come to town after nine weeks' absence. I am grown fat, but you know I was born with somewhat of a round belly. . . . Think of me as I am, nothing extenuate. My service to Robin, who would laugh to see me puzzled to buckle my shoe, but I'll fetch it down again." This admirably fits with the picture one would choose to have of the comfortable author, who, only twenty years later, addressed to Cobham the *Epistle of Improving the Present Time*:

> Come see thy friend, retired without regret,
> Forgetting care, or striving to forget,
> In easy contemplation soothing time,
> With morals much, and now and then with rhyme ;
> Not so robust in body as in mind,
> And always undejected, tho' declined :
> Not wondering at the world's new wicked ways,
> Compared with those of our forefathers' days.
> For virtue now is neither more nor less,
> And vice is only varied in the dress.
> Believe it, men have ever been the same.

Congreve's friendship with Keally is undoubtedly most precious for those who would know what manner of man he was. Congreve had greater, but not better, friends than Joseph Keally. His more illustrious friendships, part of his public life, tell us more about the author but less about the man. Swift, Gay, Pope, Southerne, Dryden, and Steele have all recorded their opinions of Congreve and his work. Possibly these opinions would best appear in an estimate of Congreve's position in English letters ; but we are also able to detect a personal note.

Swift helps us considerably on the personal side, especially in the period after 1710 when Congreve was nearly blind with cataract, and afflicted with gout. In the *Journal to Stella* (26 October, 1710) there is a lively picture of our author cheerful in despite of his misfortunes : " I was to-day to see Mr. Congreve, who is almost blind with cataracts growing on his eyes; and his case is, that he must wait two or three years, until the cataracts are riper, and till he is quite blind, and then he must have them couched ; and besides, he is never rid of the gout, yet he looks young and fresh, and is as cheerful as ever. He is younger by three years or more than I, and I am twenty years younger than he. He gave me a pain in the great toe, by mentioning the gout."

Thirteen years later (February, 1723) Gay, writing to Swift, almost repeats him : " Mr. Congreve I see often. He always mentions you with the strongest expressions of esteem and friendship. He labours still under the same afflictions as to his sight and gout ; but, in his intervals of health, he has not lost anything of his cheerful temper. I passed all last season with him at the Bath, and I have great reason to value myself upon his friendship, for I am sure he sincerely wishes me well. We pleased ourselves with the thoughts of seeing you there."

Swift, in a sense, has written the epitaph of Congreve. He records for himself, putting reputation aside, the loss of a friend. In February, 1729 (*Journal to Stella*), he writes : " This renews the grief for the death of our friend Mr. Congreve, whom I loved from my youth, and who, surely, besides his other talents, was a very agreeable companion. He had the misfortune to squander away a very good constitution in his younger days ; and I think a man of sense and merit like him is bound in conscience to preserve his health for the sake of his friends, as well as of himself. Upon his own account I could not much desire the continuance of his life, under so much pain and so many infirmities. Years have not yet hardened me, and I have an

addition of weight on my spirits since we lost him,
though I saw him seldom, and possibly, if he had
lived on, should never have seen him more."

There is unmistakably a personal note in
Dryden's eulogium of the *The Double Dealer* :

> Already I am worn with cares and age,
> And just abandoning the ungrateful stage. . . .
> But you, whom every Muse and Grace adorn,
> Whom I foresee to better fortune born,
> Be kind to my remains; and, oh defend,
> Against your judgment, your departed friend !
> Let not the insulting foe my fame pursue,
> But shade those laurels which descend to you :
> And take for tribute what these lines express ;
> You merit more, nor could my love do less.

This is deeper than compliment. The affection
was genuine. " I am Mr. Congreve's true lover,"
Dryden wrote to Tonson in August, 1693, "and
desire you to tell him how kindly I take his often
remembrance of me. I wish him all prosperity and
hope I shall never lose his affection."

Congreve himself undoubtedly read into Dryden's
lines more than the official commendation of a
laureate; and spent the late years of his leisure
editing the plays of his dead predecessor. In his
prefatory dedication of the edition to the Duke of
Newcastle he recalls the friendly charge which
Dryden had laid upon him twenty-three years ago.
" In some very elegant though very partial verses
which he did me the honour to write to me, he
recommended me to 'be kind to his remains.' I
was then and have been ever since most sensibly
touched with that expression, and the more so
because I could not find in myself the means of

satisfying the passion which I felt in me to do something answerable to an injunction laid upon me in
so pathetic and amiable a manner."

We may infer from a letter of Congreve to
Pope (May, 1726) that he, too, was of the
inner circle. "Here is not one creature." says
Congreve, "that I know which, next to the few
I would choose, contributes very much to my satisfaction." Macaulay has found, in the splendid compliment of Pope's dedication of the *Iliad* to Congreve,
evidence rather of the poet's shrewdness than his
affection. To whom should he dedicate the trumpeted *Homer ?* Dedication to a political patron
would have been invidious. A neutral person was
best ; and Congreve was harmless, elderly, and
quite out of the literary and political fray. All this
is misplaced ingenuity to establish an inference
that Congreve was not so estimable in the eyes
of his friends as the dedication implies. Yet the
dedication is every way fitting. Dryden, dedicat-
ing his *Æneid* years before to the Marquis of
Normanby had written of Congreve : "I shall
never be ashamed to own that this excellent young
man has showed me many faults which I have
endeavoured to correct." Pope was Dryden's successor in the enterprise of nationalising the classics.
Congreve was the link between them. Pope's
dedication requires no explanation beyond the one
he himself has clearly offered. "Let me," he
writes, "leave behind a memorial of my friendship
with one of the most valuable men, as well as finest
writers, of my age and country ; one who has tried
and known by experience how hard an undertaking

it is to do justice to *Homer*, and who, I am sure, sincerely rejoices with me at the period of my labours. To him, therefore, having brought this long work to a conclusion, I desire to dedicate it, and to have the honour and satisfaction of placing together in this manner the names of Mr. Congreve and of A. Pope."

"Friendly Congreve ; unreproachful man "— Prior's line recurs continually as we read almost any one of these commendations in prose or verse.

> 'Tis something to be willing to commend
> But my best praise is that I am your friend

concludes Southerne's epistle to Mr. Congreve on *The Old Bachelor*. Dick Steele, likewise, ends upon the personal note in his celebration of Congreve, author of *The Mourning Bride* and *The Way of the World*.

> You give us torment, and you give us ease,
> And vary our afflictions as you please.
> Is not a heart so kind as yours in pain,
> To load your friends with cares you only feign ;
> Your friends in grief, composed yourself, to leave?
> But 'tis the only way you'll e'er deceive.

Fame more often spoils good manners than good morals. But Congreve seems to have lost neither outwardly nor inwardly by his early extravagant success. He remained for his acquaintances an agreeable companion, and for his friends kept unspoiled his ability to feel "very sensibly and silently."

One more personal fact needs here to be recorded. Congreve wrote four comedies and a tragedy. That Congreve wrote a tragedy will not critically concern us; but as a personal fact it is highly important. *The Mourning Bride* was every way the greatest success of Congreve's dramatic career. Distinctly it was an episode. The majority of Congreve's contemporaries, having to choose, would almost certainly have preserved the tragedy, and destroyed the comedies. This would probably hold good of most critics up to the time of Garrick. It is, perhaps, unnecessary here to record that Dr. Johnson found in *The Mourning Bride* the "most poetical paragraph" in the whole mass of English poetry, and that he was afterwards at some pains to qualify a eulogy which startled even the eighteenth century. To-day, while we have entirely lost the point of view from which Dr. Johnson scheduled a poet's reputation, we are happily still accessible to the appeal of Congreve's exquisite prose. All we are able to find in *The Mourning Bride* is an interesting proof that, even when he was writing metrically, Congreve was unable entirely to omit from his verse some of the necessary qualities of good prose. For this reason, if for none other, an historian of English tragedy in the seventeenth century would be compelled to regard *The Mourning Bride* as of almost equal importance with *Venice Preserved*.

Congreve's first comedy *The Old Bachelor* was produced at Drury Lane in 1693. It is said to have been revised for the stage by Southerne, with Dryden's help; but we need not suffer ourselves to be disturbed into detecting the consequences of this

Joseph Harris speaking the Epilogue to "Unhappy."

revision. The writing is plainly Congreve. The play, as we have already seen, was immediately successful. The spectators might feel that happiest of sensations—the sensation of meeting with something new, but at the same time, familiar. Here was the vein they had welcomed in Etherege more surely and firmly pursued ; together with the vivid, voluble buoyancy and keen touches of character they had applauded in Wycherley. The play was brilliantly acted by Mrs. Bracegirdle, Mrs. Barry, Mrs. Mountfort, Betterton and Dogget. It ran for fourteen nights. Southerne was expressing the general view :

> Dryden has long extended his command,
> By right divine, quite through the Muses' land
> Absolute lord ; and holding now from none,
> But great Apollo, his undoubted crown. . . .
> His eldest Wycherley, in wise retreat,
> Thought it not worth his quiet to be great.
> Loose, wandering Etherege, in wild pleasures tost
> And foreign interest, to his hopes long lost :
> Poor Lee and Otway dead ! Congreve appears,
> The darling and last comfort of his years.
> Mayst thou live long in thy great Master's smiles,
> And growing under him, adorn these isles :
> But when—when part of him (be that but late)
> His body yielding must submit to fate,
> Leaving his deathless works and thee behind,
> (The natural successor of his mind),
> Then mayst thou finish what he has begun ;
> Heir to his merit, be in fame his son.

Is it entirely an accident that the opening lines of Congreve's first comedy are a manifesto ?

BELLMOUR *and* VAINLOVE *meeting.*

Bell. Vainlove, and abroad so early ! good morrow. I thought a contemplative lover could

172 THE COMEDY OF MANNERS

no more have parted with his bed in a morning,
than he could have slept in't.

Vain. Bellmour, good morrow—Why, truth on't
is, these early sallies are not usual to me, but
business, as you see, sir—[*Showing letters.*] And
business must be followed or be lost.

Bell. Business!—and so must time, my friend, be
close pursued, or lost.   Business is the rub of life,
perverts our aim, casts off the bias, and leaves us
wide and short of the intended mark.

Vain. Pleasure, I guess, you mean.

Bell. Ay, what else has meaning?

Vain. Oh, the wise will tell you—

Bell. More than they believe—or understand.

Vain. How, how, Ned, a wise man say more
than he understands?

Bell. Ay ay; wisdom's nothing but a pretending
to know and believe more than we really do.   You
read of but one wise man, and all that he knew
was, that he knew nothing.   Come, come, leave
business to idlers, and wisdom to fools: they have
need of 'em: wit, be my faculty, and pleasure my
occupation; and let father Time shake his glass.

If this be not malice aforethought, it is at any
rate no accident that Bellmour and Vainlove are
soon talking as if they had walked out of the last
comedy of Etherege into the first comedy of his
successor.

Bell. Why, faith, I think it will do well enough,
if the husband be out of the way, for the wife to
show her fondness and impatience of his absence by
choosing a lover as like him as she can; and what
is unlike, she may help out with her own fancy.

Vain. But is it not an abuse to the lover to be made a blind of?

Bell. As you say, the abuse is to the lover, not the husband : for 'tis an argument of her great zeal towards him, that she will enjoy him in effigy.

Etherege continually recurs in passages which irresistibly appeal to be quoted. The following short passage between Bellmour and Belinda is Sir Frederick Frollick and his widow in transmutation to something finer. The spirit is Etherege. The manner begins to be Congreve :

Belin. Prithee, hold thy tongue !—Lard, he has so pestered me with flames and stuff, I think I shan't endure the sight of a fire this twelvemonth !

Bell. Yet all can't melt that cruel frozen heart.

Belin. O gad, I hate your hideous fancy ! you said that once before.—If you must talk impertinently, for Heaven's sake let it be with variety ; don't come always, like the devil, wrapped in flames. —I'll not hear a sentence more, that begins with an " I burn "—or an " I beseech you, madam."

Bell. But tell me how you would be adored ; I am very tractable.

Belin. Then know, I would be adored in silence.

Bell. Humph ! I thought so, that you might have all the talk to yourself.

Wycherley recurs in scenes less susceptible of quotation. We detect him in the rough-and-tumble of the Fondlewife passages, and in the implicit satire of Heartwell's Comedy of Courtship. But Congreve has refined upon his model. There is less rapidity of merriment and less vigour of thrust, but a more deliberate expression. The satire is calculated,

tolerant, delivered with the irritating superiority
of an even temper. In the scene where Heartwell,
the surly bachelor, hovers before the door of his
enchantress, Congreve owes much to the models of
his predecessor. But even as we recognise the
debt, we feel how differently Wycherley would have
used—or misused—the opportunities of Heartwell's
misogamy.

Enter HEARTWELL, VAINLOVE *and* BELLMOUR
following.

Bell. Hist, hist, is not that Heartwell going to
Silvia ?

Vain. He's talking to himself, I think : prithee
let's try if we can hear him.

Heart. Why, whither in the devil's name am I
a-going now ? Hum—let me think—is not this
Silvia's house, the cave of that enchantress, and
which consequently I ought to shun as I would
infection ? To enter here, is to put on the en-
venomed shirt, to run into the embraces of a fever,
and in some raving fit be led to plunge myself into
that more consuming fire, a woman's arms. Ha!
well recollected, I will recover my reason, and
begone.

Bell. Now, Venus forbid !

Vain. Hush !

Heart. Well, why do you not move ? Feet, do
your office—not one inch ; no, foregad, I'm caught !
There stands my north, and thither my needle
points.—Now could I curse myself, yet cannot
repent. O thou delicious, damned, dear, destruc-

tive woman! 'Sdeath, how the young fellows will hoot me! I shall be the jest of the town. Nay, in two days I expect to be chronicled in ditty, and sung in woeful ballad, to the tune of *The Super-annuated Maiden's Comfort*, or *The Bachelor's Fall;* and upon the third I shall be hanged in effigy, pasted up for the exemplary ornament of necessary-houses and cobblers' stalls. Death, I can't think on't!—I'll run into the danger to lose the apprehension. [*Enters* SILVIA's *lodgings.*

In later scenes Congreve stands almost unsupported, a little too consciously aware, perhaps, that Wycherley was young ambition's ladder.

Belin. [*To* BELLMOUR.] O' my conscience, I could find in my heart to marry thee, purely to be rid of thee: at least thou art so troublesome a lover, there's hopes thou'lt make a more than ordinary quiet husband.

Bell. Say you so? is that a maxim among you?

Belin. Yes; you fluttering men of the mode have made marriage a mere French dish. . . . You are so curious in the preparation, that is, your courtship, one would think you meant a noble entertainment; but when we come to feed, 'tis all froth, and poor, but in show; nay, often only remains which have been I know not how many times warmed for other company, and at last served up cold to the wife.

Bell. That were a miserable wretch indeed, who could not afford one warm dish for the wife of his bosom.—But you timorous virgins form a dreadful chimera of a husband, as of a creature contrary to that soft, humble, pliant, easy thing, a lover; so guess at plagues in matrimony, in opposition to the pleasures of courtship. Alas! courtship to marriage, is but as the music in the playhouse till the curtain's drawn; but that once up, then opens the scene of pleasure.

Belin. Oh, foh! no; rather courtship to marriage, is as a very witty prologue to a very dull play.

Finally, in a bravura passage, entirely dissociated from the rest of the play, Congreve definitely announces himself. We no longer detect the faintest accent of another voice. Belinda is describing to Araminta how in the Royal Exchange she had encountered a countryman come up to town with his wife and daughters:

ARAMINTA *and* BELINDA *meeting.*

Belin. Lard, my dear, I am glad I have met you!—I have been at the Exchange since, and am so tired.

Aram. Why, what's the matter?

Belin. Oh, the most inhuman barbarous hackney-coach! I am jolted to a jelly!—Am I not horribly toused? [*Pulls out a pocket-glass.*

Aram. Your head's a little out of order.

Belin. A little! O frightful! what a furious phiz I have! O most rueful! ha! ha! ha! O gad, I hope nobody will come this way, till I have put myself a little in repair.—Ah, my dear, I have seen such unhewn creatures since!—ha! ha! ha! I can't for my soul help thinking that I look just like one of 'em.—Good dear, pin this, and I'll tell you. —Very well—so, thank you, my dear.—But as I was telling you—pish! this is the untowardest lock!

—So, as I was telling you—how d'ye like me now?
hideous, ha? frightful still? or how?

Aram. No, no; you're very well as can be.

Belin. And so—but where did I leave off, my
dear? I was telling you——

Aram. You were about to tell me something,
child—but you left off before you began.

Belin. Oh; a most comical sight: a country
squire, with the equipage of a wife and two
daughters, came to Mrs. Snipwell's shop while I was
there.—But, oh gad! two such unlicked cubs!

Aram. I warrant, plump, cherry-cheeked country
girls.

Belin. Ay, o' my conscience, fat as barn-door
fowl; but so bedecked, you would have taken 'em
for Friesland hens, with their feathers growing the
wrong way.—O, such outlandish creatures! Such
tramontanæ, and foreigners to the fashion, or anything in practice! I had not patience to behold—I
undertook the modelling of one of their fronts, the
more modern structure.

Aram. Bless me, cousin, why would you affront
anybody so? They might be gentlewomen of a
very good family.

Belin. Of a very ancient one, I dare swear, by
their dress.—Affront! pshaw, how you're mistaken!
The poor creature, I warrant, was as full of curtsies
as if I had been her godmother: the truth on't is,
I did endeavour to make her look like a Christian,
and she was sensible of it; for she thanked me and
gave me two apples, piping hot, out of her under-
petticoat pocket—ha! ha! ha! And t'other did so
stare and gape! I fancied her like the front of her

father's hall; her eyes were the two jut-windows, and her mouth the great door, most hospitably kept open for the entertainment of travelling flies.

Aram. So then, you have been diverted.

The Double Dealer is every way an advance. We have already seen that at its first production at Drury Lane in 1694 it fell flat upon the town. Dryden wrote of it to Walsh: " Congreve's *The Double Dealer* is much censured by the greater part of the town, and is defended only by the best judges, who, you know, are commonly the fewest. Yet it gains ground daily, and has already been acted eight times. . . . My verses which you will find before it were written before the play was acted; but I neither altered them nor do I alter my opinion of the play."

Dryden's verses, prefixed to *The Double Dealer*, definitely place Congreve in just relation with his contemporaries. They are excellent criticism, marred only by that blindness to the merits of the great Elizabethans which persisted in English opinion from Dryden to Coleridge :

To my dear Friend Mr. CONGREVE, *on his Comedy called* " The Double Dealer."

WELL, then, the promised hour is come at last ;
The present age of wit obscures the past :
Strong were our sires, and as they fought they writ,
Conquering with force of arms and dint of wit,
Theirs was the giant race before the flood ;
And thus, when Charles returned, our empire stood.
Like Janus, he the stubborn soil manured,
With rules of husbandry the rankness cured:
Tamed us to manners, when the stage was rude ;
And boisterous English wit with art endued.

Our age was cultivated thus at length ;
But what we gained in skill we lost in strength.
Our builders were with want of genius curst ;
The second temple was not like the first : . . .
In easy dialogue is Fletcher's praise ;
He moved the mind, but had not power to raise.
Great Jonson did by strength of judgment please ;
Yet doubling Fletcher's force, he wants his ease.
In differing talents both adorned their age ;
One for the study, t'other for the stage.
But both to Congreve justly shall submit,
One matched in judgment, both o'ermatched in wit.
In him all beauties of this age we see,
Etherege his courtship, Southerne's purity ;
The satire, wit, and strength of manly Wycherley.
All this in blooming youth you have achieved ;
Nor are your foiled contemporaries grieved ;
So much the sweetness of your manners move,
We cannot envy you, because we love. . . .
Yet this I prophesy. Thou shalt be seen
(Though with some short parenthesis between),
High on the throne of wit ; and seated there,
Not mine (that's little) but thy laurel wear.
Thy first attempt an early promise made,
That early promise this has more than paid ;
So bold, yet so judiciously you dare,
That your least praise is to be regular.
Time, place, and action may with pains be wrought,
But genius must be born and never can be taught.
This is your portion, this your native store ;
Heaven, that but once was prodigal before,
To Shakespeare gave as much ; she could not give him more.

The merits of *The Double Dealer* are accurately contrasted with the merits of *The Old Bachelor* in the circumstance that the earlier play won for its author the general and easy fame of public approbation, whereas the later play won for him the suffrage of the lettered few. Swift, in 1694, chimes harmoniously with Dryden—

God-like the force of my young Congreve's bays ;

and it is even more significant that Addison, also in
1694, thus congratulated Dryden upon his heir :

> How might we fear our English poetry,
> That long had flourished, would decay with thee,
> Did not the Muse's other hope appear,
> Harmonious Congreve, and forbid our fear ;
> Congreve! whose fancy's unexhausted store
> Has given already much, and promised more.
> Congreve shall still preserve thy fame alive,
> And Dryden's praise shall in his friend survive.

The Double Dealer is a masterpiece—with reser-
vations. Congreve definitely appears. The play's
defects are not, as were those of *The Old Bachelor*,
a consequence of the incomplete assimilation of his
models. The lighter scenes are as perfect Congreve
as any in *The Way of the World*. But the play fails
in equability. The tempestuous wickedness of Lady
Touchwood, and the deliberate villainy of Maskwell
are out of the picture. Save that he seldom
neglects to speak exquisite prose, Maskwell is anybody's property. Only occasionally he belongs to
Congreve. " For your honest man, as I take it, is
that nice, scrupulous, conscientious person who will
cheat nobody but himself : such another coxcomb
as your wise man, who is too hard for all the
world, and will be made a fool of by nobody but
himself." This is obviously a personage of Congreve.
But for the most part, Maskwell walks through the
play disguised in heavy eyebrows and a scowl.

We at once appreciate the immense advance
in maturity of style between the first and second
of Congreve's comedies. No longer are we dis-
concerted with memories, as in *The Old Bachelor*.
Congreve, of course, accepted precedents. He is

still the heir of his predecessors. Etherege continues to be the model of his style ; and the invocation of his comic mood. Wycherley continues to furnish him with many of his comic figures and situations. All this holds as definitely of *The Double Dealer* as of *The Old Bachelor*. But the difference is immense. The Fondlewife passages of *The Old Bachelor* were an absolute echo of Wycherley's lively, impudent and breathless theatre. Compare with these either of the passages where my lady Plyant, the familiar false prude of Wycherley's aversion, is so entertainingly divided between her honour and her necessity. " Etherege, his courtship," has fused with the " satire, wit and strength of manly Wycherley "; and the fusion is chemical, not mechanical, the compound being quite unlike either of its constituents.

The Double Dealer is, of all Congreve's plays, the fullest of quotations. The few here selected are chosen not alone for their merit. They are a necessary preface to a general criticism of Congreve's work.

Mellefont's dialogue with Cynthia in the Second Act is the germ of that more brilliant scene between Mirabell and Millamant in *The Way of the World* —perhaps the most perfect scene in English comedy. This earlier scene is but a shadow ; but the delicate superiority of Congreve's attitude towards the chapters of life which are commonly regarded as of some importance to mankind is already conspicuous :

Mel. You're thoughtful, Cynthia ?

Cyn. I'm thinking, though marriage make man

and wife one flesh, it leaves them still two fools; and they become more conspicuous by setting off one another.

Mel. That's only when two fools meet, and their follies are opposed.

Cyn. Nay, I have known two wits meet, and by the opposition of their wit render themselves as ridiculous as fools. 'Tis an odd game we're going to play at; what think you of drawing stakes, and giving over in time ?

Mel. No, hang't, that's not endeavouring to win, because it's possible we may lose ; since we have shuffled and cut, let's e'en turn up trump now.

Cyn. Then I find it's like cards : if either of us have a good hand, it is an accident of fortune.

Mel. No, marriage is rather like a game at bowls ; Fortune indeed makes the match, and the two nearest, and sometimes the two farthest, are together ; but the game depends entirely upon judgment.

Cyn. Still it is a game, and consequently one of us must be a loser.

Mel. Not at all ; only a friendly trial of skill, and the winnings to be laid out in an entertainment.

Since we are very gravely to consider the objections which many of Congreve's critics have scored against him on moral grounds, it may be well to choose for our text, where it is possible, passages that have actually offended, especially where these passages are diverting, easily lifted from their context, and characteristic of their author. Two such passages of *The Double Dealer* at once suggest themselves.   Mr. Brisk is Sparkish of *The Country Wife*.   It has been objected that Congreve has spoiled the encounters between Mr. Brisk and my Lady Froth by allowing them to misconduct themselves in the prevailing fashion of the comedy. Let us very solemnly reflect that the loves of Mr. Brisk and my Lady Froth have very solemnly been censured.   Then let us read the passage wherein they are discovered :

Lady Froth. O Parnassus! who would have thought Mr. Brisk could have been in love, ha! ha! ha!   O Heavens, I thought you could have had no mistress but the nine Muses.

Brisk. No more I have, egad, for I adore 'em all in your ladyship.   Let me perish, I don't know whether to be splenetic or airy upon 't ; the deuce take me if I can tell whether I'm glad or sorry that your ladyship has made the discovery.

Lady Froth. O be merry by all means!   Prince Volscius in love! ha! ha! ha!

Brisk. O barbarous, to turn me into ridicule! Yet, ha! ha! ha!—the deuce take me, I can't help laughing myself, ha! ha! ha!—yet by Heavens! I have a violent passion for your ladyship, seriously.

Lady Froth. Seriously? ha! ha! ha!

Brisk. Seriously, ha! ha! ha!   Gad, I have, for all I laugh.

Lady Froth. Ha! ha! ha!   What d'ye think I laugh at? ha! ha! ha!

Brisk. Me, egad, ha! ha!

Lady Froth. No, the deuce take me if I don't laugh at myself ; for, hang me! if I have not a violent passion for Mr. Brisk, ha! ha! ha!

Brisk. Seriously?

Lady Froth. Seriously, ha! ha! ha!

It is a grave text indeed.

Another passage, which seems painfully to have disturbed Sir Richard Steele, is a duologue between Sir Paul Plyant and his daughter Cynthia. Sir Paul has been censured for indelicately assuming that a possible result of his daughter's marriage will be an heir:

Sir Paul. [*To* Cyntha.] He! and wilt thou bring a grandson at nine months' end, he!—a brave chopping boy? I'll settle a thousand pound a year upon the rogue, as soon as he looks me in the face; I will, gadsbud! I'm overjoyed to think I have any of my family that will bring children into the world. For I would fain have some resemblance of myself in my posterity, hey, Thy? Can't you contrive that affair, girl? do, gadsbud, think on thy old father, he? make the young rogue as like as you can.

Cyn. I'm glad to see you so merry, sir.

Sir Paul. Merry! gadsbud, I'm serious; I'll give thee five hundred pounds for every inch of him that resembles me; ah, this eye, this left eye! a thousand pound for this left eye. This has done execution in its time, girl; why thou hast my leer, hussy, just thy father's leer:—let it be transmitted to the young rogue by the help of imagination; why 'tis the mark of our family, Thy; our house is distinguished by a languishing eye, as the house of Austria is by a thick lip.—Ah! when I was of your age, hussy, I would have held fifty to one I could have drawn my own picture.—Gadsbud! I could have done—not so much as you neither,—but—nay, don't blush—

Cyn. I don't blush, sir, for I vow I don't understand—

Sir Paul. Pshaw! pshaw! you fib, you baggage; you do understand, and you shall understand.

This passage, transcribed *literatim,* is not precisely in late nineteenth century phrase or taste; but the old gentleman who jokes at the marriage feast about a christening is encountered outside the licentious comedies of the Restoration.

In many scenes of *The Double Dealer* "manners" alone are the theme. Of these, two at least may profitably be cited here. The first is a dialogue on laughter between Lord Froth, Brisk, Careless and Mellefont:

Lord Froth. I assure you, Sir Paul, I laugh at nobody's jest but my own or a lady's: I assure you, Sir Paul.

Brisk. How? how, my lord? what, affront my wit! let me perish, do I never say anything worthy to be laughed at?

Lord Froth. O foy! don't misapprehend me: I don't say so, for I often smile at your conceptions. But there is nothing more unbecoming a man of quality than to laugh; 'tis such a vulgar expression of the passion! everybody can laugh. Then, especially to laugh at the jest of an inferior person, or when anybody else of the same quality does not laugh with one; ridiculous! To be pleased with what pleases the crowd! Now when I laugh, I always laugh alone.

Mel. But does your lordship never see comedies?

Lord Froth. O yes, sometimes;—but I never laugh.

Mel. No?

Lord Froth. O no;—never laugh indeed, sir.

Care. No? why, what d'ye go there for?

Lord Froth. To distinguish myself from the commonalty, and mortify the poets.

The second is a dialogue wherein is devised between Mr. Brisk and my Lady Froth the celebrated heroic poem of Jehu, formerly a hackney-coachman. It recalls, certainly not to its disadvantage, a classic passage of Molière.

Lady Froth. Then you think that episode between Susan, the dairymaid, and our coachman is not amiss; you know, I may suppose the dairy in town as well as in the country.

Brisk. Incomparable, let me perish! But then being an heroic poem, had not you better call him a charioteer? Charioteer sounds great; besides your ladyship's coachman having a red face, and you comparing him to the sun; and you know the sun is called Heaven's charioteer.

Lady Froth. Oh, infinitely better! I am extremely beholden to you for the hint; stay, we'll read over those half a score lines again. [*Pulls out a paper.*] Let me see here, you know what goes before,—the comparison, you know.

[*Reads.*] For as the sun shines every day,
So, of our coachman I may say—

Brisk. I'm afraid that simile won't do in wet weather; because you say the sun shines every day.

Lady Froth. No, for the sun it won't, but it will do for the coachman : for you know there's most occasion for a coach in wet weather.

Brisk. Right, right, that saves all.

Lady Froth. Then, I don't say the sun shines all the day, but that he peeps now and then ; yet he does shine all the day too, you know, though we don't see him.

Brisk. Right, but the vulgar will never comprehend that.

Lady Froth. Well, you shall hear.—Let me see.

[*Reads.*] For as the sun shines every day,
So, of our coachman I may say,
He shows his drunken fiery face,
Just as the sun does more or less.

Brisk. That's right, all's well, all's well!—" More or less."

Lady Froth.

[*Reads.*] And when at night his labour's done,
Then too, like Heaven's charioteer the sun—

Ay, charioteer does better.

Into the dairy he descends,
And there his whipping and his driving ends ;
There he's secure from danger of a bilk,
His fare is paid him, and he sets in milk.

For Susan, you know, is Thetis, and so—

Brisk. Incomparably well and proper egad !— But I have one exception to make :—don't you think bilk (I know it's good rhyme), but don't you think " bilk " and " fare " too like a hackney-coachman ?

Lady Froth. I swear and vow, I am afraid so.—
And yet our Jehu was a hackney-coachman when
my lord took him.

Brisk. Was he? I'm answered, if Jehu was a
hackney-coachman.—You may put that in the
marginal notes though, to prevent criticism.—Only
mark it with a small asterism, and say, " Jehu was
formerly a hackney-coachman."

Congreve's next play, *Love for Love*, was his
most successful comedy. It held the stage to the
time of Hazlitt, who has eloquently described
Munden in the part of Foresight. Its success upon
the stage is easily understood. It has a better
plot ; and a better selection of what, in slang of
the theatre, are called " character " parts than any
other comedy of the period. Ben, "the absolute
sea-wit ;" Foresight, the astrologer ; Sir Sampson,
the travelled ass ; Tattle, who kept his secrets so
mysteriously that all the town had wind of them ;
Miss Prue, the rustic ingénue, as forward as she
is innocent—all are admirably of the stage. It is
characteristic of *Love for Love* that one remembers
the persons and story of the play, which is neither
possible nor necessary in the majority of Restoration
comedies.

Nevertheless, *Love for Love*, as Congreve knew,
is infinitely less admirable than *The Double Dealer*
or *The Way of the World.* It may reasonably be
urged that comedies are built for the stage, and
that if *Love for Love* acts better than *The Way of
the World*, it is therefore a better play. But this
argument begs the question. Whether a play *acts*
better or worse than another, entirely depends upon

the audience, and the particular qualities in a play
which the audience is expecting. Every audience
to-day expects in a play the qualities in which *Love
for Love* is stronger than *The Way of the World.*
They expect an intelligible story, characters strongly
marked, and diverting situations, not too elaborately
prepared. But the audiences of the Restoration
period were being educated into expecting a different
sort of merit. The tendency from Etherege to Congreve was to encourage the qualities in which *The
Way of the World* excels every English comedy.
Plot counts hardly at all; characters are finely
shaded; manners are the principal theme; style is
the necessary excellence. This type of comedy has
never succeeded in England with a popular audience.
Undoubtedly it would have done so, had the Restoration influence survived; but causes, hereafter to be
examined, were already at work, which damned the
current of English comedy.

In *Love for Love*, Congreve turned aside from
the natural development of his style. It is the
most loosely written of his comedies. The best
scenes are a bright effervescence of that style of
which the full body is Millamant and Mirabell. In
one or two scenes—notably the scene where Miss
Prue receives a first lesson in love from Mr. Tattle
—Congreve goes negligently back to the tumbling
comedy of Wycherley. The whole play is so
obviously a backwater of the authentic stream,
that it scarcely pays to dwell upon it very particularly. As a specimen of the light running style
of its dialogue—written, as it seems, joyously,
currente calamo—we may with advantage read

the celebrated passage between Mrs. Foresight and Mrs. Frail :

Mrs. Fore. You never were at the World's-End?

Mrs. Frail. No.

Mrs. Fore. You deny it positively to my face?

Mrs. Frail. Your face! what's your face?

Mrs. Fore. No matter for that, it's as good a face as yours.

Mrs. Frail. Not by a dozen years' wearing.— But I do deny it positively to your face then.

Mrs. Fore. I'll allow you now to find fault with my face; for I'll swear your impudence has put me out of countenance :—but look you here now— where did you lose this gold bodkin?—O sister, sister!

Mrs. Frail. My bodkin?

Mrs. Fore. Nay, 'tis yours, look at it.

Mrs. Frail. Well, if you go to that, where did you find this bodkin?—O sister, sister!—sister every way.

The Way of the World was produced in 1700. Betterton, Mrs. Barry, Mrs. Bracegirdle, and Mrs. Leigh were in the cast; and Congreve wrote a prologue, in which the verdict of his audience was asked, with a confession that the play had cost him dear. The respectful irony of this appeal was too fine to be resented, even had it been perceived. But the verdict was against him.

The Comedy of Manners, as we have followed it from Etherege through Wycherley, to Congreve, has been a reflexion of contemporary life. Congreve has left, in his dedication of *The Way of the World* to Montague, unmistakable evidence of his intention.

" If," says Congreve, " it has happened in any part of this comedy, that I have gained a turn of style or expression more correct, or at least, more corrigible, than in those which I have formerly written, I must, with equal pride and gratitude, ascribe it to honour of your Lordship's admitting me into your conversation, and that of a society where everybody else was so well worthy of you, in your retirement last summer from the town ; for it was immediately after that this comedy was written."

We are now upon the summit of our theme. *The Way of the World* is a perfect expression of the temperament whose origins we have studied in the letters and plays of Sir George Etherege. Life is accepted and observed—not as a problem, but a pageant. The earlier author's impudent and bustling hedonism has, in his successor, grown to a calm and finished superiority to all that life can offer of good or bad. Etherege accepted life as the raw material of good manners. He asked no questions of Fate ; life should minister to him occasions which he would improve as became a gentleman. He was the cheerful philosopher, as yet unthinking, innocent of a system, obeying his appetite for the day, keeping no account of himself for the satisfaction of an imaginary creditor. In Congreve, this life of the superficies has grown into a principle. Existence is an agreeable pageant. Microcosm and macrocosm are justified in that they are plain to the senses. The whole duty of man is to talk, when he can, like Mirabell. The cheerful wickedness of Etherege has given place to a more rounded and systematic iniquity ;

Congreve's characters are epicures in pleasure,
exquisites in villainy. Their morality is as smoothly
asserted in conduct and precept as the philosophy of
Pope, which confines the universe in a couplet, and
dismisses its ruler in an epigram. Congreve's muse
is the full-blooded jade of Etherege and Wycherley
come to discretion. Coleridge was right. Congreve's
theme is often but simple wickedness, empty of
pleasure or lust. There is an equable finality about
the morality of *The Way of the World*—a dead level
of conscience against which is vividly thrown a
brilliant variety of manners and habits. It is a final
assertion of that noble laziness of the mind which
began with Etherege, in accepting and enjoying
the vicissitudes of fortune, and ended, with Congreve,
in despising them. Congreve seems ever to be
passing his creatures in review with faint, expressive
smiles of disdain.

Congreve's finished wickedness, of a world that
has refined upon its worldliness, is admirably
sampled in the opening scene of our comedy:

[MIRABELL *and* FAINALL, *rising from cards.*]

Mir. You are a fortunate man, Mr. Fainall!

Fain. Have we done?

Mir. What you please : I'll play on to entertain
you.

Fain. No, I'll give you your revenge another
time, when you are not so indifferent ; you are
thinking of something else now, and play too
negligently; the coldness of a losing gamester
lessens the pleasure of the winner. I'd no more
play with a man that slighted his illfortune than

I'd make love to a woman who undervalued the loss of her reputation.

Mir. You have a taste extremely delicate, and are for refining on your pleasures.

Even more significant is the dialogue between Mirabell and his cast mistress in the Second Act.

Mrs. Fain. While I only hated my husband, I could bear to see him; but since I have despised him, he's too offensive.

Mir. Oh, you should hate with prudence.

Mrs. Fain. Yes, for I have loved with indiscretion.

Mir. You should have just so much disgust for your husband, as may be sufficient to make you relish your lover.

Mrs. Fain. You have been the cause that I have loved without bounds, and would you set limits to that aversion of which you have been the occasion? Why did you make me marry this man?

Mir. Why do we daily commit disagreeable and dangerous actions? to save that idol, reputation. If the familiarities of our loves had produced that consequence of which you were apprehensive, where could you have fixed a father's name with credit, but on a husband? I knew Fainall to be a man lavish of his morals, an interested and professing friend, a false and a designing lover; yet one whose wit and outward fair behaviour have gained a reputation with the town enough to make that woman stand excused who has suffered herself to be won by his addresses. A better man ought not to have been sacrificed to the occasion; a worse had not answered to the purpose. When you are weary of him you know your remedy.

Mirabell here justifies himself by the code, striking in cold blood a profit-and-loss account of what, if we invoke the moral values of a later period, is inexcusable, perfidious villainy.

Lady Wishfort, Mirabell, and Millamant of *The Way of the World* are the three most brilliant and equably sustained comic figures of the Restoration theatre. Lady Wishfort is presented as a portrait; but she is in every stroke impressed with the style of her master. It is not easy to recover the mood in which Congreve conceived her. We are persistently troubled with intrusions of pity or disgust, equally remote from the contemptuous ironical detachment of her author:

Mrs. Fain. Female frailty! we must all come to it, if we live to be old, and feel the craving of a false appetite when the true is decayed.

Mir. An old woman's appetite is depraved like that of a girl—'tis the green sickness of a second childhood; and, like the faint offer of a latter spring, serves but to usher in the fall, and withers an affected bloom.

Mirabell and Millamant are gallantry upon the heights. Millamant makes love with the tips of her fingers; Mirabell with the finished decorum of the man who has in this world nothing to learn or to lose. In the last encounter of Mirabell and Millamant, Congreve's comedy reaches a full close. " Here," in the words of Mirabell, "the chase must end," though Millamant would be followed to the last:

Mrs. Mil. Though I am upon the verge of

matrimony, I expect you should solicit me as much as if I were wavering at the grate of a monastery, with one foot over the threshold. I'll be solicited to the very last, nay, and afterwards.

Mir. What, after the last?

Mrs. Mil. Oh, I should think I was poor and had nothing to bestow, if I were reduced to an inglorious ease, and freed from the agreeable fatigues of solicitation. . . . I hate a lover that can dare to think he draws a moment's air, independent of the bounty of his mistress. There is not so impudent a thing in nature, as the saucy look of an assured man, confident of success. The pedantic arrogance of a very husband has not so pragmatical an air. Ah! I'll never marry, unless I am first made sure of my will and pleasure.

Mir. Would you have 'em both before marriage? or will you be contented with the first now, and stay for the other till after grace?

Mrs. Mil. Ah! don't be impertinent.—My dear liberty, shall I leave thee? my faithful solitude, my darling contemplation, must I bid you then adieu? Ay-h adieu—my morning thoughts, agreeable wakings, indolent slumbers, all ye *douceurs*, ye *sommeils du matin*, adieu?—I can't do't, 'tis more impossible—positively, Mirabell, I'll lie abed in a morning as long as I please.

Mir. Then I'll get up in a morning as early as I please.

Mrs. Mil. Ah! idle creature, get up when you will—and d'ye hear, I won't be called names after I'm married; positively I won't be called names.

Mir. Names!

Mrs. Mil. Ay, as wife, spouse, my dear, joy,
jewel, love, sweetheart, and the rest of that
nauseous cant, in which men and their wives are
so fulsomely familiar—I shall never bear that—
good Mirabell, don't let us be familiar or fond, nor
kiss before folks, like my Lady Fadler and Sir
Francis : nor go to High-Park together the first
Sunday in a new chariot, to provoke eyes and
whispers, and then never to be seen there together
again ; as if we were proud of one another the first
week, and ashamed of one another ever after. Let
us never visit together, nor go to a play together ;
but let us be very strange and well bred : let us be
as strange as if we had been married a great while ;
and as well bred as if we were not married at all.

Mir. Have you any more conditions to offer ?
Hitherto your demands are pretty reasonable.

Mrs. Mil. Trifles ! As liberty to pay and
receive visits to and from whom I please ; to write
and receive letters without interrogatories or wry
faces on your part ; to wear what I please ; and
choose conversation with regard only to my own
taste ; to have no obligation upon me to converse
with wits that I don't like, because they are your
acquaintance : or to be intimate with fools, because
they may be your relations. Come to dinner when
I please ; dine in my dressing-room when I'm out
of humour, without giving a reason. To have my
closet inviolate ; to be sole empress of my tea-table,
which you must never presume to approach without first asking leave. And lastly, wherever I am,
you shall always knock at the door before you come
in. These articles subscribed, if I continue to

endure you a little longer, I may by degrees dwindle
into a wife.

Mir. Your bill of fare is something advanced in
this latter account. Well! have I liberty to offer
conditions—that when you are dwindled into a
wife, I may not be beyond measure enlarged into a
husband?

Mrs. Mil. You have free leave; propose your
utmost, speak and spare not.

Mir. I thank you. *Imprimis* then, I covenant,
that your acquaintance be general; that you admit
no sworn confidant, or intimate of your own sex;
no she-friend to screen her affairs under your countenance, and tempt you to make a trial of a mutual
secrecy. No decoy duck to wheedle you a fop-
scrambling to the play in a mask.

Mrs. Mil. Detestable *imprimis!* I go to the
play in a mask!

Mir. *Item,* I article, that you continue to like
your own face, as long as I shall; and while it
passes current with me, that you endeavour not to
new-coin it. To which end, together with all
vizards for the day, I prohibit all masks for the
night. *Item,* when you shall be breeding——

Mrs. Mil. Ah! name it not.

Mir. Which may be presumed with a blessing
on our endeavours.

Mrs. Mil. Odious endeavours!

Mir. I denounce against all strait-lacing, squeez-
ing for a shape, till you mould my boy's head like
a sugar-loaf, and instead of a man-child, make me
father to a crooked-billet. Lastly, to the dominion
of the tea-table I submit—but with proviso, that

you exceed not in your province; but restrain yourself to native and simple tea-table drinks, as tea, chocolate, and coffee: as likewise to genuine and authorised tea-table talk—such as mending of fashions, spoiling reputations, railing at absent friends, and so forth—but that on no account you encroach upon the men's prerogative, and presume to drink healths, or toast fellows; for prevention of which I banish all foreign forces, all auxiliaries to the tea-table, as orange-brandy, all aniseed, cinnamon, citron, and Barbadoes waters. These provisos admitted, in other things I may prove a tractable and complying husband.

Mrs. Mil. O horrid provisos! filthy strong-waters! I toast fellows! odious men! I hate your odious provisos.

The Way of the World but rarely falls beneath the level of this passage. It is equably brilliantly, monotonously fine. Comic dialogue can no further go. This may seem an extravagant opinion to such as may not have sufficiently reflected upon the necessary qualities of style, conditioned by conversation. But it is a measured extravagance—an opinion uttered by Hazlitt, and echoed in our own time by George Meredith. "The style of Congreve," says Hazlitt, "is inimitable, nay perfect. It is the highest model of comic dialogue. Every sentence is replete with sense and satire, conveyed in the most polished and pointed terms. Every page presents a shower of brilliant conceits, is a tissue of epigrams in prose, is a new triumph of wit, a new conquest over dulness. . . . Sheridan will not bear a comparison with him in the regular

antithetical construction of his sentences and in the
mechanical artifices of his style, though so much
later, and though style in general has been so
much studied, and in the mechanical part so much
improved since then. It bears every mark of being
what he himself in the dedication of one of his
plays tells us that it was, a spirited copy taken off
and carefully revised from the most select society
of his time, exhibiting all the sprightliness, ease,
and animation of familiar conversation with the
correctness and delicacy of the most finished composition. His works are a singular treat to those
who have cultivated a taste for the niceties of
English style; there is a peculiar flavour in the very
words which is to be found in hardly any other
writer. To the mere reader his writings would be
an irreparable loss."

Meredith is equally emphatic. "Where Congreve excels all his English rivals," he says, "is in
his literary force and a succinctness of style peculiar
to him. He hits the mean of a fine style and a
natural in dialogue. He is at once precise and
voluble. If you have ever thought upon style
you will acknowledge it to be a signal accomplishment. In this he is a classic, and worthy of tread-
ing a measure with Molière. Sheridan imitated
but was far from surpassing him. The flow of
boudoir Billingsgate in Lady Wishfort is unmatched
for the vigour and pointedness of the tongue. It
spins along with a final ring, like the voice of
nature in a fury, and is, indeed, racy eloquence of
the elevated fish-wife. Millamant is an admirable,
almost a lovable heroine. It is a piece of genius

in a writer to make a woman's manner of speech
portray her. You feel sensible of her presence in
every line of her speaking. An air of bewitching
whimsicality hovers over the graces of this comic
heroine, like the lively conversational play of a
beautiful mouth."

Congreve has not missed his due as a stylist.
His height, breadth, and depth as a comic dramatist
will more clearly appear as we follow the falling
career of English comedy through the works of
Vanbrugh and Farquhar.

VANBRUGH.
From the Painting in the National Portrait Gallery.

CHAPTER VI

SIR JOHN VANBRUGH

SIR JOHN VANBRUGH was coeval with Congreve. His first comedies appeared contemporaneously with *The Double Dealer* and *The Way of the World.* This is one of the curiosities of literature. It is a paradox in the evolution of English comedy that Congreve, who brought it to perfection, outlived his successor, who urged it to decline. Vanbrugh is emphatically a generation beyond the point at which we arrived in the preceding chapter. Already the movement in conscience and philosophy fore-run by Jeremy Collier was astir.

The difference between the pre-Collier and the post-Collier period of English comedy will not be perceived by anyone who still thinks of Congreve as an immoral author. The plays of Congreve are a faithful reflexion—the summation—of a whole period. They are studies in a particularly elaborate and a very positive *morality.* They may be regarded, justly perhaps, as wicked and vicious; they are, beyond all doubt, packed with offence for those who cannot in imagination recover the attitude in which they were conceived. But they are not *immoral.* Immorality implies a conscious defiance of the right rules of social conduct. Congreve's plays are positively *wicked* from the point of view that regards virtue as a well-conducted six months in the life of a modern Englishman, and vice as an occasional week-end in Paris. They would be positively *immoral* if Congreve himself had looked upon society as an ill-regulated conflict between honour and necessity. But Congreve's society is all of a piece; undesignedly consistent. His plays are studies in late seventeenth-century morality: Macaulay has criticised them as studies in early nineteenth-century immorality. This is no subtle or arbitrary distinction. It is critically at the root of a just estimate.

Jeremy Collier's *Short View of the Profaneness and Immorality of the English Stage* was published in 1698. An historian in love with simplicity would like to discover that every comedy which reflects the morality of Congreve's theatre preceded the *Short View*, and that every comedy of the fall followed it. But history is never quite so simple. The mere publication of Collier's tract did not immediately change the face of society, and the heart of man. Nevertheless, Collier's view of morality as a narrow way between pleasant meadows where trespassers will be prosecuted, definitely enters English comedy of the first-class in the plays of Sir John Vanbrugh. It enters positively and negatively. The dialogue between Constant and Heartfree of *The Provoked Wife* upon the topic of a happy marriage could have appeared in no comedy of any one of Sir John Vanbrugh's predecessors. We rub our eyes suddenly to discover morality of the Victorian fireside intruding into the morality of Spring Garden:

Constant. Though marriage be a lottery, in which there are a wondrous many blanks, yet there is one inestimable lot, in which the only heaven on earth is written. Would your kind fate but guide your hand to that, though I were lapped in all that luxury itself could clothe me with I should still envy you.

Heartfree. And justly too : for to be capable of loving one, is better than to possess a thousand.

But for the most part, Vanbrugh, as a witness that times are about to change, is revealed in a wilful reaction against the new morality—a reaction which testifies that he has fallen beneath its influence. Vanbrugh is an *immoral* author. He was sufficiently Collier's contemporary to disagree with him, to dislike him, to contradict him in precept and example. He understands Collier. He knows how Collier may be shocked and exasperated. Congreve and Wycherley were unable even to see what Collier was driving at. When Congreve is wicked, his wickedness *expresses* the morality of his period. When Vanbrugh is wicked, his wickedness *outrages* the morality of his.

Sir John Vanbrugh was born in 1663, of a middle-class or merchant family that had a generation previously married into nobility. He is said to have had a "liberal" education, with a French finish. Anyhow he was at the King's School, Chester ; and in February, 1692, he was locked up in the French Bastile as an English spy. Up to the date of his first appearance as a playwright, he seems to have lived the life of independent means. Of his career in the army nothing is known. Cibber

in his apology has described how in the early days
when Vanbrugh was an ensign he "had a heart
above his income."

His first comedy was written as a *jeu d'esprit*.
Many critics have sensibly wondered how long the
happy ending of a comedy would last if the curtain
were raised upon a sequel. Few comedies survive
an examination into the loose adieu with which the
spectators are in the final act dismissed—certainly
not *Love's Last Shift or The Fool in Fashion* of Colley
Cibber. Vanbrugh was present at this production
in 1696 ; and his sensible blunt humour refused
to credit the lasting reformation of Cibber's hero.
Within a few weeks he had posted to the managers
at Drury Lane *The Relapse or Virtue in Danger*,
being the play that would logically ensue from the
position at the fall of Cibber's curtain.

Thus, in 1696, began Vanbrugh's career as a
dramatist. Characteristically he forewent all profit.
Drury Lane was far from prosperous at this time ;
and an old friend of Vanbrugh, Sir Thomas Skip-
with, was a shareholder of the theatrical patent.
Vanbrugh resigned his rights. The action was
significant. Vanbrugh, first to last, made next to
nothing as an author. His plays were an avocation,
which it pleased him to pursue for eleven years of
his leisure. At the end of this period he virtually
retired as an author for twenty years.

Vanbrugh's period of authorship falls into two
chapters. His first group of plays were produced
at the two theatres in Drury Lane and Lincoln's Inn
Fields. *Æsop, The Pilgrim, The Country House*,
and *The False Friend* appeared at Drury Lane ;

The Provoked Wife and *Squire Trelooby* at Betterton's theatre in Lincoln's Inn Fields. Of these plays
only *The Provoked Wife*, Vanbrugh's third play, was
original work.

The second group of plays was written by
Vanbrugh for his own theatre in the Haymarket.
This included *The Confederacy*, *The Cuckold in
Conceit*, and *The Mistake*—all adaptations or free
translations from the French, and produced before
the end of 1707. In addition to these plays,
Vanbrugh, dying in 1726, left behind, a portion of
an original comedy entitled *The Journey to London*.
This, with a piece of *Miscellaneous Verse*, and the
Vindication against Jeremy Collier, completes the
list of his literary accomplishments.

Vanbrugh's active life, apart from the theatre,
was divided between his offices as herald, civil
servant and architect. Cutting midway into his
career as an author came the commission from Lord
Carlisle for the building of Castle Howard. This
was the beginning of Vanbrugh's career as the
friend and correspondent of noble families—an
intimate of the society and public life of his time.
His post at the Board of Works ; his appointment
as Clarencieux herald ; his architectural duties at
Blenheim and Greenwich Hospital, together with his
private building commissions, not only brought him
into touch with the highest political and literary
circles, but enabled him to live up to them.

Vanbrugh touches his period at many points.
His letters to Lord Carlisle, to the Duke of
Newcastle, and to the Duke of Marlborough are
packed with politics—the latest " dark stroke of the

Cabinet," the talk of lobbies, the who's in who's out of public life. For the purposes of this volume we will select the passages of Vanbrugh's career wherein his character is most conspicuously revealed. Especially valuable for our purpose are the episodes of his career which may be illustrated from his letters.

One of the earliest of Vanbrugh's extant letters is one of 13 July, 1703, to Tonson, publisher, Kitcat, and friend of all the poets. It relates to his first appointment as herald—scandalously, a job. Vanbrugh knew nothing whatever of heraldry at the time; he had even ridiculed the mystery in his comedy of *Æsop*. To aggravate the scandal, Gregory King, whom he displaced, was, after Dugdale, perhaps the most accomplished alumnus of the college. Lord Carlisle was the culprit. He very keenly appreciated Vanbrugh's work at Castle Howard; and to make of his architect a herald was equally a good joke and a means of repayment. Vanbrugh's account admirably fits this scandalous solemnity. " Carlisle," he tells Tonson, " stayed in town a good while about our herald's business. There was a good deal of saucy opposition, but my Lord Treasurer set the Queen right, and I have been soused a Herald Extraordinary in order to be a King at Easter. Lord Essex did the feat, which he did with a whole bowl of wine about my ears instead of half a spoonful." Writing in October, 1725, Vanbrugh records : " I got leave to dispose in earnest of a place I got in jest." It was a jest that lasted for 23 years of Vanbrugh's life, and got him a knighthood in the end. George I., on his

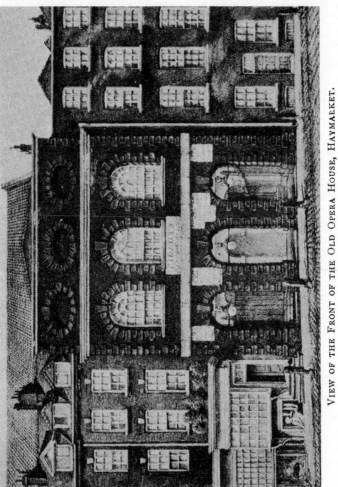

VIEW OF THE FRONT OF THE OLD OPERA HOUSE, HAYMARKET.

Built by Sir John Vanbrugh.

From an original drawing by Capon, made in 1783.

accession, commendably knighted the man whose
least honour was to have carried over the Garter to
him in 1706.

Next in date of the incidents for which Vanbrugh himself is an authority was the building of
the Haymarket Theatre, and the first attempt at
naturalising Italian opera in England. The best
account is a letter of Vanbrugh's to the Earl of
Manchester. The whole enterprise is eloquently a
comment upon the rash, resourceful, sanguine, and
virile temperament of its author. The fortunes of
Betterton's company at the small, inconvenient
theatre in Lincoln's Inn were rapidly sinking before
the energetic competition of Cibber's younger men
at the Theatre Royal. "To recover them, therefore, in their due estimation," Cibber tells us in his
Apology, "a new project was formed of building
them a stately theatre in the Haymarket, by Sir
John Vanbrugh, for which he raised a subscription
of thirty persons of quality at one hundred pounds
each, in consideration whereof every subscriber, for
his own life, was to be admitted to whatever entertainments should be publicly performed there without further payment for his entrance." The theatre
was built and opened in 1705. It was indeed a
"stately" theatre—so stately that the voices of the
actors "sounded like the gabbling of so many
people in the lofty aisles in a cathedral." In vain
did Vanbrugh put forward the best adaptation of
his life, *The Confederacy*. Mrs. Barry and Mrs.
Bracegirdle in vain wasted their sweetness. *The
Mistake*, which followed, and ran for nine nights,
labelled the whole undertaking. *The Provoked*

Wife and *Squire Trelooby* would not be repeated in a new success. Congreve, who had lent his name, retired from the enterprise in 1705 ; and Vanbrugh, in the following year, withdrew from active management. Henceforth the Haymarket, under Mr. Rich, of Drury Lane, was run as a complementary entertainment (of singers and dancers) to the Theatre Royal.

It was at this point that Vanbrugh's interest in Italian opera breaks into his correspondence with the Earl of Manchester. His seasons at the Haymarket were variegated light comedy and Italian opera ; and the principal subject of his correspondence with Manchester is his plan for bringing over Santini and Nicolini. Thus began the importation of foreign singers, whose evil result is, after two hundred years, not yet extinguished. Vanbrugh writes to Manchester of the result, 7 July, 1708 : " I lost so much money by the opera this last winter that I was glad to get quit of it, and yet I do not doubt that opera will settle in London. The occasion of the loss was three things "— briefly, that the season was started too late, that the salaries given were exorbitant, and that there were not subscribers enough. Also there was a falling off of "the gallery people who hitherto only thronged out of curiosity, not taste." The same month in which Vanbrugh described his failure to Manchester, Mainwaring wrote concerning Vanbrugh to the Duchess of Marlborough : " I am sorry for him, because I believe he is unhappy through his own folly, and I can see no reasonable way to help him. What I mean by his folly is his building the playhouse, which certainly cost him a good deal more than was subscribed."

Vanbrugh's troubles at the Haymarket were as nothing compared with his twenty years' anxiety and conflict in the building of Blenheim. The story belongs to histories of the period, and has more than once been well told since Isaac Disraeli inserted it among his *Curiosities of Literature*. Here we will select only such passages as illustrate the position and temper of our author.

Blenheim was voted by Parliament to the Duke of Marlborough in the spring of 1705. Vanbrugh, as Comptroller of the Board of Works, prepared the design, and the first stone of the palace was laid in June of the same year. Supplies were charged upon the Civil List, and their regularity was largely determined by the political situation. Thus, in 1710, when the Whigs went out, and again in 1711, when Marlborough was dismissed from every one of his posts, the supplies for Blenheim might conceivably have dried up altogether. The duke and duchess were continually in alarm at the way in which Vanbrugh set about spending the money before it was due. Friction was in any case bound to arise between an architect with generous ideas and mean-fisted clients. As a result of this, Blenheim stood still in 1710, and again in 1712. In 1716, the duke having fallen into his last sickness, the continuous bickering between Vanbrugh and the duchess broke into an open quarrel.

We may infer from a paper of Vanbrugh's, printed in Mrs. Thomson's *Memoirs of the Duchess*, that from the accession of George I. to the time of

the duke's seizure, Vanbrugh was not entirely unhappy at Blenheim. "I made no step," he writes,
"without the duke's knowledge while he was well;
and I made none without the duchess's after he fell
ill; and was so far, I thought, from being in her ill
opinion, that even the last time I waited on her and
my Lord Duke at Blenheim, she showed no sort of
dissatisfaction with anything I had done." Probably the duke, at any rate less irredeemably
vulgar than his wife, had hitherto saved Vanbrugh
from the worst of his dealings with a woman who in
1709 had imputed, from Vanbrugh's laudable desire
to save the ancient manor of Woodstock from the
housebreakers, that he wanted to live there himself!

War was upon her side declared with great
suddenness in the autumn of 1716. Vanbrugh was
engaged at the time in forwarding a match on her
behalf between the Duke of Newcastle and the
duchess's grand-daughter, Lady Henrietta Godol-
phin. At the precise moment when Vanbrugh was
serving her in a very difficult and delicate business
the duchess was secretly preparing the document
so rudely and unexpectedly fired upon him in
November. Thus, Vanbrugh innocently writes to
her on the 6th, puzzled to guess why he had not
received any further intimation from the duchess
that his good offices with Newcastle in behalf of
her family were agreeable to herself. Vanbrugh
was not a little hurt at her silence. "I do not," he
says, "court being farther employed in this matter;
for a match maker is a dam'd trade, and I never
was fond of meddling with other people's affairs.
But, as in this, on your own motion, and your own

desire, I had taken a good deal of very hearty pains
to serve you, and I think with a good deal of hearty
success, I cannot but wonder (though not be sorry)
you should not think it right to continue your
commands upon your obedient humble servant."

Two days later the bomb has burst. On the
8th Vanbrugh writes to the duchess a letter in
which anger visibly strains at the leash of polite
formality :

"Whitehall, Nov. the 8th, 1716.

" When I writ to your Grace on Tuesday last, I
was much at a loss, what could be the ground of
your having dropped me in the service I had been
endeavouring to do you and your family with ——
upon your own sole motion and desire.

" But having since been shown by Mr. Richards
a large packet of building papers, sent him by
your Grace, I find the reason was, that you had
resolved to use me so ill, in respect of Blenheim, as
must make it impracticable to employ me in any
other branch of your service.

" These papers, Madam, are so full of far fetched
laboured accusations, mistaken facts, wrong infer-
ences, groundless jealousies, and strained construc-
tions, that I should put a very great affront upon
your understanding if I supposed it possible you
could mean anything in earnest by them, but to put
a stop to my troubling you any more.

" You have your end, Madam, for I never will
trouble you more ; unless the Duke of Marlborough
recovers so far, to shelter me from such intolerable
treatment.

"I shall in the meantime have only this concern on his account (for whom I shall ever retain the greatest veneration) that your Grace, like the Queen, having thought fit to get rid of a faithful servant, the Tories will have the pleasure to see your Glass-maker Moor make just such an end of the Duke's building, as her minister Harley did of his victories, for which it was erected. I am, etc.

"If your Grace will give me leave to print your papers, I'll do it very exactly, and without any other answer or remarks, but this short letter tacked to the tail of them, that the world may know I desired they might be published."

Considering the provocation he had received—the full extent of it will in a moment appear—it is agreeable to find Vanbrugh honourably sticking to his point with Newcastle as to the match. The duchess would not have had the project miscarry; she even seems to have deferred her quarrel with Vanbrugh till the match was safe. Vanbrugh himself explains it: "As in all her other traffic, so in a husband for her grand-daughter she would fain have him good and cheap." Vanbrugh kept Newcastle posted in his quarrel with the duchess, but generously urged him not to weigh it against his estimate of her grand-daughter:

"*To the Duke of Newcastle.*

"London, Nov. the 10th, 1716.

"MY LORD DUKE,—I sent your Grace last post a copy of what I had writ to my Lady Marlborough.

"I have since I saw you had a sight of the load of papers she had sent up to Richards, for a foundation (though a very rotten one) to quarrel with me. I therefore writ to her, by Thursday's post, the letter which I here enclose a copy of.

"I have this afternoon had one from her, in answer to that I writ about your Grace, in which she says I have no cause to complain of her not speaking to me and that I should have done it first to her. In short her letter is mere banter; and by a few words at the latter end about the building, she shows quite plain, that she was resolved to get me out of that, and so judged it impossible to concern me any longer in t' other affair. I need make no remarks to your Grace upon this abominable woman's proceeding, which shall not however lessen my regard to my Lord Duke, nor good opinion of his grand-daughter, who I do not think has one grain of this wicked woman's temper in her; if I did, I would not advise you to take her though with the allay of a million.

  "Your Grace's ever faithful and
    "obedient servant
      "J. VANBRUGH."

In 1718, the duchess conceived the honourable design of turning upon Vanbrugh the whole burden of the debt still due upon Blenheim. The duchess lost her case, though it went as far as the House of Lords before Vanbrugh was able to feel safe. Even so he had to give up all hope of his fees as architect. Vanbrugh writes of his misadventures to Tonson : "I have the misfortune of losing, for I now see little hope of ever getting it, near two thousand pounds, due to me for many years' service, plague and trouble at Blenheim, which that wicked woman of Marlborough is so far from paying me, that, the duke being sued by some of the workmen for work done there, she has tried to turn the debt due to them upon me, for which I think she ought to be hanged."

Vanbrugh, through statement and counter statement and an interminable suit, maintained a cheerful habit of irony, interrupted with an occasional honest burst of indignation. In the midst of these encounters he came to Woodstock with his wife and a party from Castle Howard, which included the Countess of Carlisle. "We stayed," Vanbrugh writes to Tonson, "two nights in Woodstock, the ladies having a mind to view Blenheim in every part with leisure. But for my own share there was an order to the servants, under her Grace's own hand, not to let me enter Blenheim; and lest that should not mortify me enough, she having somehow learned that my wife was of the company, sent an express the night before we came there with orders that if *she* came with the Castle Howard ladies, the servants should not suffer her to see either house, garden, or even to enter the park; so she was forced to sit all day long, and keep me company at the inn."

It is a tribute to the easy humour of "Brother Van" that under insults like these he was able to conduct himself with an admirable dignity. Privately with his friends he was vigorously outspoken; but he is never spiteful or scurrilous. He splutters in good-natured rage. The last letter we have upon the matter was written to Tonson in 1725.

In a new campaign the duchess had successfully
suborned the rascal Macclesfield. Vanbrugh de-
feated the conspiracy with Walpole's help, which
apparently ended the whole business. Vanbrugh
writes :

"I have been forced into Chancery by that
B.B.B.—old *B.*—the Duchess of Marlborough,
where she has got an injunction upon me by her
friend the late good Chancellor (Earl of Macclesfield), who declared that I never was employed by
the duke, and therefore had no demand upon his
estate for my services at Blenheim. Since my
hands were thus tied up from trying by law to
recover my arrears, I have prevailed with Sir
Robert Walpole to help me in a scheme which I
proposed to him, by which I got my money *in spite
of the hussy's teeth*—and that out of a sum she
expected to receive into her hands, towards the
discharge of the Blenheim debts, and of which she
resolved I should not have a farthing. My carry-
ing this point enrages her much, and the more
because it is of considerable weight in my small
fortune, which she has heartily endeavoured so to
destroy."

These incidents help to determine Vanbrugh's
position in society and his character as a man.
Socially Vanbrugh was in the direct tradition of the
English comic school—the school of which Horace
Walpole wrote to the Countess of Ossory in June,
1787. He was really a part of the social life he
painted in his comedies. "Who should act genteel
comedy perfectly," says Walpole, "but people of
fashion that have sense ? Actors and actresses can

only guess at the tone of high life, and cannot be inspired with it. Why are there so few genteel comedies, but because most comedies are written by men not of that sphere. Etherege, Congreve, Vanbrugh and Cibber wrote genteel comedy because they lived in the best company; and Mrs. Oldfield played it so well because she not only followed but often set the fashion."

Vanbrugh was largely indebted to Carlisle for his social career. For Carlisle, as we have seen, he had in 1702 built Castle Howard, the "top seat and garden of England," so keenly admired by Horace Walpole. Some twenty years later Carlisle stood godfather to Vanbrugh's little son. The two men were fast friends from their first meeting to Vanbrugh's death in 1726. Carlisle was a Kitcat. In a letter of October, 1725, Vanbrugh writes to Tonson (himself a Kitcat, at whose house the club had frequently met) of how pleasantly my Lord remembered his Kitcat days, before death had thinned the meetings. "You may believe me," said Vanbrugh, "when I tell you you were often talked of both during the journey and at Stowe; and our former Kitcat days were remembered with pleasure. We were one night reckoning who were left, and both Lord Carlisle and Cobham expressed a great desire of having one meeting next winter, if you come to town, not as a club, but old friends that have been a club, and the best club that ever met."

A picture of the social life in which Vanbrugh so brilliantly shared is vividly described in a letter to the Duke of Newcastle written from Castle

Howard in August, 1721. Vanbrugh begins with
a description of the house, already famous for its
country parties :

" Many new charms open this year, that never
appeared before, and many more will next, that
people do not dream of now . . . I believe here will
be (beyond all content) the top seat and garden of
England. Of the house I say nothing : The others
I may commend, because nature made them ; I
pretend to no more merit in them than a midwife,
who helps to bring a fine child into the world, out
of bushes, bogs and briars.

" I was at York all last week. A race every
day, and a ball every night ; with as much well
looked company, as ever I saw got together. The
ladies I mean in chief. As to the men the Duke
of Wharton was the top gallant. The entertainments ending on Friday, he declared if the company
would stay in town one day more, he would treat
the jockeys with a plate, the ladies with a ball, and
all together with a supper. 'Twas done accordingly,
and my Lady Milner who had all along been his
partner, was now his Queen. When supper was
ended, he invited all the good company to meet
him again that day twelve month, on the same
terms ; with many decent and good compliments
to the inhabitants of York and Yorkshire for the
honour they did him, and hoped would do him
again. To which they gratefully bowed, as who
would say, yes. But his Grace then bethought
himself of one civil thing more, and said : that
unless my Lady Milner would absolutely engage to
be there too, he was off, as to the rest of the

company. Upon which she looked she did not know how, and all went home to sleep."

In a letter to Newcastle, written in August of the previous year, Vanbrugh strikes a more personal note:

"What I mentioned of my hard luck was far from being meant any sort of complaint, either of your Grace, or those others you name, who, I am entirely satisfied, do bear me all good will, and do neither trick me nor neglect me. There is nothing your Grace has said, in stating my small affairs, but what is just and true; and I have (in my own thoughts) never once stated them otherwise, so that I have no other meaning, in what I say about them, but to set forth my ill fortune by way of a little vent for ease. But I am not one of those who drop their spirits, on every rebuff; if I were, I had been under ground long ago. I shall therefore go on, in hopes fortune will one day or other let those help me, who have a mind to it."

Already Vanbrugh appears beneath the social personage, a sincere, patient, and kindly man—in public figuring true to his character of a young architect who, as Surveyor of Works, refused to be put over the head of his respected predecessor Sir Christopher Wren. The lampoons of Swift and Prior (not to mention Dr. Evans, who otherwise would be lost to fame) show him to have been an ideal butt for the wits of his generation. Clearly he had humour and good-humour; a capacity for solid friendships. The Homeric epithet for Vanbrugh seems as clearly to have fitted him as the Homeric epithets for his predecessors. It was

Easy Etherege, Manly Wycherley, Friendly Congreve; but it was Brother Van. The suitability
of this more clearly appears in his married life
with Harriet Yarborough.

Sir John Vanbrugh married in 1718 the eldest
daughter of Colonel Yarborough of Heslington.
There is virtually no doubt as to the date of the
marriage; and it is equally certain that, eight years
before this, Vanbrugh was in Yorkshire courting a
Miss Yarborough. It would seem that for eight
long years the lady eluded him. The evidence of
a courtship in 1710 is a letter of Lady Mary
Montagu, a product of her delicate maiden years :

"I can't forbear entertaining you with our York
lovers (strange monsters, you'll think, love being as
much forced up here as melons). In the first form
of these creatures is even Mr. Vanbrugh. Heaven,
no doubt, compassionating our dulness, has inspired
him with a passion that makes us all ready to die
with laughing : 'tis credibly reported that he is
endeavouring at the honourable state of matrimony,
and vows to lead a single life no more. Whether
pure holiness inspires his mind, or dotage turns
his brain, is hard to find. 'Tis certain he keeps
Monday and Thursday market (*assembly*-day) constantly ; and for those that don't regard worldly
muck, there's extraordinary good choice indeed.
I believe last Monday there were two hundred
pieces of women's flesh (fat and lean): but you
know Van's taste was always odd : his inclination
to ruins has given him a fancy for Mrs. Yarborough :
he sighs and ogles so, that it would do your heart

good to see him ; and she not a little pleased, in so
small a proportion of men amongst such a number of
women, that a whole man should fall to her share.
My dear, adieu.   My service to Mr. Congreve.

"M. P. (MARY PIERREPONT)."

A Restoration dramatist faithfully persisting in
love for eight years has so staggered the critics that
they have invented a supposititious Miss Yarborough
for 1710, a different person from the Miss Yarborough
whom Vanbrugh married in 1718. May we not
rather assume that here, privately, was precisely
the equable, persistent, and sincere fellow who kept
his temper and his courage for twenty years at
Blenheim, who was the ideal butt of his witty
friends, who thought neither time nor energy
wasted when the object was worth while? Miss
Yarborough was almost certainly worth while.
Lady Mary Montagu's "ruin" was about thirty to
Vanbrugh's forty-five at the time she wrote. The
marriage was very happy.

Vanbrugh's letters upon his marriage bring us
intimately into touch. They are not all equally
familiar. His letter to Newcastle, for instance, is
more a public proclamation than an intimate confession. Vanbrugh wears but little of his heart in
public. "I have no care now left," he writes from
Nottingham, in January, 1718–9, "but to see the
Duchess of Newcastle as well pleased with it (the
Castle) as your Grace is. I hope she won't have
the less expectation from my judgment in choosing a
seat from *my having chosen a wife*, whose principal
merit in my eye has been some small distant shadow

of those valuable qualifications, in her, your Grace
has formerly with so much pleasure heard me talk of.
The honour she likewise has *of being pretty nearly
related to the Duchess* gives me the more hopes I
may not have been mistaken. If I am, 'tis better
however to make a blunder towards *the end of one's
life* than at the beginning of it. But I hope all will
be well; it can't at least be worse than most of my
neighbours which every modest man ought to be
content with and so I'm easy. . . .

"J. VANBRUGH.

"Jacob [Tonson] will be frightened out of his
wits and his religion too when he hears I'm gone
at last. If he is still in France, he'll certainly give
himself to God, for fear he should now be ravished
by a gentlewoman. I was the last man left between
him and ruin."

Vanbrugh writes here as a man of the politest
world. More familiar letters show us more
truly the temper of his marriage. They are a
delightful blending of Vanbrugh's mental attitude
—humorous, detached, equably sensible—and the
homely sentiments of a householder, not without
pride in his nursery. In 1722 he writes to Carlisle
of the small boy to whom the Earl stood godfather:
"He talks everything, is much given to rhyming,
and has a great turn to dry joking. What the
seeds may grow to, God knows, they being of a
kind that may do his business up hill or down hill,
so perhaps upon the whole he were as well without
them. They serve, however, to make himself and
other people sport at present."

It is in the letters to Tonson that we get
nearest the heart of " Brother Van." Tonson was
abroad in 1718–19 ; and Vanbrugh sends word of his
marriage in July. " Here," he writes in allusion to
the death of many Kitcats, "has been so great a
slaughter of old friends since you went, I wish those
who are left may have share enough in your affections to incline you to think of England with any
pleasure. I don't know whether you'll reckon me
amongst the first or last, since I have taken that
leap in the dark—marriage. But though you should
date me with the former, I know at least you
would be glad to know how 'tis in this (perhaps)
your future state ; for you have not forgot it ever
was agreed, if I fell, you'd tremble. Don't be too
much dismayed however. . . . I have not yet re-
pented. Thus far 'tis possible you may believe me ;
if I offer at more 'tis like you won't, so I have done."

In November he writes more explicitly. " I am
much obliged to your good wishes in my matrimonial
state ; and encouraged by your opinion that it may
possibly do me as much good as it has mischief to
many a one that we know. I'll give you, however,
no other account of it till we meet than that I have
a good-humoured wife, a quiet house, and find
myself as much disposed to be a friend and servant
to a good old acquaintance as ever."

Later in the same month Vanbrugh writes to
Tonson with his wife, as we imagine, looking over
his shoulder ; for the script runs on in another
handwriting to a paragraph signed Harriet V. : " I
desire to make no such correction of your manners
as to stifle one of your jokes upon matrimony ; for

though the chain should happen to hang a little easy about me . . . I shall always think of my neighbours as I used to do.   And if I should chance at last to come in for a share of their disappointment, I don't know whether I could not rouse up a little, give the matter a new turn, and reckon, when my joke was thrown into the fund, I had a better title to a little merriment upon the stock than before. At least that I always thought I could do, or I had never wed.   But more of that if it comes to the trial.   I have only to tell you how my wife returns your compliments.   She says she is sorry she has not a sister for you ; but she knows them that have. And if you'll give her a commission she'll answer to provide at least as well for you as she has done for me.   She . . . accepts of your dinner at Barnes, and of your purpose to accept of hers at Greenwich, where she will treat you with the best of her good (Yorkshire) housewifery.

"*And if you will make one at cards, as I understand you have often done with much finer ladies than I am, I give you my word that I will neither cheat nor wrangle.   Your servant, Harriet V.*"

This letter of Sir John—read, attested, and improved by Harriet V.—allows us a glimpse of a very pleasant domestic interior.   Vanbrugh was happy enough in 1722 to wish that his friend Tonson would follow his example.   "I am now," he writes, "two boys strong in the nursery.   It would be a great comfort to me if you (the only one left) were to come in too, and pin the basket. Have a care of this retired country life.   We shall hear of some Herefordshire nymph in your solitary walks bounce out upon your heart from under an apple-tree and make you one of us; but end it so or not, a married man or a bachelor, while you and I are in the world I shall continue both your friend and humble servant."

The plays of Vanbrugh are a natural fruit of the temperament illustrated for us in these letters and episodes of his life. They are precisely the plays we should expect from a mischievous, tolerant and kind man of humour. Vanbrugh accepted the convention of Restoration comedy, but leavened it with an element of feeling and the harmless pleasure of an old dog playing with hell-fire. His gallants are no longer of a world whose moral values are consistently those of Congreve or Wycherley. Promiscuous gallantry is no longer a matter of course—the proviso of a well-regulated career. In the plays of Vanbrugh it is a yielding to temptation. Adultery is no longer treated in the dry light of comedy. It is passionate; it takes to itself fine names. It is a comedy of heaving bosoms, and seductive phrase. Vanbrugh, in fact, killed the comedy of sex for the English theatre. In his own plays the disaster that arises so soon as art is divorced from life is not yet obtrusively palpable; but the comic treatment of adultery was doomed from the moment when in *The Relapse*, Berinthia was borne off by Loveless, faintly protesting, in a bed-chamber scene which persists to this day as the *scène-à-faire* of English comedy.

In his preface to *The Relapse*, Vanbrugh says of his comedy: "There is not one woman of a real reputation in town, but when she has read it impartially over in her closet, will find it so innocent she will think it no affront to her prayer-book to lay it upon the same shelf." Later he continues : " As for the saints (your thorough-paced ones, I mean, with screwed faces and wry mouths) I despair of them ; for they are friends to nobody ; they love nothing but their altars and themselves ; they have too much zeal to have any charity ; they make debauches in piety, as sinners do in wine ; and are as quarrelsome in their religion, as other people are in their drink." Vanbrugh is here declaring the impatience of an easy-natured, tolerant man of this world with a zealot of the next. In Congreve this had been a declaration of faith ; in Vanbrugh it is a declaration of indulgence.

Vanbrugh wrote but two complete original plays, and part of a third. The rest were closely adapted or translated from the French. Vanbrugh was the perfect translator. He was easily fired with the dramatic possibilities of a situation. In every case his adaptations from Dancourt, Boursault, even Molière, are better than their originals. Moreover, one of his two original and complete comedies was suggested by the conclusion of another play. These facts are a key to the quality of Vanbrugh's work. Vanbrugh drew his inspiration more from the theatre than from life. His best original creations, like Foresight and Ben Legend of *Love for Love*, are cleverly sketched, effective stage figures ; and one of his best-known characters, Lord Foppington of *The Relapse*, is Cibber's Sir Novelty Fashion theatrically improved precisely in the same way in

which *The Confederacy* is improved from *Les Bour-
geoises à la Mode*. Vanbrugh's spirit of authorship
is hereby admirably illustrated. He accepted the
material of his comedy with little care for its moral
or social significance; his one aim was to amuse
honest gentlemen of the town—"to divert (if
possible) some part of their spleen in spite of their
wives and their taxes"—a task for which his agreeable style, his gift of wise humour, his instinct for
the theatre excellently qualified him.

We will here confine ourselves to a consideration
of Vanbrugh's three original contributions to
English comedy—*The Relapse*, produced with
success at Drury Lane in 1696; *The Provoked
Wife*, produced with equal success at Covent
Garden in 1698; *The Journey to London*, left
unfinished. A brief examination of these three
plays declares the insincerity that has already
entered into English comedy.

The Relapse, as we have seen, was Vanbrugh's
continuation of *Love's Last Shift* by Colley Cibber.
The play falls into two plots or sections—one
presenting the moral adventures of Loveless and
Amanda; the other introducing Sir Tunbelly
Clumsey and his daughter Hoyden. The two plots
are to the last moment almost entirely disconnected,
but when Collier, in this regard, attacked Vanbrugh's construction he missed the really serious
blemish. Vanbrugh answered Collier quite
reasonably that "whether it be right to have two
distinct designs in one play, I'll only say I think
when there are, if they're both entertaining, then
they're right, if they are not, 'tis wrong."

AT THE

QUEEN'S THEATRE,
In the HAY-MARKET.

To morrow being Tuesday, the Sixth Day of November, 1705, will be presented, A New Comedy call'd,

The CONFEDERACY.

With several Entertainments of DANCING by the Famous Monsieur DESBARQUES and others, Newly Arriv'd from PARIS.

Boxes Five Shillings, Pit Three Shillings, First Gallery Two Shilings.

No Money to be Return'd after the Curtain is Drawn up. Beginning exactly at Five of the Clock.

By Her Majesty's Servants.   VIVAT REGINA.

[From the original Play-bill, in the Possession of JOHN NIXON, Esq.]

FARQUHAR'S CONFEDERACY PLAY BILL.

" Entertaining " requires a commentary. If we are first entertained with a scene in which the moral struggles of a wedded pair to preserve their virtue are presented with an assumption that virtue is from heaven, and should certainly prevail in the best of possible worlds ; and, immediately upon this, are asked to be equally well entertained with scenes imitated from the theatre of Congreve and Wycherley, where wedded virtue is, at most, the better part of discretion—then we may be allowed to inquire whether the entertainment is not a little too freely mixed.

The Relapse opens with a soliloquy of Loveless —the reformed rake of Cibber's comedy. The confusion of Vanbrugh's moral postulates is unconsciously reflected in the style of their delivery. In the scenes wherein Loveless and Amanda importantly figure Vanbrugh is not sure whether his creatures are talking verse or prose. Let us assume that the opening lines of the comedy are verse :

> How true is that philosophy which says
> Our heaven is seated in our Minds !
> Through all the roving pleasures of my youth,
> (Where nights and days seem all consum'd in joy,
> Where the false face of luxury
> Display'd such charms,
> As might have shaken the most holy hermit,
> And made him totter at his altar)
> I never knew one moment's peace like this.
> Here—in this little soft retreat,
> My thoughts unbent from all the cares of life,
> Content with fortune,
> Eas'd from the grating duties of dependence,
> From envy free, ambition under foot,
> The raging flame of wild destructive lust
> Reduc'd to a warm pleasing fire of lawful love,
> My life glides on, and all is well within.

Note that the wheel is almost full circle here. Etherege delivered his first comedy in mixed prose and verse, and with an equally disastrous confusion of romantic and comic threads. The rise of English comedy was determined when, in his second play, Etherege discarded the pretences of verse. The decline of English comedy is determined when in his first play Vanbrugh restored confusion. The mischief of this confusion is the pause it gives to the reader, breaking his illusion of an ordered comic world, wherein it would be impertinent for his private sense of moral values to intrude. The reader is in the plays of Vanbrugh frequently arrested and compelled to ask himself, what is the law and the prophets of this curious tribe ? Inconsistency in the artist sends the spectator for a standard rudely back to his own experience—a test which the plays of Vanbrugh are not able to sustain. Nor would they be required to sustain it, but for their own lack of coherence.

Vanbrugh's true character appears most clearly in touches of humorous observation equally independent of the two hemispheres of his comedy. When neither the moral standards of his home-life at Greenwich, nor the moral standards of the comedy of Congreve are at issue, Vanbrugh falls back upon a vein of native humour in which he quite easily excels everyone of his predecessors. These touches, as all Vanbrugh's happiest effects, are usually suggested by the flow of the scene :

Wor. What ! she runs, I'll warrant you, into that common mistake of fond wives, who conclude themselves virtuous, because they can refuse

a man they don't like, when they have got one
they do.

Ber. True, and there I think 'tis a presumptuous
thing in a woman to assume the name of virtuous,
till she has heartily hated her husband, and been
soundly in love with somebody else. Whom if she
has withstood—then—much good may it do her!

The Relapse, in the majority of its scenes, is the
product of these three suggested elements: Loveless's
soliloquy is Vanbrugh, the husband-to-be of Harriet
Yarborough, the contemporary of Jeremy Collier;
the passage between Worthy and Berinthia is
Vanbrugh, shrewd, fluent, and witty, as the poets
loved him; then there is Vanbrugh, the successor
of Congreve and Wycherley, who accepted the convention of Restoration comedy without being of
the Restoration world. This last is he of whom
Hazlitt wrote that certain of his conversations in
The Relapse and *The Provoked Wife* "will do to
compare with Congreve in the way of wit and
studied raillery; but they will not stand the comparison."

The passages referred to by Hazlitt as suggesting the manner of Congreve are those between
Amanda and Berinthia. But how differently would
Congreve have handled them! Berinthia's design
of corrupting her friend would by Congreve, as by
Wycherley, have been presented with dry veracity;
it would naturally express the sex-morality of the
world we had entered and for the moment accepted.
But Vanbrugh merely sketches in Berinthia an agreeable weakness of the flesh. Fluently and lightly
he ignores precisely the elements of her design

which Congreve would clearly have underlined. We feel that Vanbrugh has but accepted a situation, which for his predecessors would have been blood and bone of their comedy, that he might use it as vehicle for light and agreeable passages delivered in the idiom of his personal temperament. So long as the scene is lightly handled, with facts avoided and motives slurred, the result is not artistically disastrous. But it is inevitable that, so soon as Vanbrugh's comedy comes to a strict issue, there intrudes a suspicion of uncertainty and unreality.

Two passages may here be cited as examples of Vanbrugh's comic manner in the shoes of Congreve. The first should be read closely in connexion with the foregoing paragraph :

Ber. Quarrel or not, smile or frown, I must tell you what I have suffered upon your account.

Aman. Upon my account !

Ber. Yes, upon yours ; I have been forced to sit still and hear you commended for two hours together, without one compliment to myself ; now don't you think a woman has a blessed time of that ?

Aman. Alas ! I should have been unconcerned at it ; I never knew where the pleasure lay of being praised by the men : but pray who was this that commended me so ?

Ber. One you have a mortal aversion to—Mr. Worthy : he used you like a text, he took you all to pieces, but spoke so learnedly upon every point, one might see the spirit of the Church was in him : if you are a woman, you'd have been in an ecstasy to have heard how feelingly he handled your hair,

your eyes, your nose, your mouth, your teeth, your
tongue, your chin, your neck, and so forth. Thus
he preached for an hour : but when he came to use
an application, he observed that all these, without a
gallant, were nothing—Now consider of what has
been said, and heaven give you grace to put it in
practice !

Aman. Alas! Berinthia, did I incline to a
gallant (which you know I do not), do you think
a man so nice as he, could have the least concern
for such a plain unpolished thing as I am? It is
impossible!

Ber. Now have you a great mind to put me
upon commending you.

Aman. Indeed that was not my design.

Ber. Nay, if it were, it's all one, for I won't
do't, I'll leave that to your looking-glass. But to
shew you I have some good-nature left, I'll commend him, and may be that may do as well.

Aman. You have a great mind to persuade me
I am in love with him.

Ber. I have a great mind to persuade you, you
don't know what you are in love with.

The ensuing passage between Tom Fashion
and Miss Hoyden should be read as a successor of
at least half a dozen similar scenes in the plays of
Wycherley and Congreve. Miss Hoyden is Vanbrugh's contribution to the Restoration literature
of the *ingénue*—the young woman whose coming-
on disposition had proved so fruitful a source of
comedy for his predecessors. Miss Hoyden is the
successor of Mrs. Pinchwife and of Prue :

Young Fash. Your servant, madam. I'm glad to

find you alone ; for I have something of importance to speak to you about.

Miss. Sir (my lord, I meant), you may speak to me about what you please, I shall give you a civil answer.

Young Fash. You give me so obliging a one, it encourages me to tell you in few words, what I think both for your interest and mine. Your father, I suppose you know, has resolved to make me happy in being your husband, and I hope I may depend upon your consent, to perform what he desires.

Miss. Sir, I never disobey my father in any thing but eating of green gooseberries.

Young Fash. So good a daughter must needs be an admirable wife ; I am therefore impatient till you are mine, and hope you will so far consider the violence of my love, that you won't have the cruelty to defer my happiness so long as your father designs it.

Miss. Pray, my lord, how long is it ?

Young Fash. Madam, a thousand year—a whole week.

Miss. A week !—why, I shall be an old woman by that time.

Young Fash. And I an old man, which you'll find a greater misfortune than t'other.

Miss. Why I thought it was to be to-morrow morning, as soon as I was up ; I'm sure nurse told me so.

Young Fash. And it shall be to-morrow morning still, if you'll consent.

Miss. If I'll consent ! Why I thought I was to obey you as my husband.

Young Fash. That's when we are married; till then I am to obey you.

Miss. Why then if we are to take it by turns, it's the same thing : I'll obey you now, and when we are married you shall obey me.

Vanbrugh's *The Provoked Wife* and the unfinished draft of *A Journey to London,* are less obviously open to charges of indecision and confusion of style than the play we have been discussing. This is more the result of finished workmanship than of any fundamental reconciliation of Vanbrugh's attitude towards life with the morality of his borrowed theatre. Vanbrugh is himself aware of the inconsistency between the character with which he personally would like to have invested his men and women and the character they actually bore in deference to the convention of Restoration comedy. Vanbrugh's best scenes, in fact, are those in which this inconsistency is itself humorously observed and exploited :

Constant. 'Tis now two years since that damned fellow her husband invited me to his wedding ; and there was the first time I saw that charming woman, whom I have loved ever since, more than ever a martyr did his soul ; but she is cold, my friend, still cold as the northern star.

Heartfree. So are all women by nature, which makes them so willing to be warmed.

Constant. O don't profane the sex ! Prythee, think them all angels for her sake, for she's virtuous even to a fault.

Hartfree. A lover's head is a good accountable thing truly ; he adores his mistress for being virtuous, and yet is very angry with her because she won't be lewd.

In another passage of this kind, between Constant and Lady Brute, it is curious to observe the author abandoning in mid-career the casuistical pretences of his hero, to write in his broadest and most humorous vein of the social basis of chastity.

Const. True virtue, wheresoever it moves, still carries an intrinsic worth about it, and is in every place, and in each sex, of equal value. So is not continence, you see : that phantom of honour, which men in every age have so contemned, they have thrown it amongst the women to scrabble for.

Lady Brute. If it be a thing of so little value, why do you so earnestly recommend it to your wives and daughters ?

Const. We recommend it to our wives, madam, because we would keep 'em to ourselves ; and to our daughters, because we would dispose of 'em to others.

Lady Brute. 'Tis, then, of some importance, it seems, since you can't dispose of them without it.

Const. That importance, madam, lies in the humour of the country, not in the nature of the thing.

Compare this with Sir Charles' observation upon the chastity of prudes who " indulge themselves in everything else that is vicious." " These women," says Sir Charles, " keep their chastity only because they find more pleasure in doing mischief with it than they should have in parting with it." All the touches in which Vanbrugh is happiest are where he escapes into neutral territory between the world to which he by temperament belonged, and the world he accepted from Congreve and his predecessors.

How far Vanbrugh was from the positive values of Congreve's world appears as clearly in his latest as his earliest work. A passage between Lord Loverule and Sir Charles in *A Journey to London*, is of an age with Sheridan. We find in this passage precisely the feeling which for English comedy was mortal sickness :

Lord Love. 'Tis pity anything that's bad should come from women.

Sir Charles. 'Tis so indeed, and there was a happy time when both you and I thought there never could.

Lord Love. Our early first conceptions of them, I well remember, were that they never could be vicious, nor never could be old.

Sir Charles. We thought so then ; the beauteous form we saw them cast in, seemed designed a habitation for no vice, nor no decay ; all I had conceived of angels, I conceived of them ; true, tender, gentle, modest, generous, constant, I thought was writ in every feature ; and in my devotions, Heaven, how did I adore thee, that blessing like them should be the portion of such inferior creatures, as I took myself and all men else (compared with them) to be— but where's that adoration now ?

Lord Love. 'Tis with such fond young fools as you and I were then.

Sir Charles. And with such it ever will be.

We may seem to have valued the work of Vanbrugh below its merit, for we have hitherto insisted upon the negative side of his genius.

Vanbrugh belongs to the fall.   There intrudes into his
comedy an element which was to kill it.   He hesitates
between two kingdoms.   Society was in revolution,
and Vanbrugh belonged to the new period.   But
he accepted for his models a comedy based upon
the old.   His theatre no longer reflects the moral
values of life.   The connexion is broken, and
confusion has ensued.   But we must not dwell
upon this aspect of the plays of Vanbrugh to the
exclusion of his undoubted merits.   Vanbrugh had
so shrewd a penetration into motive and character,
so level a judgment, so embracing a humour, that
had he taken the theatre more seriously than he
did, he might have founded a new school of English
comedy in strict relation with the new social period
that was setting in.   He might, in a word, have
started English comedy upon a fresh career.   But
he idly chose to continue an exhausted vein.   He
accepted a convention that he could not honestly
employ.   He was content to be inspired by the old
theatre rather than by the new life to which he
belonged.

Vanbrugh's positive merits were suggested in
his first play.   In his later work they are empha-
sised.   Sir John Brute and Lady Fanciful are
among the most effective stage figures of English
Comedy.   Sir John appears complete in the scene
of his introduction ; and never once recedes :

Enter Sir JOHN.   *Solus.*

Sir John. What cloying meat is love—when
matrimony's the sauce to it !   Two years' marriage
has debauched my five senses.   Everything I see,

everything I hear, everything I feel, everything I smell, and everything I taste—methinks has wife in't. No boy was ever so weary of his tutor, no girl of her bib, no nun of doing penance, or old maid of being chaste, as I am of being married. Sure, there's a secret curse entailed upon the very name of wife. My lady is a young lady, a fine lady, a witty lady, a virtuous lady,—and yet I hate her. There is but one thing on earth I loathe beyond her : That's fighting. Would my courage come up to a fourth part of my ill-nature, I'd stand buff to her relations, and thrust her out of doors. But marriage has sunk me down to such an ebb of resolution, I dare not draw my sword, though even to get rid of my wife. But here she comes.

Enter Lady BRUTE.

Lady Brute. Do you dine at home to-day, Sir John ?

Sir John. Why, do you expect I should tell you what I don't know myself ?

Lady Brute. I thought there was no harm in asking you.

Sir John. If thinking wrong were an excuse for impertinence, women might be justified in most things they say or do.

Lady Brute. I'm sorry I have said anything to displease you.

Sir John. Sorrow for things past is of as little importance to me, as my dining at home or abroad ought to be to you.

Lady Brute. My enquiry was only that I might have provided what you liked.

Sir John. Six to four you had been in the wrong there again ; for what I liked yesterday I don't like to-day ; and what I like to-day, 'tis odds I mayn't like to-morrow.

Lady Brute. But if I had asked you what you liked ?

Sir John. Why then there would have been more asking about it than the thing was worth.

Lady Brute. I wish I did but know how I might please you.

Sir John. Ay, but that sort of knowledge is not a wife's talent.

Lady Brute. What is it that disturbs you ?

Sir John. A parson.

Lady Brute. Why, what has he done to you ?

Sir John. He has married me. [*Exit* Sir JOHN.]

Lady Fanciful is drawn with equal facility and strength. From her first confession she takes and fills the stage : " I'm nice, strangely nice, mademoiselle ; I believe were the merit of whole mankind bestowed upon one single person, I should still think the fellow wanted something to make it worth my while to take notice of him ; and yet I could love ; nay, fondly love, were it possible to have a thing made on purpose for me : For I'm not cruel, mademoiselle ; I'm only nice."

" Lard, why was I formed to make the whole creation uneasy," she cries, a little later. Every scene in which she bears a part flows with a tide of fun reaching perhaps its most finished perfection of stage-craft in the debate with mademoiselle whether she shall rebuke the insolent Heartfree :

Lady Fan. Why, truly, satire has ever been of

wondrous use to reform ill-manners. Besides, 'tis
my particular talent to ridicule folks. I can be
severe, strangely severe, when I will, mademoiselle
——Give me the pen and ink——I find myself
whimsical——I'll write to him——Or I'll let it alone,
and be severe upon him that way. [*Sitting down to
write, rising up again.*]——Yet active severity is
better than passive. [*Sitting down.*]——'Tis as
good let it alone, too; for every lash I give him
perhaps he'll take for a favour. [*Rising.*]——Yet
'tis a thousand pities so much satire should be lost.
[*Sitting.*]——But if it should have a wrong effect
upon him, 'twould distract me. [*Rising.*]——Well,
I must write, though, after all. [*Sitting.*]——Or I'll
let it alone, which is the same thing. [*Rising.*]

Madam. La voilà déterminée. [*Exeunt.*

That Vanbrugh might have started English
comedy afresh is clear from one or two brilliant
passages, like these, of his later plays in which the
old convention is forgotten and Vanbrugh's personal
humour finds honest expression. It is curious to
come upon isolated passages to whose effect the
mood or convention of Restoration comedy is quite
unessential. To conclude upon an example of
Vanbrugh at his best, there is a scene of *A Journey
to London* where the Lady Arabella and Clarinda
discuss the pleasures of married life. The Lady
Arabella has just had a violent altercation with her
husband, who bids her to amend her extravagance
and late hours. He departs in anger; and when
Clarinda enters she finds her friend a little flushed
with the encounter.

Enter CLARINDA.

Clar. Good-morrow, Madam; how do you do to-day? you seem to be in a little fluster.

Lady Ara. My lord has been in one, and as I am the most complaisant poor creature in the world, I put myself into one too, purely to be suitable company to him.

Clar. You are prodigious good; but surely it must be mighty agreeable when a man and his wife can give themselves the same turn of conversation.

Lady Ara. Clarinda, you are the most mistaken in the world; married people have things to talk of, child, that never enter into the imagination of others. Why, now, here's my lord and I, we haven't been married above two short years you know, and we have already eight or ten things constantly in bank, that whenever we want company, we can talk of any one of them for two hours together, and the subject never the flatter. It will be as fresh next day, if we have occasion for it, as it was the first day it entertained us.

Clar. Why that must be wonderful pretty.

Lady Ara. O, there's no life like it. This very day now, for example, my lord and I, after a pretty cheerful *tête-à-tête* dinner, sat down by the fire-side, in an idle, indolent, pick-tooth way for a while, as if we had not thought of one another's being in the room. At last (stretching himself, and yawning twice), my dear, says he, you came home very late last night. 'Twas but two in the morning, says I. I was in bed (*yawning*) by eleven, says he. So you are every night, says I. Well, says he, I am amazed, how you can sit up so late. How can you

be amazed, says I, at a thing that happens so often ?
Upon which we entered into conversation. And
though this is a point has entertained us above fifty
times already, we always find so many new pretty
things to say upon't, that I believe in my soul it
will last as long as we live.

Clar. But in such sort of family dialogues (though
extremely well for passing of time) doesn't there now
and then enter some little witty sort of bitterness ?

Lady Ara. O yes ; which doesn't do amiss at
all ; a little something that's sharp, moderates the
extreme sweetness of matrimonial society, which
would else perhaps be cloying. Though to tell you
the truth Clarinda, I think we squeezed a little too
much lemon into it, this bout ; for it grew so sour
at last, that I think I almost told him he was a fool ;
and he talked something oddly of turning me out
of doors.

In this scene the breach which Vanbrugh made
in English comedy is imperceptible, and there are
many such passages scattered through his plays.
But Vanbrugh's great gifts and his positive achiev-
ments must not blind us to his real place in the
history of English comedy. He is a dramatist of
the fall. He accepted a tradition ; and shattered it.
This will appear even more clearly as we proceed
to consider the work of George Farquhar. Farquhar
was very definitely Vanbrugh's successor. It is one
of the necessary results of a study in evolution that
any particular stage of development is more clearly
understood when the stage which follows it is
examined. Vanbrugh made the breach whereby
Farquhar entered in and destroyed the citadel.

CHAPTER VII

GEORGE FARQUHAR

FARQUHAR is the last of the five principal figures in the half century of English comedy that began with Etherege. Facts continue to be kind. We have found in the lives and works of the four conspicuous predecessors of Farquhar an uninterrupted story of the development of a definite type of comedy. In Farquhar the story continues without a break. The comedy of manners, reaching perfection in Congreve, perceptibly droops in Vanbrugh, and in Farquhar is extinguished. It was no accident of history that Farquhar had no successor. Farquhar killed the comedy to which he contributed the last brilliant examples.

Farquhar's position in English comedy has not yet been historically considered. Critics have approached Farquhar from many points of view; never as the heir of Congreve. That Farquhar was the last of the comic dramatists, that he really succeeded Etherege and Wycherley, is one of those too obvious facts which invariably escape. Between the lines of most criticisms of the plays of Farquhar, more especially those which were written in the late nineteenth century—we detect an indulgence, a determination to make the most of his good, and

GEORGE FARQUHAR.

From an old print.

the least of his bad qualities, which contrasts remarkably with the treatment usually bestowed upon his predecessors. The explanation of this is that Farquhar is invariably approached as a late nineteenth-century author, who, from youth, inexperience, hot blood, and high spirits, did not quite come off either morally or artistically. His heart is felt to be in the right place. He introduced, it is said, fresh air into the theatre. He took a serious interest in moral problems. The nauseous comedy of Wycherley; the heartless comedy of Congreve, is abandoned. Farquhar, in fact, has been treated as a reformer of the old theatre; and as the possible founder of a better type of play.

This is history inverted. When we come to consider his plays in detail we shall find in Farquhar precisely that acceptance of an outgrown convention which mars the comedy of Vanbrugh. Where the critics find in Farquhar humanity and fresh air we shall detect an emotional and romantic treatment of sex stifling the parent stem of a comedy whose appeal depended upon an entirely different system of moral and imaginative values. Farquhar's comedies are the direct result of an author, whose temperament and environment were not much unlike those of his nineteenth-century critics, trying to write comedies like Congreve. The consequent inconsistencies, often resulting in serious moral and artistic offence, are more patent than in Vanbrugh's case; for Farquhar was more careless a writer than his predecessor, and never really discovered in his art a neutral territory where

244 THE COMEDY OF MANNERS

the values he borrowed were reconciled with the values he contributed.

The evidence upon which an idea of the life and character of Farquhar may be constructed is unhappily slender. Etherege, Wycherley, Congreve, and Vanbrugh had brilliant social careers, and touched the life of their time at many points. We have been able to form an idea of their personalities from the impression they made upon their contemporaries. Concerning Farquhar the "records of wit" are curiously silent. Nearly all our information as to the facts of his life is derived from a memoir for which his friend the actor Wilks supplied the details. So meagre are the sources for an appreciation of Farquhar that perhaps one of the most striking pieces of evidence for our purpose here is precisely this silence of the time in his regard. A few scraps of positive biography, and a handful of published letters, put beside the rather striking fact that the most successful dramatic author of his generation has scarcely left a trace of his passage upon the social life of his time, allow us vaguely to recover him.

Farquhar was an Irishman, born at Londonderry in 1678. His father was a poor clergyman with a family of seven children to bring up on £150 a year. Chetwood, in his *History of the Stage*, using a memoir based upon the testimony of Wilks, tells us that Farquhar's parents "could bestow no fortune upon him further than a genteel education." It is said that this education (at Trinity College, Dublin) was nipped untimely. Farquhar, required to write an essay upon the

subject of Christ's walking on the water, flippantly
suggested the proverb about "a man born to be
hanged." The ribaldry was every way unfortunate.
Farquhar was rusticated ; but the habit persisted of
clumsily forcing himself to an impudence which
bore no honest relation to his character. His
career at college was typical of the man as we may
venture to see him. He was a sizar at Trinity,
and tradition varies as to whether he were a "dull"
fellow or whether he "acquired a considerable reputation." With a little licence of imagination—without
which Farquhar must remain for ever indistinct—
we may picture him as a sensitive young man,
whose gifts, though they were recognised by his
companions and his teachers, were under a cloud.
He was poor. His position was inferior. The
irritating disproportion between the man he would
wish to be and the man he was would tend to make
him socially diffident, clumsy of address, apt to
vary between the extremes of irresponsiveness and
geniality, of humility and impudence.

Farquhar "began very early to apply himself
to the stage." He became an actor at the Smock
Alley Theatre, Dublin ; and acted with Robert
Wilks, then rising into fame. The friendship that
ensued between them determined Farquhar's career.
It was Wilks who persuaded Farquhar to come
to London and to write a play ; who "created"
the part of Sir Harry Wildair; and spurred the
dying author into producing his last and best play.

Farquhar did not succeed as an actor. Theophilus Cibber, following Wilks, tells us that
Farquhar "had a ready memory, proper gesture,

and just elocution, but then he was unhappy in his voice, which had not power enough to rouse the galleries, or to rant with any success. Besides he was defective in point of assurance, nor could ever enough overcome his natural timidity." Here, in Farquhar the actor, we seem to detect a temperament shrinking and ineffective, as in Farquhar the sizar of Trinity. He seems to have lacked the self-certainty and decision which is necessary to the man who would be a striking figure upon any stage. Even in the circumstance which ended his acting career there is an element of *gaucherie*. Playing Guyamon in Dryden's *Indian Emperor* he accidentally stabbed a fellow-player.

Farquhar's first play, *Love and a Bottle*, was produced in 1698. He had come to London at the instance of Wilks, who invited him to write a comedy. *Love and a Bottle* was well acted and well received. Farquhar's next four comedies followed at regular intervals. *The Constant Couple* in 1699, *Sir Harry Wildair* (sequel to *The Constant Couple*) early in 1701, *The Inconstant* (an adaptation of Fletcher's *Wild Goose Chase*) in 1702, *The Twin Rivals* later in the same year. At this point there is a gap of nearly four years. (We may reasonably except his share in the adaptation of *Les Carosses D'Orléans*.) Farquhar's next play, *The Recruiting Officer*, appeared in 1706 ; followed in the spring of 1707 by *The Beaux' Stratagem*.

Farquhar lived upon the profits of his plays and his commission in the army. He had already received his commission, through the kind offices of the Earl of Orrery, before the production of his

first play.   Nothing is known of his military duties
or achievements, save that he spent some weeks
with a recruiting party in Shropshire.   Probably
his journey to Holland in 1701 had something to
do with his military employment, for Farquhar could
scarcely afford to travel at his own expense.   The
gap in his dramatic activities between 1702 and
1706, broken at last with a military comedy, may
also be accounted for in this way; though it may as
possibly be due to the dubious success of the 1702
productions.   The comparative ill-success of these
plays would damp their author the more, as their
predecessor had been wildly fortunate.   *The Constant Couple* brought "some fifty audiences in five
months."   "Never did anything such wonders,"
says Gildon.   *The Inconstant* was played six times,
but the public preferred French dancing.   "The
charm of Gallic heels was too hard for an English
brain," says Farquhar in his preface.   They "left a
poor fellow—without one farthing for half-a-year's
patience."   For *The Twin Rivals* "the galleries
were thin."

   The period of Farquhar's silence of four years
was broken in 1703 by his marriage.   The story is
that a young lady of Yorkshire, to make herself the
more eligible, reported herself an heiress, and that
Farquhar thought he was marrying £700 a year.
"To his honour be it spoken," said Wilks, "though
he found himself deceived and his circumstances
embarrassed, yet he never upbraided her for the
cheat, and behaved to her with all the delicacy
and tenderness of an indulgent husband."   True
or false, this story supports the picture we have

imagined of Farquhar, the awkward amateur of success, trying to live up to the happy and impudent heroes of his comedy. Farquhar seems ever to be hanging desperately by the skirts of fortune, but is never in the midst of her favours.

The tragic story of his last years fits with a melancholy and thwarted career. His luck at the theatre returned with *The Recruiting Officer*. " It had powerful helps to set it forward," says Farquhar in his preface. " The Duke of Ormond encouraged the author, and the Earl of Orrery approved the play. My recruits were reviewed by my general and my colonel, and could not fail to pass muster." But *The Recruiting Officer* did not fill the author's purse. It is said that the Duke of Ormond advised him to sell his commission to meet his immediate necessities, promising to provide him with another at the earliest opportunity. Farquhar sold his commission; but the Duke of Ormond did not keep his word. Farquhar was without a prospect or a penny. His will seems utterly to have broken down.

Wilks discovered him in a back garret in St. Martin's Lane. The story in all its forms obviously derives from the version said to be furnished by Wilks himself:

" Mr. Farquhar was a constant attendant on the theatre; but Mr. Wilks, having missed him there for upwards of two months, went to the house where he lodged in York Buildings to enquire for him, and was informed that he had left it, but could not learn where he lived. Mr. Wilks a few days after received a letter from Farquhar desiring to see

him at his lodgings in St. Martin's Lane. Wilks
went there and found him in a most miserable
situation, lodged in a back garret, and under the
greatest agitation of mind. Wilks enquired the
reason of his distress, and Farquhar acquainted him
with the whole affair of the commission. . . . Wilks
advised him to write a play, and that it should be
brought on the stage with all expedition. 'Write!'
says Farquhar, ' it is impossible that a man can write
common sense who is heartless, and has not a
shilling in his pocket.' 'Come, George,' replied
Wilks, ' banish melancholy, draw your drama, and I
will call on you this day week to see it; but as an
empty pocket may cramp your genius, I desire you
will accept of my mite,'—and gave him twenty
guineas. Mr. Farquhar immediately drew up the
drama *The Beaux' Stratagem*, which he delivered
to Mr. Wilks, and it was approved by him and the
managers, and finished in six weeks. Mr. Farquhar,
during his writing this play, had a settled sickness
on him, and most part of it he wrote in his bed, and
before he had finished the second act he perceived
the approaches of death. The first night that it
was performed, his good friend Mr. Wilks came to
give him an account of its great success. . . . On
the third night of its being performed, which was
for his benefit, he died, which was the last week in
April, 1707."

This story may in the main be trusted ; though
it is clearly a little embellished. Farquhar lived
long enough, at any rate, to realise the success of his
play. He even seems to have witnessed it. To
the first edition, "as it is acted at the Queen's

Theatre in the Haymarket," he prefixed the following advertisement : " The reader may find some faults in this play, which my illness prevented the amending of ; but there is great amends made in the representation, which cannot be matched, no more than the friendly and indefatigable care of Mr. Wilks, to whom I chiefly owe the success of the play."

The printed epilogue, "designed to be spoke " in *The Beaux' Stratagem*, opens with an appeal to the audience in which is exploited, in doubtful taste, the author's pitiful condition :—

> If to our play your judgment can't be kind,
> Let it's expiring author pity find :
> Survey his mournful case with melting eyes,
> Nor let the bard be damned before he dies.
> Forbear, you fair, on his last scene to frown,
> But his true exit with a plaudit crown.

It is at any rate clear that Farquhar wrote the lightest and merriest of his comedies with the full knowledge that death was upon him.

A last pathetic touch is added to the story by the tradition that from the first year of his unlucky marriage Farquhar was troubled with the dread of leaving his family unprovided for. " Dear Bob," he wrote to Wilks at the last, " I have not anything to leave thee to perpetuate my memory but two helpless girls ; look upon them sometimes and think on him that was to the last moment of his life thine." Wilks obtained a benefit for Farquhar's family, and apprenticed his daughters to mantua-makers. Mrs. Farquhar died in extreme poverty ; one of her daughters married a tradesman ; the other became, it is said, a domestic servant. The contradictions of which his life was fashioned ended only with his latest recorded breath. The man who bequeathed his daughters poverty and ill-success died with a merry jest. It was reported to him that Mrs. Oldfield objected that in his play Mrs. Sullen had not been furnished with a plausible divorce from her husband. "To solve that," said Farquhar, "I'll marry her myself, and give my bond she shall be a real widow in less than a fortnight."

When we turn from the few and not too well attested facts of the life of Farquhar to the handful of letters and papers definitely his, the impression grows of a man ineffectual in spite of his gifts, unhappy in spite of his flaunted liveliness. Farquhar has published a prose portrait of himself entitled *The Picture*. He writes with an affectation of detachment, through which there peeps an engaging sincerity. "As to the mind," he tells us, "'tis generally dressed like my person in black. Melancholy is its everyday apparel; and it has hitherto found few holidays to make it change its clothes. In short, my character is very splenetic and very amorous."

Amorous of life, yet cursed with diffidence which holds him perpetually from life's feast—such is our picture of Farquhar—precisely the temperament which most aspires to be fortunate, but which fortune invariably shuns; too careful of happiness to be truly happy. "I am very sparing," he writes, "in my praises and compliments to a lady, possessed with a fear that they may affect myself more than her; for the idols that we worship are generally of our own making: and though at first men may not speak what they think, yet truth may catch them t'other hand, and make them think what they speak. . . . I am cautious of promising, especially upon the weighty article of constancy, because in the first place I have never tried the strength of it in my own experience, and secondly, I suppose a man can no more engage for his constancy than for his health, since I believe they both equally depend upon a certain constitution of the body." This man fears his fate too much.

Nor would he be of an open accessible spirit. "I have something in my outward behaviour," he tells us, "which gives strangers a worse opinion of me than I deserve. . . . I have many acquaintances, very few intimates. I have no secret so weighty but what I can bear in my own breast, nor any duels to fight but what I may engage in without a second, nor can I love after the old romantic discipline. I would have my passion, if not led, yet at least waited on by reason; and the greatest proof of my affection that a lady must expect is this, I would run any hazard to make us both happy, but would not for any transitory pleasure make either of us miserable."

The glimpses we get in Farquhar's letters of the author in love confirms the outlines of his *Picture*. Most of the letters are undated and unaddressed; and it is not possible to read them as a connected series. There is a tradition that Penelope of the letters was the celebrated Mrs.

Oldfield, whom Farquhar had discovered and
introduced to the stage; but we may not with
certainty assume it. All we really know of the
letters Farquhar tells us himself—that they were
"brought from a lady's cabinet to the Press."
Whether this were the cabinet of Mrs. Oldfield,
or of the future Mrs. Farquhar, and whether all
the letters are addressed to the same person, is not
clear.

One of the earliest letters to Penelope is the
literary embellishment of a mood which must have
been very general with Farquhar. We obtain of
him a picture that haunts the mind, of a sober
figure, enviously looking into a world of pleasure,
sustaining his spirits in his own despite with
wine and hungry fancies. "I went to the play
this evening, and the music raised my soul to such
a pitch of passion that I was almost mad for
melancholy. I flew thence to Spring Garden, where
with envious eyes I saw every man pick up his
mate whilst I alone walked like solitary Adam
before the creation of his Eve, but the place was
no Paradise for me. . . . Thence I retired to the
tavern where methought the shining glass represented your fair person, and the sparkling wine
within it looked like your lovely wit and spirit.
I met my dear mistress in everything; and I
propose presently to see her in a lively dream,
since the last thing I do is to kiss her dear letter,
clasp her charming idea in my arms, and so fall
fast asleep." A passage of *The Picture* here recurs
where Farquhar talks of waiting and hoping—"'tis
keeping the springs of desire so long upon the

rack till at last they grow loose and enervate; besides, anyone of a creative fancy by a duration of thought will be apt to frame too great an idea of the object, and so make the greater part of his hopes end in a disappointment." *Tendebantque manus* is the burden of Farquhar's life—a wistful figure, habited in black, looking indecisively on while every man picks up his mate.

Significantly, Farquhar is usually alone when the picture is more than usually clear. In a letter to Penelope, bravely whimsical, we again recover an impression of emptiness and melancholy. "Your indisposition last night when I left you," he writes, "put me into such disorder that, not finding a coach, I missed my way, and never minded whither I wandered till I found myself close by Tyburn. When blind love guides, who can forbear going astray? Instead of laughing at myself I fell to pitying poor Mr. Farquhar, who, whilst he roved abroad amongst your whole sex, was never out of his way, and now by a single she, was led to the gallows—from the thoughts of hanging I naturally entered upon those of matrimony—why should I not hazard the noose to ease me of my torment?"

Farquhar was unfortunate even in a little wine. His temperament seems, indeed, to have been largely determined by a frail physical constitution. A melancholy habit of thought and feeling united with a lively intelligence, and a quick eye for the humours and splendours of life, is frequently found in persons of delicate health. They are, as it were, perpetually convalescent, forever recovering to the joys and uses of life, but lacking the virility of perfect health. Farquhar seems never to have been robust. Penelope discouraged him from pretending that he could be a good fellow with impunity. She probably feared his hours of repentance more than his hours of riot. Farquhar, in one of his letters, certainly justifies the advice she seems to have previously bestowed. " I can no more keep the discovery of my faults from you than from my own conscience," he writes, " because you comprise so great a part of my devotion. Let me, therefore, confess to my dearest angel how last night I sauntered to the *Fountain*, where some friends waited for me. . . . The searching wine has sprung the rheumatism in my right hand, my head aches, my stomach pukes ; I dreamed all this morning of fire, and waked in a flame. To complete my misery I must let you know this and make you angry with me. . . . I'll put on the resolution of amending my life to fit me for the joys of heaven and you."

Two letters are of biographical interest. In one of them Farquhar proposes marriage to a lady, unnamed ; in the other he solemnly bids farewell to a lady, unnamed. Whether these letters were addressed to Penelope, or who Penelope was, is mysterious. We cannot even discover whether the proposal and the farewell are intended for the same person. Did we yield to temptation of the picturesque, we should assume that both letters were written to Mrs. Oldfield, and that here we have a record of Farquhar's supreme disappointment.

It seems that the lady in question had a little

previously been robbed of her jewels. Farquhar condoles with her upon the event, and concludes : " I think a lady without a husband is very much exposed to abuses from the rude world ; that the weakness of her constitution is a sufficient proof that her Maker designed man for her guard. Now, if a lady will neglect the protection which Providence has designed her, when there is one that begs so very earnestly, and has so long solicited the place, 'tis but just, I think, that she should meet with some small rubs to mind her of her insufficiency."

Farquhar's farewell certainly reads like a sequel to this : " Madam, 'tis a sad misfortune to begin a letter with an adieu ; but when my love is crossed, 'tis no wonder that my writing should be reversed. I would beg your pardon for the other offences of this nature which I have committed, but that I have so little reason to judge favourably of your mercy. I can assure you, madam, that I shall never excuse myself my own share of the trouble, no more than I can pardon myself the vanity of attempting your charms, so much above the reach of my pretensions. . . . May you be as happy, madam, in the enjoyment of your desires as I am miserable in the disappointment of mine."

In all that vaguely appears of Farquhar we have left the world of Etherege and his con-temporaries infinitely far behind. Etherege and Farquhar are antithetical. For the one playwriting, or diplomacy—life itself—was an agreeable diversion. All was accepted in the sanguine faith that the ready and present sensation, idea, or adventure, would in its passing be justified. For the other life was rather a pilgrimage than a play ; fortune was suspected ; the present was marred with gain-giving. The contrast between the temperaments of these two men is fundamental to an understanding of Farquhar's position as an English comic writer. Farquhar accepted the tradition of Etherege. He is expressing himself in a foreign language, an attempt which was equally disastrous for his message and for his idiom.

Let us pause for a moment upon Farquhar's *Discourse upon Comedy*, less for its excellent sense and nimble style than for the light it throws upon the decay of the comic idea. Farquhar's *Discourse upon Comedy* was written primarily as an attack upon the pedants who objected to the loose construction of his plays. There are many wholly admirable passages of this essay, wherein Farquhar discusses the use and abuse of dramatic conventions. We will linger only upon two points. First, Farquhar puts forward a definition of comedy which Jeremy Collier himself might approve—" a well-framed tale handsomely told as an agreeable vehicle for counsel or reproof." Æsop, he tells us, was the first comedian—" where should we seek for a foundation but in Æsop's symbolical way of moralising upon tales and fables, with this difference, that his stories were shorter than ours? He had his tyrant Lion, his statesman Fox, his beau Magpie, his coward Hare, his bravo Ass, and his buffoon Ape—with this distinction, nevertheless, that Æsop made his beasts speak good Greek and our heroes sometimes can't talk English." Whatever difference time has made in the form, Farquhar continues, we must stick to the end and intention of *Æsop's Fables* which was to school mankind into better manners.

Second, Farquhar definitely refers himself for his rules to the "Pit, Box and Galleries" of the English theatre. He would "examine into the humour of an English audience." We must not too heavily insist upon this; but it is the beginning of the new fashion for dramatic authors. The old idea of the fine gentleman writing plays in recovery from a fit of sickness for the easing of his wit is rapidly passing. Farquhar wrote to please an English audience rather than to please himself. He came to the theatre as a professional author, accepting the conventions that he found, perverting them, sometimes to fit his personal temperament, sometimes to fit his idea of what the public required of him. English comedy is at point of becoming a business, conducted with due regard for the moral susceptibilities of the public : in a word, English comedy is at point of death.

Farquhar's first play, *Love and a Bottle,* clearly pointed the characteristics of his comedy. Roebuck, the gallant hero of the tale, is the predecessor of Sir Harry Wildair, Captain Plume and Mr. Archer. He is the Restoration gentleman at point of being redeemed to a reluctant and uncertain belief in the virtues of monogamy. He is Farquhar's attempt to realise and consistently to deal with a figure which he had mechanically accepted from the theatre of his predecessors. In Roebuck the insincerity of Farquhar's effort to project himself into the comic world of Congreve glares obviously through the lines of his pert cynicism. His author's

brutality is forced. Roebuck is a tedious hypocrite,
feigning harder to be bad than Alderman Gripe
feigned to be good. Farquhar himself feels the
contradiction between his personal instincts and
the conduct of his heroes. Every now and then
he pauses vaguely to justify himself and smooth
out the inconsistencies of his comedy. Leanthe
says of Roebuck : " Wild as wind and unconfined
as air ! Yet I may reclaim him. His follies are
weakly founded upon the principles of honour,
where the very foundation helps to undermine the
structure. How charming would virtue look in
him whose behaviour can add a grace to the
unseemliness of vice." This passage has been
quoted as putting Farquhar morally above his predecessors. Merely it is an attempt to justify in
his conscience the motives of a stage-figure he had
picked up from Congreve and Wycherley at second-
hand. Roebuck corresponds to nothing truthful
or real in Farquhar. Seen through these words
of Leanthe he is a dishonest attempt to graft on
to the unimpassioned comedy of the Restoration,
based upon the morality of Charles II., the emotional
comedy of the Revolution, based upon the immorality of William III. Sexual irregularity is
now explained as an amiable excess of the qualities
which make a devoted husband. Moreover, con-
comitant with this confusion of moral values, there
proceeds that other degradation of comedy which
we noted in the plays of Vanbrugh—a " passionate
and luscious " treatment of sex. In *Love and a
Bottle* we meet the stock phrases of the theatre
of Aphrodite—" Soft, melting, white and yielding

waist"; "folded fast"; "broken sighs"; "heat of love," and so forth—the whole being intended to convey a correct and Victorian impression that nothing more nor less than an interchange of souls is in question.

Farquhar had but one avenue of escape from the perplexities of a comic world whose laws were in revolution. His style was light and rapid as a bird's wing. His best scenes are those in which ease and rapidity of motion defeat the critical eye. They are sleight-of-hand. *Sir Harry Wildair* completely sums the qualities of Farquhar. The confusion of values, noted in the character of Roebuck, is in Wildair worse confounded. But Sir Harry is ever so "brisk and airy," that to offer a serious indictment would seem like taxing the air. He bustles happily through two consecutive plays— *The Constant Couple* and *Sir Harry Wildair*. He is never out of spirits or countenance. Impudence is his most engaging quality. In Sir Harry, Farquhar almost escapes the rocks on which his comedy is invariably wrecked. Sir Harry is rarely a victim of Farquhar's moral and artistic inconsistency. He avoids exhibiting himself as a contradiction in terms by refusing to be anything whatever explicitly, save an incarnation of irresponsible high spirits.

Sir Harry is introduced in a passage not altogether innocent of an uneasy preliminary attempt to justify, or, at any rate, to remove the sting of his irregularity: "He's a gentleman of most happy circumstances, born to a plentiful estate, has had a genteel and easy education, free from the rigidness

of teachers and pedantry of schools. His florid
constitution being never ruffled by misfortune, nor
stinted in its pleasures, has rendered him entertaining to others, and easy to himself:—turning all
passion into gaiety of humour, by which he chooses
rather to rejoice his friends than be hated by any."

His virtue is never to be serious, never to be
abashed, rarely to disturb the reader. Even a
challenge he refuses to accept, save as an opportunity
to be gay:

Standard. I hope you're no coward, sir.

Sir Har. Coward, sir! I have eight thousand
pounds a year, sir.

Stand. You fought in Flanders to my knowledge.

Sir Har. Ay, for the same reason that I wore a
red coat, because 'twas fashionable.

Stand. Sir, you fought a French count in Paris.

Sir Har. True, sir; he was a beau like myself.
Now you're a soldier, Colonel, and fighting's your
trade; and I think it downright madness to contend
with any man in his profession.

Stand. Come, sir, no more dallying: I shall take
very unseemly methods if you don't show yourself
a gentleman.

Sir Har. A gentleman! why there again now?
A gentleman! I tell you once more, Colonel, that
I am a baronet, and have eight thousand pounds
a year. I can dance, sing, ride, fence, understand
the languages. Now, I can't conceive how running
you through the body should contribute one jot
more to my gentility. But pray, Colonel, I had
forgot to ask you: what's the quarrel?

Stand. A woman, sir.

Sir Har. Then I put up my sword.—Take her.

Stand. Sir, my honour's concerned.

Sir Har. Nay, if your honour be concerned with a woman, get it out of her hands as soon as you can.

In a passage like this Sir Harry carries himself off successfully. He keeps the reader at arm's length, pleased with his pleasant and dazzling exterior. Even his marriage is credible in the rush of high spirits and happy speech in which it is celebrated :

Sir Har. Canst thou not guess, my friend? Whence flows all earthly joy? What is the life of man and soul of pleasure?—woman! What fires the heart with transport, and the soul with raptures?—lovely woman! What is the master-stroke and smile of the creation, but charming, virtuous woman? When nature, in the general composition, first brought woman forth, like a flushed poet ravished with his fancy, with ecstasy she blessed the fair production!

Nevertheless Sir Harry is not entirely proof. In the scenes between Wildair and Angelica, we are often conscious of the insincerity and make-believe of a comedy where all the postulates are at issue. We have no right to insist that Farquhar's moral values should square with our own, but we have every right to insist that, in one and the same artistic presentment of life, the values should not be slurred, confused, or inter-destructive. Farquhar has cleverly minimised the peril into which his comedy necessarily falls whenever Sir Harry

encounters Angelica. He has allowed Sir Harry
to believe that Angelica is a daughter of Paphos.
Primed with Burgundy, and believing Angelica
to be within compass of his purse, he jests with
her virtue without losing the sympathy of his
nineteenth-century critics :

Angel. What madness, Sir Harry, what wild
dream of loose desire could prompt you to attempt
this baseness ? View me well. The brightness
of my mind, methinks, should lighten outwards,
and let you see your mistake in my behaviour.
I think it shines with so much innocence in my
face,

That it should dazzle all your vicious thoughts.
Think not I am defenceless 'cause alone.
Your very self is guard against yourself :
I'm sure, there's something generous in your soul ;
My words shall search it out,
And eyes shall fire it for my own defence.

Sir Harry's retort, in liquor and under a false
impression as to Angelica's social position, is a
telling commentary upon the next two centuries
of English comedy. "This is the first whore in
heroics," said Sir Harry, "that I have met with."
Sir Harry had to be drunk to be so perspicacious
and so honest. Had he said anything so true to
the morality of his immediate ancestors when sober,
he would not have married Angelica. It would
then have been too painfully clear that Angelica
and Sir Harry belonged to two different worlds.
Presenting Sir Harry in this scene as drunk and
deceived is Farquhar's ingenious device to make

a gentleman, of whom Dick Steele might approve, behave like the friend of Etherege and Rochester.

Farquhar's next original comedy—we may safely omit *The Inconstant*, Farquhar's adaptation of Fletcher's *The Wild Goose Chase*—was *The Twin Rivals*, produced in 1702. Nemesis has definitely overtaken him. Farquhar is here revealed in a deliberate attempt to reconcile the theatre of Congreve with the preaching of Jeremy Collier. The general result is a wavering of his comedy between two irreconcilable conventions, and in the end a pitiful descent into scenes where the feeling is utterly false, and where the expression sinks below the level of anything we have yet read. Hermes Would-be, hero of the piece, enters after a long absence. He discovers Aurelia and Constance in conversation. Is Constance faithful to his memory? In the scene which ensues the English comic theatre visibly flickers towards extinction :

Enter HERMES WOULD-BE *unperceived.*

Herm. Would. In tears! perhaps for me! I'll try.

> [*Drops a miniature, and goes back to the entrance, and listens.*

Aur. If there be aught in grief delightful, don't grudge me a share.

Con. No, my dear Aurelia, I'll engross it all. I loved him so, methinks I should be jealous if any mourned his death besides myself. What's here!—[*Takes up the miniature.*] Ha! see, cousin —the very face and features of the man! Sure, some officious angel has brought me this for a companion in my solitude! Now I'm fitted out for sorrow! With this I'll sigh, with this converse, gaze on his image till I grow blind with weeping!

Aur. I'm amazed! how came it here?

Con. Whether by miracle or human chance, 'tis all alike; I have it here: nor shall it ever separate from my breast. It is the only thing could give me joy, because it will increase my grief.

Herm. Would. [*Coming forward.*] Most glorious woman! now I am fond of life.

Aur. Ha! what's this!—Your business, pray, sir?

Herm. Would. With this lady.—[*Goes to* CONSTANCE, *takes her hand, and kneels.*] Here let me worship that perfection whose virtue might attract the listening angels, and make 'em smile to see such purity, so like themselves in human shape!

Con. Hermes!

Herm. Would. Your living Hermes, who shall die yours too!

Con. [*Aside.*] Now passion, powerful passion, would bear me like a whirlwind to his arms!—But my sex has bounds.—[*Aloud.*] 'Tis wondrous, sir!

Herm. Would. Most wondrous are the works of fate for man; and most closely laid is the serpentine line that guides him into happiness!

Even more significant is the final repentance of Richmore, the professing rake. Caught by his friend Trueman red-handed in the act of ravishing

Aurelia he improves the shining moment with a declaration : " Your youthful virtue warms my breast, and melts it into tenderness." For which Trueman suitably returns : " Indulge it, sir ; justice is noble in any form."

Farquhar in his next play, *The Recruiting Officer*, sets off his comedy with the humours of country life and manners. Here definitely was Farquhar's opportunity to shake off the influences that thwarted him, and to find for himself a new convention. But the change of scene is all. Captain Plume is again Sir Harry Wildair—Congreve's libertine playing, in the teeth of his character, for the sympathy of Collier's parishioners. Having for a while consistently lived up to his reputation as the successor of Mr. Horner, he suddenly asserts for the comfort of his audience : " I'm not that rake that the world imagines ; I have got an air of freedom, which people mistake for lewdness in me, as they mistake formality in others for religion. The world is all a cheat; only I take mine, which is undesigned, to be more excusable than theirs, which is hypocritical. I hurt nobody but myself, and they abuse all mankind."

Farquhar's last and best play, *The Beaux' Stratagem*, shows at their highest power all the qualities that make and mar his comedy. To pick holes is an ungrateful enterprise. This play is an act of splendid courage—a conspicuous triumph of the author over the man. Farquhar was dying, haunted with fears for his family left without provision. He was looking back upon a life of which the leitmotiv was hope unsatisfied :

Serjeant Kite & Bullock, in the Recruiting Officer Act 3 Scene I.
Why Roast, Sister Roast 29 MA 55

ENGRAVING OF A SCENE FROM FARQUHAR'S RECRUITING OFFICER.

Aim. But did you observe poor Jack Generous in the Park last week?

Arch. Yes, with his autumnal periwig, shading his melancholy face, his coat older than anything but its fashion, with one hand idle in his pocket, and with the other picking his useless teeth ; and, though the Mall was crowded with company, yet was poor Jack as single and solitary as a lion in the desert.

Aim. And as much avoided, for no crime upon earth but the want of money.

Jack Generous is the only spot of gloom in *The Beaux' Stratagem.* It is the sunniest of his plays. For the circumstances of its writing alone it deserves a high place in our regard. But we must not, therefore, falter in our analysis. The play shows no development upon any one of its predecessors. Archer is again Sir Harry Wildair, straight out of Congreve or Etherege. Archer delivers himself in a speech upon the five senses in the absolute manner of Sir Frederick Frollick : " Give me a man that keeps his five senses keen and bright as his sword; that has 'em always drawn out in their just order and strength, with his reason as commander at the head of 'em; that detaches 'em by turns upon whatever party of pleasure agreeably offers, and commands 'em to retreat upon the least appearance of disadvantage or danger! For my part, I can stick to my bottle while my wine, my company, and my reason, holds good ; I can be charmed with Sappho's singing without falling in love with her face; I love hunting, but would not, like Actæon, be eaten up by my own dogs; I love a fine house, but let another keep it; and just so I love a fine woman."

This single speech is a perfect expression of the attitude which determined the half-century of life and literature which preceded its delivery. Nevertheless, in the same play are collected sentiments and motives which are directly contrary. Consider the root question of marriage. Farquhar has been commended for his insistence in marriage upon an alliance of spirit:

Dor. But how can you shake off the yoke? Your divisions don't come within the reach of the law for a divorce.

Mrs. Sul. Law! what law can search into the remote abyss of nature? What evidence can prove the unaccountable disaffections of wedlock? Can a jury sum up the endless aversions that are rooted in our souls, or can a bench give judgment upon antipathies?

Farquhar here restores to English comedy the normal English idea of sex-relationship. Restoration Society, as we have seen, dissociated the act of sex from sentiments of friendship or the transports of romantic exaltation. Farquhar has outlived the influences which determined the Restoration attitude. His comedy unhappily divides itself into scenes where the Restoration attitude is for the form's sake accepted, and scenes where for the moral's sake it is condemned. It is significant that, unconsciously torn between two irreconcilable alternatives, he finally resorts, in his happiest manner, for refuge to his old device of lightly skimming the surface of his theme for fear of tumbling into a pitfall:

Sir Chas. You promised last night, sir, that you would deliver your lady to me this morning.

Squire Sul. Humph!

Arch. Humph! what do you mean by humph? Sir, you shall deliver her! In short, sir, we have saved you and your family; and if you are not civil, we'll unbind the rogues, join with 'em, and set fire to your house. What does the man mean? not part with his wife!

Count Bel. Ay, garzoon, de man no understan common justice.

Mrs. Sul. Hold, gentlemen! All things here must move by consent; compulsion would spoil us. Let my dear and me talk the matter over, and you shall judge it between us.

Squire Sul. Let me know first who are to be our judges. Pray, sir, who are you?

Sir Chas. I am Sir Charles Freeman, come to take away your wife.

Squire Sul. And you, good sir?

Aim. Charles, Viscount Aimwell, come to take away your sister.

Squire Sul. And you, pray, sir?

Arch. Francis Archer, esquire, come——

Squire Sul. To take away my mother, I hope. Gentlemen, you're heartily welcome; I never met with three more obliging people since I was born! —And now, my dear, if you please, you shall have the first word.

Arch. And the last, for five pound! . . .

Mrs. Sul. How long have we been married?

Squire Sul. By the almanac, fourteen months; but by my account, fourteen years.

Mrs. Sul. 'Tis thereabout by my reckoning. . . .

Mrs. Sul. Pray, spouse, what did you marry for?

Squire Sul. To get an heir to my estate.

Sir Chas. And have you succeeded?

Squire Sul. No.

Arch. The condition fails of his side.—Pray, madam, what did you marry for?

Mrs. Sul. To support the weakness of my sex by the strength of his, and to enjoy the pleasures of an agreeable society.

Sir Chas. Are your expectations answered?

Mrs. Sul. No. . . .

Sir Chas. What are the bars to your mutual contentment?

Mrs. Sul. In the first place, I can't drink ale with him.

Squire Sul. Nor can I drink tea with her.

Mrs. Sul. I can't hunt with you.

Squire Sul. Nor can I dance with you.

Mrs. Sul. I hate cocking and racing.

Squire Sul. And I abhor ombre and piquet.

Mrs. Sul. Your silence is intolerable.

Squire Sul. Your prating is worse.

Mrs. Sul. Have we not been a perpetual offence to each other? a gnawing vulture at the heart?

Squire Sul. A frightful goblin to the sight?

Mrs. Sul. A porcupine to the feeling?

Squire Sul. Perpetual wormwood to the taste?

Mrs. Sul. Is there on earth a thing we could agree in?

Squire Sul. Yes—to part.

Mrs. Sul. With all my heart.

Squire Sul. Your hand.

Mrs. Sul. Here.

Squire Sul. These hands joined us, these shall part us—Away!

Mrs. Sul. North.

Squire Sul. South.

Mrs. Sul. East.

Squire Sul. West—Far as the Poles asunder.

Count Bel. Begar, the ceremony be vera pretty.

Everyway *The Beaux' Stratagem* is well fitted to close the story of the fall of English comedy. The " passionate and luscious " treatment of sex which entered with Vanbrugh reaches a climax in the interrupted bedchamber scene between Archer and Mrs. Sullen. The lamentable obverse of this is Aimwell's fifth-act repentance in the act of deceiving Dorinda :

Aim. [*Aside.*] Such goodness who could injure! I find myself unequal to the task of villain; she has gained my soul, and made it honest like her own—I cannot, cannot hurt her. Madam, behold your lover and your proselyte, and judge of my passion by my conversion!—I'm all a lie, nor dare I give a fiction to your arms; I'm all counterfeit, except my passion.

Dor. Forbid it, Heaven! a counterfeit!

Aim. I am no lord, but a poor needy man, come with a mean, a scandalous design to prey upon your fortune; but the beauties of your mind and person have so won me from myself, that, like a trusty servant, I prefer the interest of my mistress to my own.

Dor. Sure I have had the dream of some poor mariner, a sleepy image of a welcome port, and wake involved in storms!—Pray, sir, who are you ?

Aim. Brother to the man whose title I usurped, but stranger to his honour or his fortune.

Dor. Matchless honesty!—Once I was proud, sir, of your wealth and title, but now am prouder that you want it : now I can show my love was justly levelled, and had no aim but love.

To end upon a note so false as this would be flat injustice. Let us, as brief examples of a better Farquhar, read of Mr. Archer's " Howd'ye," and how the count nearly came to be hidden in Mrs. Sullen's closet. Archer was at this time a pretended footman :

Mrs. Sul. I suppose you served as footman before ?

Arch. For that reason I would not serve in that post again ; for my memory is too weak for the load of messages that the ladies lay upon their servants in London. My Lady Howd'ye, the last mistress I served, called me up one morning, and told me : Martin, go to my Lady Allnight with my humble service ; tell her I was to wait on her ladyship yesterday, and left word with Mrs. Rebecca, that the preliminaries of the affair she knows of are stopped till we know the concurrence of the person that I know of, for which there are circumstances wanting which we shall accommodate at the old place ; but that in the meantime there is a person about her ladyship, that, from several hints and surmises, was accessory at a certain time to the

disappointments that naturally attend things, that
to her knowledge are of more importance—

Mrs. Sul. and Dor. Ha, ha ha! where are you
going, sir?

Arch. Why, I haven't half done!—The whole
howd'ye was about half an hour long; so I
happened to misplace two syllables, and was turned
off, and rendered incapable.

"The pleasantest fellow, sister, that I ever saw,"
Dorinda's comment is justified. Foigard, the hero
of the closet, is also a pleasant fellow—like Farquhar,
an Irishman:

Gip. What would you have me do, doctor?

Foi. Noting, joy, but only hide the count in
Mrs. Sullen's closet when it is dark.

Gip. Nothing! is that nothing? It would be
both a sin and a shame, doctor.

Foi. Here is twenty Lewidores, joy, for your
shame; and I will give you an absolution for the
shin.

Gip. But won't that money look like a bribe?

Foi. Dat is according as you shall tauk it. If
you receive the money beforehand, 'twill be, *logice*,
a bribe; but if you stay till afterwards, 'twill be
only a gratification. . . .

Gip. But should I put the count into the
closet—

Foi. Vel, is dere any shin for a man's being
in a closhet? One may go to prayers in a closhet.

Gip. But if the lady should come into her
chamber, and go to bed?

Foi. Vel, and is dere any shin in going to
bed, joy?

Gip. Ay, but if the parties should meet, doctor?

Foi. Vel den—the parties must be responsable. Do you be after putting the count in the closhet, and leave the shins wid themselves.

As with Vanbrugh we have been forced in reading the plays of Farquhar to dwell unduly upon the darker side. It has been necessary to insist that these two authors, accepting a comedy which expressed the society of the Restoration, were unable consistently to present life from the point of view of the men who served as their models. Their plays are pitted with inconsistencies. They never succeeded in bridging the gulf that separated their personal convictions from the moral and artistic conventions of the theatre into which they intruded. Nevertheless their positive merits must not be neglected. Vanbrugh reaches his height in scenes where humour and insight play tolerantly between two worlds. Farquhar is able to blind us to the worst of his faults in the happy running of his speech and fancy. He is perhaps the lightest of foot of all our comic authors. Farquhar was born too late. He should have come from Ireland in the 'sixties or 'seventies and have been accepted into the company of Etherege and Sedley. He might then have had for his share a more brilliant glory—to assist the rise of English comedy; actually he assisted the fall. It must be at the charge of Farquhar himself that no successor was found to continue the tradition.

CHAPTER VIII

CRITICAL CONCLUSIONS

WE have systematically neglected perhaps the most important event of the period. The publication in 1697 of Jeremy Collier's *Short View of the Profaneness and Immorality of the English Stage* was one of the great sensations of English literature. The importance of Collier's pamphlet bears no reasonable proportion to its merit or originality. It chimed with the spirit of the year. Collier said vigorously what the great majority of people wanted at that particular moment to have said. His book was one of the journalistic successes of history. It ran immediately through several editions. It provoked a literature. The men who were attacked, though to notice it was to the last degree distasteful to them, were unable to ignore it. Moreover the spirit with which Collier was inspired profoundly influenced the work of the men who imagined they were at all points opposed to him.

Macaulay has absurdly exaggerated the merit of Collier's book. It is on the whole well written : occasionally it is witty. But one's total impression of the book is that it is over-long drawn out ; that the author has not made the most of an absurdly easy case ; that it is superfluously weighted with a clumsy display of ancient learning. Its principal fault is a complete absence of humour. Collier thrusts wittily at his adversaries; but his sense of humour does not rise above academic repartee. Collier's "humour" is that of a university professor who has wit enough to defeat a rival theory of enclitic δε with raillery of the Junior Common-room, but not wit enough to realise that enclitic δε is not really momentous.

Collier's case was proved in advance. One perpetually asks, reading the *Short View*, why, from the author's stand-point, the book needed to be written. From Collier's point of view the comic dramatists were profane, licentious, and wicked. If people in a play are to be strictly judged by the rules of life; and if the rules of life are, irrespective of period or the conventions of art, immovably what Collier believed them to be, then the *Short View* is otiose. Collier had nothing to prove. It is plain fact that Mr. Horner commits adultery, that successful gallantry is in the plays of the comic dramatists invariably rewarded; that Mr. Pinchwife is not regarded as immune from ridicule because he is legally married to Mrs. Pinchwife. If these things are "immoral," and if their presentation in a play necessarily condemns it as a form of entertain-ment, then Wycherley is an "immoral" author; and there's an end. Why Collier, and, after Collier, Macaulay, Johnson, and Swift, should trouble to argue the point is mysterious. They have already assumed what they pretend to prove. It is idle to go into the minutiæ of the argument between Collier and the poets. If Collier is right in his premises, he is right upon every page of his book. The *Short View* is a literary exercise in illustration of a foregone conclusion.

Collier, in fact, begins with a proposition which includes all that he has to say, and is nowhere justified by argument. " The business of plays," says Collier, "is to recommend virtue and discountenance vice. . . . 'Tis to expose the singularities of pride and fancy, to make folly and falsehood contemptible, and to bring everything that is ill under infamy and neglect." Thereafter Collier proceeds to show that according to his views of a well-conducted life—the finality of whose standard is also assumed without argument—the plays of the comic dramatists are "in the following particulars intolerable, viz. :—their smuttiness of expression; their swearing profaneness and lewd application of scripture, their abuse of the clergy, their making the top characters libertines, and giving them success in their debauchery."

The book may from this be entirely reconstructed by the intelligent reader. Mr. Morality, says Collier in effect, is always the same person, and the theatre is his prophet. It is assumed that Wycherley's idea of good life was Collier's idea ; that Wycherley, like Collier, ascended into the pulpit whenever he wrote a play ; that because the conduct of Wycherley's people was of a kind that would distress Collier in one of his parishioners, therefore Wycherley's aim was to debauch his hearers, and corrupt society, and consciously do the devil's work. Lest this should seem an exaggeration of Collier's attitude, a passage may be cited

from the first chapter of the *Short View* : " Here,"
says Collier, "is a large collection of debauchery ;
such pieces are rarely to be met with : 'Tis sometimes painted at length too, and appears in great
variety of progress and practice. It wears almost
all sorts of dresses to engage the fancy, and fasten
upon the memory, and keep up the charm from
languishing. Sometimes you have it in image and
description ; sometimes by way of allusion ; sometimes in disguise ; and sometimes without it. And
what can be the meaning of such a representation,
unless it be to tincture the audience, to extinguish
shame, and make lewdness a diversion ? This is
the natural consequence and therefore one would
think it was the intention too. Such licentious
discourse tends to no point but to stain the imagination, to awaken folly, and to weaken the defences
of virtue."

As typical instances of the sort of thing which
excited Collier to ungovernable indignation it will
be convenient to cite passages of the comic dramatists already met. "I am thinking," says Cynthia
of *The Double Dealer*, "that though marriage
makes man and wife one flesh it leaves them still
two fools." "Mr. Worthy used you like a text,"
says Berinthia of *The Relapse*, "he took you all to
pieces." Collier's comment upon these examples is
that they "look reeking as it were from Pande-
monium, and almost smell of fire and brimstone.
This is an eruption of hell with a witness! I
almost wonder the smoke of it has not darkened
the sun, and turned to plague and poison. These
are outrageous provocation ; enough to arm all

nature in revenge ; to exhaust the judgments of
heaven, and sink the island in the sea."

Critics have dismissed the chapters of Collier's
Short View wherein he exhibits an excessive
sensibility to imagined reflexions upon Holy writ,
or to a disrespect of his calling, as the weaker side
of his argument. Vanbrugh cleverly said of him,
"'Twas the quarrel of his gown, not of his God,
that made him take up arms against me." On this
side Collier has by mere process of time been truly
measured. It is realised that here, in Dryden's
phrase, "the parson stretched a point too far."
Really Collier's pages upon morality at large are,
as criticism, equally at fault; only the errors are
not so easily detected. We are not, in these
times, much in peril of a bias in favour of Collier's
clerical sensibilities ; but we most of us subscribe to Collier's morality, and are therefore
less likely to perceive that his mistakes are as bad
one way as the other. It will possibly help us to
realise the absurdity of applying Collier's moral
test to works of imagination, if we put aside the
comic dramatists, and inquire how Shakespeare has
fared at his hands. Seeking for authors of
approved morality to contrast with the lewd theatre
of the Restoration, Collier says of Shakespeare :
" He is too guilty to make an evidence. But I
think, he gains not much by his misbehaviour.
He has commonly Plautus' fate : where there is
most smut there is least sense." Take, for instance,
the character of Falstaff. Falstaff, it seems, is
horribly smutty. But Shakespeare is never so bad
as Congreve or Vanbrugh. Shakespeare does not

forget the moral : " The admired Falstaff goes off in disappointment. He is thrown out of favour as being a rake, and dies like a rat behind the hangings. The pleasure he had given would not excuse him. The poet was not so partial as to let his humour compound for his lewdness." Before contemptuously dismissing a piece of nonsense, which not even the darkest days of eighteenth-century Shakespearean criticism can match, let us clearly realise that Collier's view of Falstaff is based upon precisely the same method of critical approach as his view of Sir John Brute.

Collier was fortunate in his adversaries. That his position, morally, remains to-day virtually where Macaulay left it is due less to the merit of the *Short View* than to the ineffectiveness of the principal rejoinders. Congreve and Vanbrugh, answering the *Short View*, give away their case from first line to last of their argument. They accept the standard of Collier, and dispute his applications. If nothing better could be said for the comic dramatists than what they were able to say for themselves, judgment would go by default in favour of Collier. The ineffectiveness of Congreve and Vanburgh in reply is not in the least surprising. Least of any men were they likely to realise the historical value of their work, or its relation to the morality of their time. Only rarely does an artist realise the forces that move him, the tendencies that direct the manner and matter of his message. Least of all should we expect to find this species of self-knowledge in authors of a period whose temperament was the reverse of introspective. Congreve, as we have seen, was a good judge of his work. He knew he had done well, had done better, had done best. But this craftsman's sense of the value of his accomplishment is a very different thing from a reasoned knowledge of the springs of history, the definite location of one's self amid influences that determine the character of a period.

Congreve practically accepts Collier's definition of the end of comedy. "Men," he says, "are to be laughed out of their vices in comedy. . . . As vicious people are made ashamed of their follies by seeing them exposed in a ridiculous manner, so are good people at once warned and diverted at their expense." Congreve has here accepted the moral test. Thereafter his only possible line of defence is to argue that morality is not fixed but fluid; that his plays have a positive morality of their own which differs from the morality of Collier; that judged by the standard of this morality they are immune.

This, in effect, is what Congreve has attempted to say. But he has never really thought about morality. Morality, as he wrote his plays, never entered his head. All he really knows, now that Collier has challenged him, is that his plays honestly say what he had to say, and that he is unconscious of the indecencies imputed to him. He knows that he violently disagrees with Collier; but he has not sufficiently reflected upon the laws of imagination and the process of art either to challenge Collier's main assumption, or to define in opposition to Collier the moral values of the

society he had depicted. In the *Amendments to
Mr. Collier's False and Imperfect Citations*, Congreve foolishly meets Collier upon Collier's ground.
Collier quarrels with this passage or that in Congreve's plays as inconsistent with the morality of
the *Short View*. Congreve vaguely and violently
justifies these passages without either disputing
Collier's premises, or defining his own. Naturally
he gets considerably the worst of the encounter.
Collier's every point logically follows from his
premises, and Congreve could only have met him
successfully by refusing to accept them. Congreve
nowhere refuses in definite terms; but he does
so unconsciously from his simple knowledge that
Collier's conclusions are wrong. The result is that
Congreve often seems downright dishonest, where
it is quite obvious upon a closer examination that
he was merely confused.

A good illustration is afforded by a passage
from *The Old Bachelor*. It runs as follows:

Vainlove. Could you be content to go to
heaven?

Bellmour. Hum, not immediately, in my conscience, not heartily. I'd do a little more good
in my generation first to deserve it.

What is the real spirit and intention of this
passage? Really it is an excellent summation of
the Restoration spirit. It has the characteristic
faint irony of the period towards things spiritual,
and the characteristic negligent pleasure of the
period in things material. It expresses a not too
violent belief in a reasonably-conducted life of the
senses. From Collier's point of view it was the

profane expression of an infidel who believed in nothing. From Congreve's point of view it was the conscientious expression of a believer who did not believe in very much.

The argument between Collier and Congreve as to this passage, perfectly illustrates the merits of their controversy. Collier quotes it in the *Short View*, stopping at the word "heartily." His comment runs: "This is playing, I take it, with edge tools. To go to heaven in jest is the way to go to hell in earnest." Congreve's rejoinder is the extreme of futility. He objects to Collier leaving out Bellmour's concluding words: "I'd do a little more good in my generation first"; and then sets out solemnly to prove that he intended Bellmour in this sentence to be contemplating an edifying life that he might be fitter for eternal life. "'Tis one thing," says Congreve, "for a man to say positively he would not go to heaven, and another to say he does not think himself worthy till he is better prepared." At first sight this looks either like a highly finished piece of irony, or a dishonest effort to make the best both of this world and the next. Actually it is neither; but merely the controversial incompetence of an author who has never bothered his head about the moral significance of his plays. It illustrates the line taken by Congreve on every page of his *Amendments*. He sets out clumsily to justify his plays by reference to the same moral values and critical point of view from which Collier attacked them. Collier accuses him of making a jest of heaven. Instead of answering that it was in his character to make a jest of heaven, and that in any case his idea of heaven was different from Collier's, he feebly attempts to maintain that he was not making a jest of heaven; that Bellmour really wanted to go to Mr. Collier's heaven; and was contemplating a course of life which would successfully bring him there. Collier's retort was obvious and crushing. " He would do a little more good first," says Collier, "*i.e.* he would gladly be a libertine somewhat longer, and merit heaven by a more finished course of debauchery."

Sir John Vanbrugh takes precisely the same line. He is more successful because he is more alive to the significance of Collier. Congreve was utterly at a loss; his *Amendments* is the work of a man groping amid values that are unintelligible to him. But Vanbrugh, simply because he was consciously wicked (as constrasted with Congreve who was unwittingly so), is better able to measure his antagonist and meet him. Like Congreve, Vanbrugh accepts Collier's definition of the aims of comedy. " What I have done," he says in his *Vindication*, " is in general a discouragement of vice and folly; I am sure I intended it, and I hope I have performed it." The answer to this is that Vanbrugh no more set out to write comedies for the reformation of manners than Congreve; but that it similarly pleases him to assume it now that Collier has put the idea into his head. " The business of comedy," he continues, " is to show people what they should do by representing them upon the stage doing what they should not. . . . The stage is a glass for the world to view itself in.

People ought therefore to see themselves as they are; if it makes their faces too fair, they won't know they are dirty, and by consequence will neglect to wash 'em."

Vanbrugh's *Vindication* is all through an ingenious but entirely unsuccessful attempt to defeat Collier, after having accepted Collier's conditions. There are passages of the *Vindication* where Vanbrugh, consciously impudent, merrily turns Collier's weapons against Collier. Earnestly defending the moral of his tale, Vanbrugh grows quite eloquent upon the virtue of Amanda, and its effect upon libidinous Worthy. Collier had quite justly ridiculed Worthy's sudden conversion at the end of *The Relapse* to a spiritual conception of love—one of the scenes where Vanbrugh is decidedly at his worst. "His passion is metamorphosed in the turn of a hand," says Collier, "he is refined into a Platonic admirer, and goes off as like a town spark as you would wish. And so much for the poet's fine gentleman." Vanbrugh's retort admirably typifies his happy, shallow, and impertinent treatment of the whole controversy. "The world may see by this," he says, "what contempt the doctor has for a spark that can make no better use of his mistress than to admire her for her virtue. This, methinks is something so very extraordinary in a clergyman that I almost fancy that when he and I are in our graves those who shall read what we both have produced will be apt to conclude there's a mistake in the tradition about the authors; and that it was the reforming divine that writ the play and the scandalous poet the remarks upon it."

This is brilliant but quite ineffective light skirmishing about the subject; it leaves Collier's position not only unassailed, but stronger than before. Collier is right, is Vanbrugh's argument, but I am more Collier than Collier.

Vanbrugh, as in his plays, is happiest in this controversy where his shrewd humour balances the conflicting issues. He admirably says of Collier that he "always takes care to stretch that way which becomes him least, and so is sure to be in the wrong himself whether I am or not." He also says, in a passage that sums up both sides of the whole dispute: "When men fight in passion, 'tis usual to make insignificant thrusts."

The best pamphlet of the host that followed the publication of *A Short View* was an anonymous *Vindication of the Stage* which appeared in May, 1699. Mr. Edmund Gosse, upon internal evidence alone, attributes it without hesitation to Wycherley. It would be agreeable to believe that Wycherley, who in *The Plain Dealer* suggested in a single phrase a complete critical justification of his comic treatment of sex, was also the author of the only answer to Collier which tentatively questions his main assumption. The anonymous author of *A Vindication of the Stage*, citing Collier's opening definition, suggests a doubt as to whether comedies have any "business" at all. He also insists that comedy reflects life; that its chief end is delight; that, since the people must like it, it cannot debauch them with indecencies which are below the level of their culture and taste. If the theatre is indecent, he argues, it is the fault of the clergy for not instructing the people.   All this is on quite another level from the confused protests of Congreve and Vanbrugh.   The author of *A Vindication of the Stage* has evidently thought about his subject.

Nevertheless he was no match for Collier. Collier could only be met with flat denial of his main thesis.   Our anonymous author, though he clearly feels the inadequacy of Collier's proposition, was not prepared with a counter.   " Art for art's sake," the converse fallacy of " art for morality's sake," was not yet heard.   Criticism was in its nonage.   The end of comedy, concludes our author, is " to shame us out of our follies."   But he qualifies this in a way that shows him to be feeling after a more satisfactory idea.   " Comedy," he says, " like an indulgent parent, mixes something to please when it reproves."

We include this anonymous *Vindication* out of respect for the opinion of Mr. Gosse as to its authorship; but we must be careful of accepting it as the work of Wycherley.   Wycherley has written nothing so good as this in continuous prose.   It is in the form of a letter; but the style —easy and lucid—bears little resemblance to the sprawling sentences and conceits of Wycherley's authentic correspondence.   Whoever was the author, it may stand here as the nearest approach to a competent defence of the comic dramatists that was possible in a period too near to the matters at issue to perceive their real significance, and too little exercised in the art of criticism to oppose any definite obstacle to the application of the moral and logical footrule of Jeremy Collier.

It is a recognised principal of English law that the worst criminal should have counsel. It has been sensibly felt that innocence is a frail barricade against a really vigorous and alert prosecution, and that it would be grossly unjust to leave a prisoner to fend for himself against the practised onslaught of a specialist. The comic dramatists of the Restoration are in the position of criminals tried for their reputation without counsel. Surely it is grossly against even the coarse sense of justice typified in the ordinary procedure of the courts to condemn them for having failed in these circumstances to establish their innocence.

"Art for morality's sake," said Jeremy Collier; and Congreve accepted it. It is easy for a modern critic to say that Congreve should have refused. We have thought a good deal about art since 1698, and written even more than we have thought. We have tested formulæ at the opposite extreme to Collier's. It is possible to understand how Collier was wrong and how difficult it was for Congreve to perceive exactly why and where.

Art is not primarily concerned with morality. It is not the aim or business of comedy to improve the world. Good morality is not necessarily good art, else every good man would of necessity be a great artist. We are not committing ourselves to any nonsense about "art for art's sake"—really a pleonasm. When we say that art is not primarily concerned with morality, we mean that in most cases (the exceptions prove the rule) an artist is first concerned with beautifully expressing something he has felt or seen. He endeavours to give local habitation and a name to a piece of life imaginatively realised. His art is fashioned in the heat of a desire to see life in shape and form. His impulse is not the impulse of a moralist to improve the world : it is the impulse of an artist to express it.

Here, in the art of a poet or dramatist, enters a paradox and stumbling-block. Art is not primarily concerned with morality, but morality is the stuff of the poet's art. The artist is dealing with emotions and conduct which in the world whence he draws his material are determined by a positive morality. Morality is his subject, though it is not his object. The critics of Collier's generation, and incompetent critics of every generation, invariably confuse the subject with the object—worse, they mistake the subject of a picture or a poem for the work itself.

The problem is further confused by the continuous inter-influence of subject and object. The artist's purpose is to give form and imaginative reality to a piece of life—beauty is his object. But just as the beauty which a worker in marble and bronze aims at expressing is conditioned by his material, so is the poet's work conditioned by the period in which he lives, the moral laws which his moods and characters unconsciously obey. He does not aim at enforcing or weakening the moral code ; but in the result he necessarily does so. The moralist, Jeremy Collier for instance, perceives the result; and mistakes it for the intention. The artist himself, working intuitively, if he is not also a critic, is equally liable to mistake it.

The most difficult question remains. Can good art be bad morality? If Collier has proved that the result of Congreve's impulse to express beautifully the life of his time is morally vicious, has he also proved that it is bad art? First we must be quite clear as to what morality means. If it means the definite system of moral values from which Collier attacked the plays of Congreve, then it is immediately obvious that bad morality as Collier understood it is quite consistent with good art as any artist understands it. It is not necessarily bad art—nor ever was—to suggest that man and wife though they be made one flesh will often remain two fools. If by morality is understood the minutiæ of the contemporary code, then obviously bad morality may be not only good art but better manners.

But there is a higher morality than that of Jeremy Collier—a plane upon which Plato and S. Francis, Confucius and Elijah may meet. Without being a Manichee one may reasonably see in the history of mankind an angel of darkness in conflict with an angel of light; and without in the least circumscribing the sphere of the artist one may confidently assert that the highest art has invariably expressed the highest morality. A great artist does not consciously intend to be a great prophet. His prophesying comes by the way. His impulse is to create imaginatively in the likeness of things felt and seen; but precisely in proportion to the strength of his artistic impulse he sees clearer and feels deeper into life than common folk. He aims at winning from the chaos of life one more province for the imagination of man; but the province when put upon the map is perceived to be in the loftiest sense a moral as well as an imaginative triumph. "Art for art's sake" is in the event, "Art for morality's sake." The greatest artists are also those who have contributed most to the morality of the Commonwealth. Morality is an accident of the artist's accomplishment, though it is not the intention. It is required of the artist that he should sincerely live for his art alone. These other things are, thereafter, added unto him.

This is the heart of the matter. The artist must himself be sincere. Only so long as he obeys an impulse to express the thing he sees, reaching into the unconquered spaces of life, is he protected against falsehood. Responding to a genuine inspiration he will leave the moral result of his endeavours to look after itself. But if he is, as an artist, immoral; if he repeats a message which he has not himself realised imaginatively, he is then at the mercy of mischance. Congreve, though not one of the very great artists of the world, was within his limits sincere. He is therefore saved not only artistically but morally. Vanbrugh, who accepted without examination artistic conventions which had no real relation to the truth he might otherwise have expressed, is, both ways, as inevitably damned.

How shall we at last decide the critical and moral questions raised in the course of this study? The evidence is before us; and some liberty of dogmatism may, after so long an argument, be permitted. What is the position of Etherege, Wycherley, Congreve, Vanbrugh and Farquhar in the light of all we have been able to see and hear ?

We have looked into a period of our social history unlike any that preceded it or followed. We found in Etherege a man who in temperament and mind accurately reflected this period in his personal character, and received a sincere impulse to reflect it artistically in his comedies. His sincerity as an artist has met the inevitable reward. His plays are morally as well as artistically sound. He felt and saw the comedy of contemporary life ; and he honestly sought and found the means to express it. The result of his honesty and purity of motive as an artist is that, as soon as we enter the imaginative regions of his comedy, we are sensible that the laws are harmonious and just ; they will bear inspection. We are sensible of a strange land ; but it does not occur to us to question the finality of its laws so long as we remain within its bounds. They are not laws with which we are familiar to-day in the homes of Kensington or Mayfair ; but having submitted our imagination to the author in the act of consenting to read his comedy, that suggestion can only intrude when the comedy is put away. Moreover, when the comedy is put away, we are aware that the morality of this strange country, just because Etherege was as an artist sincerely endeavouring to see life and express it, has a positive value of its own. We have contemplated a phase of human experience ; realised it imaginatively. We have explored a mood of the human spirit which is in every age, though in this particular age it was more conspicuous. Etherege, aiming at beauty, has brought down truth as well; and, if from the standpoint of the narrow morality of this or that generation, truth may often seem an angel of darkness, from the standpoint of the higher morality of all time it is seen as an angel of light.

Wycherley followed. The truth of Wycherley is in the main the truth of Etherege. He was sufficiently the man of his period to enter and possess as his artistic right the comic world which Etherege had opened up before him. His comedies admirably illustrate the main point of our argument, that in art he who would save his moral shall lose it, and he that would lose his moral for art's sake shall find it. So long as Wycherley obeys a simple impulse to express the attitude towards life of his time the reader who enters his comedy from another world instinctively accepts the picture and is not offended. But when the singleness of Wycherley's artistic purpose is confused by a malignant puritanism, inconsistent with the temper of his comedy, then we are immediately arrested. Wycherley's whole fabric tumbles about us.

Wycherley's lapses are the exception. His plays are masterpieces of sustained comedy, broken only very rarely by the intrusions of the shorter catechist. *The Country Wife*, for example, is almost perfect. With the exception of the tea-drinking scene between Mr. Horner and the Fidgets it answers the severest test of imaginative sincerity; and, in proportion as it does so, it equally satisfies the severest test of morality. So

long as the laws of Mr. Horner's comic kingdom
are faithfully observed, Mr. Horner is quite immune
from the attacks of Collier and his successors.
Mr. Horner is in another world, whence there is
no treaty of extradition for his attachment. When,
for instance, he is accused of indecent gallantry,
those of us who are seised of his imaginative
kingdom already know that gallantry cannot here
be indecent. It is a first law of the cloud-cuckooland of *The Country Wife* that the act of sex has
no more suggestion of the indecently amorous than
tumbling upstairs or losing one's hat in a gale.
Wycherley has already created an atmosphere
where passion is unable to ¦breathe. Mr. Horner
goes after his friend's wife precisely as boys go
after their neighbour's apples. Either you have
accepted this convention, and without further
thought of the proprieties, enter with zest into the
collection of Mr. Horner's china, or the comedy is
worse than nonsense. Lamb was entirely accurate
in this regard when he virtually describes Mr.
Horner as a fairy. He was wrong when, and if,
he assumed that Mr. Horner never had a prototype
in real life. Mr. Horner, in fact, is a perfect fairy
for the very reason that he is also a faithful
portrait. It is because Mr. Horner imaginatively
expresses his period so well that he is morally
immune from the censure of any other period.

Wycherley, on the other hand, is fairly open
to criticism when he breaks the laws of his own
comedy—when the passionate satire of *The Plain
Dealer* intrudes into the dispassionate comedy of
The Country Wife. The illusion of fairyland is lost.

Everyday values intrude into our thoughts. Mr. Horner as a comic figure is spiritually lost, in whose place we seem to see an ineligible guest for a modern house-party.

Vanbrugh and Farquhar inevitably come in here. What was accidental in Wycherley was fundamental in them. They took over the comic kingdom of Mr. Horner; but administered it according to the laws of Queen Anne. They accepted as the figures of their comedy characters which had no relation to their own imaginative vision of life, or their attitude towards society. They did not obey a simple artistic impulse to express something clearly seen and vividly felt. They accepted a formula whose significance was outworn, writing entertainingly within its bounds, and slurring where it was possible inconsistencies of which they were only half aware. The result of their artistic insincerity is, as ever, a moral as well as an imaginative degeneration. So long as Mr. Horner borrows the wives of his friends in the same spirit as he would borrow their books, he may proceed unchallenged and unashamed. But when Mr. Horner seduces one particular wife of one particular friend with every circumstance of suggestive ardour the case is different. Vanbrugh and Farquhar read romantic love into Mr. Horner's affairs. They are trying to reconcile two inconsistent attitudes. Romantic love cannot be reconciled with a comic treatment of adultery. The result upon the reader is that, driven from one convention to another, he finally retires for refuge to the conventions of his own well-regulated life of every

day. He then sees Vanbrugh's Loveless and Farquhar's Mr. Archer forcibly seducing a pretty
woman in his immediate presence.

Congreve, like Etherege and Wycherley at his
best, is immune from any such criticism. His
comedies are the perfect expression of an attitude.
They are as consistent in art as in morality. All
we have found in the Comedy of Etherege is
expressed in Congreve upon a higher imaginative
level. Congreve saw more clearly what he had
to express and drew with a firmer hand.

Congreve is the summit of our theme. He
produced the most perfect specimens of the comedy
we have studied. Nevertheless we must end upon
a statute of limitations. A critic could no more
put Congreve upon a level with Shakespeare than
he could put Catullus upon a level with Homer, or
Scarlatti upon a level with Beethoven. But if
Congreve attained the extreme limit of beauty in
the artistic expression of the life of his time, whence
comes this sense of his inferiority to the greatest?
The obvious answer is that Shakespeare's subjects
are bigger than those of Congreve; that whereas
Shakespeare expressed Falstaff and Othello, Congreve expressed Mirabell and Witwoud. But this
difference of subject is not the root of the matter.
It is a visible token of the contrast; not the contrast itself. The contrast itself is in the creative
energy of the two men. Whereas Shakespeare
was ardently impelled to look quite through the
shows of things, to penetrate into the depths of
himself and of the life he saw, to body forth in
imagination secrets he was furiously urged to

discover, Congreve was mildly driven to fashion an image of existence observed at ease, incuriously, with no ambition to pursue the spirit of truth into the dark. That almost invisible curl of the lip with which he seems to follow the movements of his creatures is not of a man who could be stirred in imagination to the depths. He is not less than Shakespeare because his subjects are less ; for an artist's subjects, be they what they may, are never by one jot less or greater than the artist. Congreve is less than Shakespeare, because the mood in which he wrote is not that of a man whose imagination is, like Shakespeare's, working at the limit of pressure. If after-generations had lost his work entirely, they would have lost a perfect artistic reflexion of English Society at a particular period. Had they entirely lost the work of Shakespeare, they would have lost an embattled fortress upon boundaries which part the waters of chaos from the solid earth redeemed by great artists for the habitation of man.

AUTHORITIES

[This is not a complete bibliography; but a list of books and papers quoted in the text, or upon which facts and arguments in the text are based.]

CHAPTER I

CRITICAL PRELIMINARIES

Leigh Hunt. *Dramatic Works of Wycherley, Congreve, Vanbrugh and Farquhar* (1849). A complete edition of the plays, containing memoirs of the dramatists and the essays of Lamb and Hazlitt.
Macaulay. *Leigh Hunt.* A review of the Leigh Hunt edition, dealing only with Wycherley and Congreve.
Pepys' Diary.. Passim. References are dated in the text.
Evelyn's Diary   „   „   „
The Tatler. (Steele).   „   „   „
The Spectator. (Addison).   „   „   „
Johnson. *Life of Congreve.*
Blackmore. *The Epic of Prince Arthur.*
The Collier Pamphlets. (See Chapter VIII.).
Thackeray. *The English Humourists.*
Meredith. *An Essay on Comedy.*

CHAPTERS II—III

SIR GEORGE ETHEREGE

Letter-Book of Sir George Etherege. Add. MSS. Brit. Mus.
Oldys. Memoir in the *Biographia Britannica.*
Langbaine. *Dramatic Poets.* Edited and Supplemented by Gildon.
Jacob. *The Poetical Register.*
Spence. *Anecdotes.*
Luttrell. *Relation of State Affairs*, ii. 171.
Hatton Correspondence (1879) i. 133 ; ii. 216.
Dryden. *State Poems* (1704).
Gildon. *The Poetical Remains of the Duke of Buckingham.*
Rochester. *Session of the Poets.*

Pepys' Diary. 1664 ; 1667.
Shadwell. Preface to *The Humourists.*
Steele. *Spectator* 51.
Anon. *A Defence of Sir Fopling Flutter* (1722).
Edmund Gosse. *Seventeenth Century Studies.*
A. W. Verity. *Works of Sir G. Etherege.* Complete Edition (with memoir) 1888.
Etherege. The Collected Editions of 1704, 1715, and 1723 are at the British Museum ; also a Collection of Poems by Sir G. E. (1701).

CHAPTER IV

WILLIAM WYCHERLEY

Leigh Hunt. *Memoir* prefixed to the edition of 1849.
Macaulay. *Essays.*
Dryden. *Prose Works* (edited by Malone): ii. 402 ; iii. 168 ; 177 ; 135.
Dennis. *Letters upon several occasions* (1696). *Select Works* (1721).
Spence. *Anecdotes.*
Pope. *Works.* (Edited by Elwin and Courthope).
Letters between Pope and Wycherley are transcribed as dated by Pope in 1735. The Longleat Versions are also given. References to Wycherley are also found in the letters : Pope to Cromwell, October 1711 ; Cromwell to Pope, October 1711 ; Pope to Blount, January 1715.
Theophilus Cibber. *Lives of the Poets.*
Wood. *Athenæ Oxonienses.*
Genest. *Some Account of the English Stage.*
Jacob. *The Poetical Register.*
Langbaine. *Dramatic Poets* (Gildon).
Lansdowne. *Works.*
Grainger. *Biographia Historica*, V. 248.
Noble. *Continuation of Grainger* (1806) i. 237-240.
Voiture. *Familiar and Courtly Letters* (1700).
Pack. *Wycherley's Posthumous Works* (with Memoir).
The Collier Pamphlets.
Voltaire. *Letters Concerning the English Nation.*
Swift. *Journal to Stella.* Works (edited by Scott) xvii. 21 ; 284 ; xix. 16 ; 245.
Notes and Queries. 4th Ser. iv. 451 ; 550 ; v. 176 ; 7th Ser. xii. 146.
Hist. MSS. Comm. 2nd *Report*, pp. 70-1.
Gentleman's Magazine. New Series (1871) vii. 823-4.
W. C. Ward. *Memoir.* Prefixed to the Mermaid Edition of Wycherley's Plays.
Wycherley. The Collected Editions of 1713 ; 1720 ; 1731 ; 1735 ; 1768 ; 1849 (Leigh Hunt) ; 1851 (Leigh Hunt) ; 1888 (Mermaid Series : W. C. Ward) ; 1903 (ditto) are at the British Museum : also the Miscellany Poems (1704).

CHAPTER V

WILLIAM CONGREVE

Leigh Hunt. *Memoir* prefixed to the edition of 1849.
Macaulay. *Essays.*
Dryden. *Rhymed Epistle to Southerne* (1692).
    Works. (Edited by Congreve) 1717.
    Letters. To Tonson: August 1693; to Walsh: 1694.
    Mr. Congreve's Last Will and Testament (with "characters"
      by Dryden, Blackmore, etc.).
    Translation of The Art of Love (Ovid) by Dryden, Con-
      greve and Tate (1709).
    Translation of The Metamorphoses (Ovid) by Dryden,
      Addison and Congreve (1717).
    Translation of Juvenal and Persius (1693) by Dryden
      and Congreve.
Malone. *Life of Dryden.*
The Collier Pamphlets.
Swift. *Journal to Stella.* October 1710; February 1729.
    Letters. Swift to Pope, 10th January 1721; 13th February
      1729; Arbuthnot to Swift, 20th September 1726; Gay to
      Swift, February 1723.
Monck Berkeley. *Literary Relics.* Letters of Congreve to Keally.
Pope. *Works.* (Edited by Elwin and Courthope).
    Letters between Congreve and Pope. Dedication of the Iliad.
Voltaire. *Lettres sur Les Anglais.*
Spence. *Anecdotes.*
Steele. *Preface to The Drummer.*
Jacob. *Poetical Register.*
Wilson. *Memoirs of the Life, Writings and Amours of William
    Congreve Esq.* (Curll).
Davies. *Dramatic Miscellanies* (1883).
Theophilus Cibber. *Lives of the Poets.*
Johnson. *Life of Congreve.*
Genest. *Some Account of the English Stage.*
Notes and Queries. 2nd Ser. ix. 418.
              3rd Ser. v. 132; xi. 280.
Dennis. *Letters upon Several Occasions.*
Nichols. *Literary Anecdotes.*
Addison. *Lines to Congreve* (1674).
Biographia Dramatica. (Baker) 1812.
Walter Moyle. *Works.* Letters from Congreve.
Leslie Stephen. *Dict. Nat. Biogr.*
Swinburne. *Encyl. Brit.*
Gosse. *Life of Congreve* (with bibliography by John P. Andersen).
A. W. Ward. *History of English Dramatic Literature.*
T. H. Ward. *English Poets.* (Essay on Congreve by Austin
    Dobson).
Congreve. *Works.* The Collected Editions of 1710; 1717; 1719-
    1720; 1730; 1753; 1761; 1773; 1774 are at the British Museum;
    also the *Collected Plays* of 1731 (Dublin); 1773; 1849 and 1851

(Leigh Hunt); 1887 (Mermaid Series: Ewald); 1895 (critical introduction by G. S. Street—the best modern edition); 1903 (Mermaid reissue); 1912 (Archer): also the *Collected Poems* of 1778 (Edinburgh: Bell); 1793 (Edinburgh: Andersen); 1810 (London: Chalmers).

CHAPTER VI

SIR JOHN VANBRUGH

Leigh Hunt. *Memoir* prefixed to the edition of 1849.
Voltaire. *Lettres sur Les Anglais.*
Dryden. *Works.* (Edited by Scott) viii. 439–64.
Chetwood. *History of the Stage.*
Genest. *Some Account of the English Stage.*
Colley Cibber. *Apology.*
Disraeli. *Curiosities of Literature.*
Lovegrove. *The Life Work and Influence of Sir John Vanbrugh* (1902).
Biographia Dramatica. (Baker).
Encyclopædia Britannica. (Arthur Ashpitel).
Noble. *The College of Arms.*
Dalton. *Army Lists,* iii. 409.
Historical MSS. Comm. *12th Report.* App. ix. 97.
                 15th Report. App. vi. (Carlisle Papers).
Add. MSS. Brit. Mus. 9011 *ff.* 346 *seq.*
                 6321 *f.* 59.
         9123 ; 19618 ; 19592–605 (Marl. Papers).
Nichols. *Select Collection of Poems* (1780) iii. 161.
Coxe. *Life of Marlborough.*
W. C. Ward. *Works of Sir J. Vanbrugh.* Collected Edition (with Memoir) 1893.
Theophilus Cibber. *Lives of the Poets.*
Langbaine. *Dramatic Poets* (Gildon).
Thompson. *Memoirs of the Duchess of Marlborough.*
Notes and Queries. 4th Ser. ix. 499.
                 7th Ser. iv. 28 ; 113.
                 8th Ser. vii. 166 ; 258 ; 509.
                 9th Ser. iv. 4.
Athenæum. 1861. i. 84–86. ⎫
           1890. ii. 289 ; 321. ⎬ Letters.
           1894. ii. 234 ; 299. ⎭
Gentleman's Magazine. 1802. ii. 1065.
                     1804. ii. 411 ; ii. 737.
                     1815. ii. 494.
                     1816. i. 37 ; 135.
                     1829. i. 42.
                     1831. i. 330.
                     1836. i. 13 ; ii. 27 ; 374 ⎫
                     1837. i. 243 ; 449   ⎬ Letters.
                     1839. i. 149   ⎭
                     1857. ii. 420.

Pope. *Works*. (Edited by Elwin and Courthope) iii. 173–176 ; 366 ; vi. 112 ; x. 106 ; 187.
Swift. *Works*. (Edited by Scott) ii. 71 ; xiii. 6 ; xiv. 80.
Swift and Pope. *Joint Preface to Prose Miscellany* (1727).
The Collier Pamphlets.
Luttrell. *Relation of State Affairs* (1857).
Horace Walpole. *Letter to the Countess of Ossory* (June 1787).
Swaen. *Sir John Vanbrugh*. Introduction and notes prefixed to the Mermaid Edition.
Vanbrugh. The Collected Editions of 1730 ; 1735 ; 1759 ; 1765 ; 1776 ; 1849 and 1851 (Leigh Hunt) ; 1893 (W. C. Ward—the best modern edition) ; 1896 (Mermaid : Swaen) are at the British Museum.

CHAPTER VII

GEORGE FARQUHAR

Leigh Hunt. *Memoir* prefixed to the edition of 1849.
Chetwood. *History of the Stage*. (A Memoir based on information supplied by Wilks).
Curll. *Life of Wilks*.
Thomas Wilks. *Memoir* prefixed to Dublin Edition (1775).
Genest. *Some Account of the Stage*.
Jacob. *The Poetical Register*.
Biographia Britannica.
Theophilus Cibber. *Lives of the Poets*.
Langbaine. *Dramatic Poets* (Gildon).
Edmund Gosse. *Gossip in a Library*.
Farquhar. The Collected Editions of 1718 ; 1728 ; 1736 ; 1742 ; 1760 ; 1772 ; 1775 (with life by Thomas Wilks) ; 1849 and 1851 (Leigh Hunt) ; 1892 (Ewald) ; 1906 (Archer) are at the British Museum : also *Love and Business* (with the Picture) 1702 ; and *Barcelona (a Poem)* 1707.

CHAPTER VIII

CRITICAL CONCLUSIONS

The Collier Pamphlets. (British Museum).
Collier. *A Short View of the Profaneness and Immorality of the English Stage* (1698).
    A Defence of the Short View etc. (A reply to Congreve and Vanbrugh) 1699.
    A Second Defence of the Short View etc. (reply to Dr. Drake) 1700.
    A Dissuasive from the Playhouse etc. (1703).
    A Letter to a Lady concerning the New Playhouse (1706).
    A Further Vindication of the Short View (reply to Filmer) 1708.
    Collected Pamphlets. (The Short View with Collier's subsequent retorts) 1853.

Congreve. *Amendments to Mr. Collier's False and Imperfect Citations* etc. (1699).
Vanbrugh. *A Vindication of the Relapse* etc. (1699).
Tenison. *A Letter from Several Members of the Society for the Reformation of Manners* (directed against Vanbrugh).
Drake. *The Ancient and Modern Stages Surveyed* (1699).
Gildon. *Phæton.* (Cf. Preface).
John Dennis. *The Usefulness of the Stage.*
Durfey. *The Campaigners.* (Cf. Preface).
Motteux. *Beauty in Distress.* (Cf. Preface) 1698.
Filmer. *A Defence of Plays* (1707).
Law. *The Absolute Unlawfulness of the Stage* (1726).
Dryden. *Epistle to Motteux* (1698).
      Fables. (Cf. Preface) 1699.
      The Pilgrim. „ „
      Cymon and Iphigenia.
Anon. *A Vindication of the Stage.* (Attributed by Mr. Gosse to Wycherley) 1698.
      The Stage Acquitted. (Edited by A. D.) 1699.
      Animadversions on Mr. Congreve's late answer.
      A letter to Mr. Congreve on his pretended amendments.
      The Stage Condemned. The Arguments of all the authors that have writ etc. (1698).

INDEX